# DEPRESSION AND CREATIVITY

# DEPRESSION AND CREATIVITY

## André Haynal

International Universities Press, Inc.
New York                    New York

*Le Sens du Désespoir*
par André Haynal
© 1976, Presses Universitaires de France

Translation Copyright © 1985, International Universities Press, Inc.

**Library of Congress Cataloging in Publication Data**

Haynal, André
  Depression and creativity.

  Translation of: Le sens du désespoir.
  Bibliography: p.
  Includes index.
  1. Creative ability. 2. Depression, Mental.
I. Title. [DNLM; 1. Creativeness. 2. Depression
WM 171 H423s]
BF408.H3413      1985        616.85'27        84-27830
ISBN 0-8236-1201-5

Manufactured in United States of America

# Contents

Foreword—Serge Lebovici vii
Preface xi
Acknowledgment xxxiii
1. Introduction 1

## PART I

2. The Depressive Affect 13
3. Childhood 36
4. Some Reflections Concerning Helplessness 49
5. Loss and Mourning 64
6. Death and Immortality 79
7. Mourning and the Psychoanalytic Process 85
8. Introjection and Identification 97
9. A Word about the Superego 114
10. Defenses against Depression 121
11. Boredom 128
12. Creativity, Culture and Civilization 140
13. Conclusions 155

## PART II

14. Freud and Depression 163
15. The Evolution of Ideas on Depression in
      the Psychoanalytic Literature 180
   References 240
   Name Index 257
   Subject Index 262

# Foreword

André Haynal's *Depression and Creativity* gives new meaning to the concept of despair. His work confirms the repeated observation that the inhibition underlying depression and shaping its various manifestations is a central feature of many psychopathological configurations, whether neurotic, psychotic, antisocial, or psychosomatic. Pierre Marty's hypothesis (1976) that such configurations reflect "essential depression," a concept elaborated by Evelyne Kestemberg (1982) under the term "blank depression," supports Haynal's contention that depressive mood plays a decisive role in mental life.

The relations between depression and creativity delineated in this book are often quite startling. Haynal notes that quite a few creative thinkers were unable to produce until after the death of their fathers. This was certainly the case with Freud, who was incapable of completing his self-analysis and his book on dreams until he had laid Jakob to rest. Haynal views artistic production as a working through of guilt feelings associated with a father's death, the same process which, under favorable circumstances, makes it possible for an analysand to achieve reparation and to transcend personal limitations. Haynal repeatedly and convincingly demonstrates that the birth of the

vii

self, which Winnicott (1949) defines as experiential feeling of "continuity of being," presupposes both concern and reparation for a gratifying object damaged by emotional stimuli not previously representable.

This view enables Haynal to deal with the universal emotion of sadness and despair in its original context. Together with others currently studying the development and psychology of infants, I have described emotions observable during interactive bathing which, with all the subtlety embodied in facial expression, body language, and verbal and preverbal communication, may occasion a depressive mood in the infant as well as the mother. A depressed mother does not respond emotionally to her baby's mood, nor does she trigger in her baby the astounding performances we have recently come to recognize and appreciate. Conversely, an infant apathetic by constitution or for any other reason will fail to react to the subtleties of its mother's delight, thereby failing to transform her emotionally into a mother and leaving her depressed. Anyone who has viewed T. Berry Brazelton's film knows the disastrous effect of instructing a baby's mother to cease her rhythmic verbalizations and remain "stillface." Under these conditions, very young babies become upset, cry, and fall asleep, withdrawing so to speak from the world of emotional interplay. It is the same when "oedipal ghosts" people the nursery (Fraiberg, 1975). The remarkable ability of mothers and their babies to harmonize their differently toned moods has been demonstrated by Daniel Stern (1971). These observations attest the remarkable quality and intensity of the emotional interplay between mother and child, an interaction so keenly sensitive to depressive withdrawal by either partner.

Whether the helplessness of the neonate is being considered, or its sensitivity to its mother's depression, one can readily follow Haynal in his efforts to make us sense the universality of depressive moods and mental anguish. Depression is linked to the feeling of helplessness, is the source of the feeling of guilt that helplessness entails, and is responsible for anxiety regarding the future.

André Haynal's work allots the concept of despair the full measure of its meaning, whether in making determinations of psychopathology or as regards its importance for both parties to an analysis. The analyst is faced with the task of mourning the feelings associated with his countertransference and interpretations, as well as the passing of his parental authority.

The book concludes with a useful and timely reminder of the development of Freud's views on depression, of the contributions to the subject made by the psychoanalytic literature of the twenties, and of the postwar literature in both English and French.

The knowledgeable will recognize in Haynal's book a truly exemplary depth of scholarship. Its originality consists in its demonstration of the universality of depressive moods and in its definition of their meaning in the psychoanalytic experience and in human encounters generally. It responds perfectly to the increasingly widespread interest in pathological depression and human despair.

Serge Lebovici, M.D.
Professor of Psychiatry (Bobigny-Paris)
Past President, International
    Psycho-Analytical Association

# References

Fraiberg, S. (1975), Ghosts in the nursery. *J. Amer. Acad. Child Psychiat.*, 14:327–341.

Kestemberg, E. (1982), Névrose de caractère: Masochisme moral et culpabilité. *Les Cahiers*, 4:53–72.

Lebovici, S. (1983), *Le nourrisson, la mère et le psychanalyste.* Paris: Le Centurion.

Marty, P. (1976), *Les mouvements individuels de vie et de mort: Essai d'économie psycho-somatique.* Paris: Payot.

Stern, D. (1971), Micro-analysis of the mother-infant interaction. *J. Amer. Acad. Child Psychiat.*, 10:501–517.

Winnicott, D.W. (1949), Mind and its relation to the psyche-soma. In: *Collected Papers*, London: Tavistock, 1958.

# Preface

In the following work I have endeavored to focus on the depressive affect as experienced primarily in psychoanalytic treatment. Affects, which Freud considered of major importance (1907a) even while acknowledging our ignorance about them (1926d), belong to the world of experience. They are apprehended through identification with the Other and may be understood when reinserted into the context of the representational world and the analysand's discourse.

There is no doubt that the depressive mood occupies an important place among our affective states, yet for many years its role did not receive the recognition it deserved. It was as if the importance properly accorded anxiety overshadowed it, as if any attention given one member of the anxiety-depression pair spelled the neglect of the other. This status of "poor relation," about which Karl Abraham complained as early as 1911 (see chapter 2), was assigned it by Freud from the outset, despite the fact that he was himself a depressive (Jones, 1953; Schur, 1972) whose self-analysis, triggered by his father's death (Anzieu, 1975) corresponded to a mourning process which bore fruit in *The Interpretation of Dreams* (1900a). But it was only gradually that the nature of the process became clear in his mind. The death theme, present in his psychoanalytic experience as the death wish *(Todeswunsch)* but to which there were only scattered references in his early writings (for instance, in "Contributions to a Discussion on Suicide" [1910g] ), was reworked under the impact of the war, with its harvest of death, destruction, separation, and the loneliness he experienced following the departure of his students for the front. The resulting "Thoughts for the Times on War and Death" (1915b) and "On Transience" (1916a), in which a series of themes relating to death were formulated and developed in greater depth, paved the way for "Mourning and Melancholia" (1917e).[1] It was during this same period that his friendship with Wilhelm Fliess was eclipsed by the relationship with Karl Abraham, and it was with the latter that he was to collaborate in developing this theme.

But the difficulty lay not merely in formulating the theme but in securing its acceptance. Can it be mere coincidence that of all Freud's concepts the death instinct was the least accepted by his students and disciples? Or that, between the extremes of the psychotic caricature of melancholia and the reassuring "normal depression" of mourning, little attention was paid to the "neurotic" depressions, that is, to *our* depressions, linked to our conflicts and casting their shadow on the psychoanalytic treatment? Can it be coincidence that Freud's remark (1916a) about death not being represented in the unconscious was seized

---

[1] "Mourning and Melancholia" was written for the most part in 1915, but was not published until 1917. "On Transience" was composed earlier in 1915.

upon as a justification for ignoring the theme entirely? Or finally, that a recent American work summarizing the psychoanalytic concepts of depression should conclude that such cases lie outside the psychoanalyst's domain? After Freud, the subject of depression was taken up by Kleinians as well as by authors either on the periphery of the Freudian current (such as Binswanger) or frankly at odds with it. Then, following the lead of Sandor Ferenczi and Imre Hermann, a number of psychoanalysts from the old Budapest school (Rado, Harnik, Gerö, Benedek, Balint, Bak) turned their attention to the relationship with the Primal Object and approached the depressive affect from that angle. Their works, followed by many others including those of contemporary French authors, have demonstrated the importance of the study of depression for elucidating the psychic apparatus in general as well as for increasing our understanding of the Other and ourselves.

Every child gradually loses his mother. Little by little, he realizes that he is separate, different from her and from the others around him. He becomes aware that he is not omnipotent, that he depends on persons outside himself for the satisfaction of needs and wishes. Once he has overcome the depression arising from this realization, he recathects himself; it is this moment that marks the birth of his individuality, of his "I" (Mahler, 1968; Mahler, Pine, and Bergman, 1975). Fantasies, nourished by longing and nostalgia for this mother growing ever more distant, will develop to fill the gap between the mother and himself. This is clearly the case with the famous orphans whose creative destinies we know so well—Descartes, Rousseau, Emily Brontë, Poe, Tolstoy (see Kanzer, 1953)—and with all motherless and abandoned children. But does it not apply equally to each one of us?

This crucial stage in human development—whether it is called the "depressive position" (Klein, 1934),[2] the "stage of concern" (Winnicott, 1954), "separation-individuation" (Mahler, 1966), or "the mirror stage" (Lacan, 1949)—coincides with the birth of the Total Object, an event that goes hand in hand with the emergence of the child's sense of responsibility for himself and his impulses. And with this awareness of responsibility comes the fear of having destroyed the increasingly separate mother through his sadistic fantasies. The child's feeling of having lost the object, or certain aspects of the object, and his resignation to that loss to the extent that he is incapable of restoring the object within himself, signals the beginning of the depressive affect and a certain susceptibility to depression. If the work of mourning is carried out harmoniously, this susceptibility can be overcome, but if it is marked by traumatic events, it gives way to a lasting depressive *vulnerability*.

The depressive affect thus emerges when omnipotence is overcome and the absolute symbiosis or fusion with the mother comes to an end; at this pivotal period the infant must of necessity grow away from the mother in order to acquire his own identity, in order to become himself.

It is my conviction that the discrepant terminology used by various schools in the attempt to grasp this

---

[2] Under the influence of Karl Abraham's "primary depression" (1911b).

crucial period of life stems mainly from the complexities of the dynamic, economic, and topographical forces at play. This is what I hoped to suggest when I chose, as the epigraph of chapter 1, Alfred North Whitehead's aphorism: "A clash of doctrines is not a disaster—it is an opportunity."

What concerns me in the present work is not so much specific external events as the child's fantasies at the time of his psychological birth. Within these fantasies lie essential "points of condensation," such as the problem of the "I" or the "self." Needless to say, these fantasies are repeated and reorganized later ("après coup") (Laplanche and Pontalis, 1967) during the oedipal phase. Consequently, our work in psychoanalysis always falls between two periods: the first establishes the anlagen, while the second, the oedipal phase, reorganizes the whole.

In Freud's language, *traurig* (sad) is associated with *Trauer* (mourning), the mourner being *trau(e)rig*. As early as 1895 Freud's writings show that he associated the depressive mood and dysphoria with mourning—in other words, with the loss of the object (Freud, 1950a). He later specified the difference between danger, which unleashes anxiety, and trauma, which results in the depressive affect (Freud, 1926d), and made the connection between trauma and the child's helplessness *(Hilflosigkeit)*. For our purposes, we shall consider the latter as the main distinguishing feature between sadness (psychic pain) and depression (sign of object loss). This helplessness goes hand in hand with powerlessness, "inferiority" (Pasche, 1969), and resignation, the feeling that nothing can be changed, *fait accompli*, that one is incapable of restoring a satisfactory inner situation.

It was Karl Abraham who first spelled out the distinction between anxiety and the depressive affect. In 1911 he wrote that anxiety refers to the future (to a potential danger), whereas the depressive affect reflects what has happened in the past: "Anxiety and depression are related to each other in the same way as are fear and grief. We fear a coming evil; we grieve over one that has occurred" (1911b, p. 137).

Loss entails change. The problem has been occupying mankind from the beginning of time: Heraclitus, for one, addressed it some twenty-five centuries ago. How does it happen, then, that we are not all depressed? It might seem impossible that the child could ever overcome his first trauma, which certain authors attribute to the actual physical rigors of birth but which seems to me rather to coincide with the child's "hatching" from the "imaginary symbiotic membrane of the mother-child dual unity," an emergence that marks the beginning of individuation (Mahler, 1966, p. 155), the birth of self-cathexis, and the shift from the narcissistic system to an object system—but only at the expense of relinquishing omnipotence and experiencing helplessness.

Freud (1908e) explained the secret by saying that everything we lose must be replaced, that we can never give anything up, but can only exchange one thing for another (p. 143). In this formulation he seems to me to have elucidated a principle of the functioning of the psychic apparatus (related to an aspect of the constancy principle) whereby everything is linked together in a continuity, from mother to wife and to the third of the three Fates, who reclaims us in the end, or from father to husband. If we could not keep within ourselves what we are likely to lose, through a ubiquitous and omnipresent introjection (in Ferenczi's meaning of the term), we could never tolerate the transitory nature of the present. *Erinnerung:* memory. The literal meaning of the German word—a taking inside—captures the sense of internalization, the constant introjection of the present. As Marcelle Spira (1968) rightly said, memory (and thoughts as well) fills in the void born of the threat of losing the present through re-creating the past in reminiscence.

Mnemosyne, the incarnation of memory, was the mother of the nine Muses, daughters of Zeus. It was she who, by filling the void through internalization and restoration of the object, gave birth to the arts, to which we shall return later.

Every original loss (breast, warmth, voice, expression, stools, urine, phallus, etc.) is experienced as a lack, as something missing. This "loss-lack," this "something missing," is replaced by the *wish*, the drive to fill the gap.

The emphasis placed on object loss and on the ubiquity of the depressive mood has shed new light on the processes of object restoration in therapy as well as in culture. Dreams, by virtue of their wish fulfillment function, are a part of these processes. According to recent neurophysiological theories, dreams are linked to the fixation of the memory, which confirms man's need to restore what he is likely to lose (the experience of the moment), even while transforming this experience through a process of assimilation into something more pleasurable, something closer to the wish. This aspect of object restoration is part of human nature or, more precisely, part of the functioning of the psychic apparatus. Thus, in addition to stressing the importance of the loss, we must underscore the importance of the internal restoration of the object through identification and creativity (Winnicott's transitional space).

It is absence which transforms the object into a mental representation: the object becomes a potential absence, and absence plays a basic formative role. "Thought," Freud (1900a) writes in the seventh chapter of *The Interpretation of Dreams*, "is after all nothing but a substitute for a hallucinatory wish" (p. 566). Or, as Thomas Mann expresses it in *Death in Venice*, "death is the birth of the image."

We shall distinguish between being helpless because rejected—a traumatic situation—and being hopeless, desperate, because "bad," castrated, a victim of the sadistic superego or the megalomanic and ruthless ego ideal.

Through *Hilflosigkeit*, helplessness, the depressive affect likewise encompasses the problem of limits—the limit to omnipotence, the transition to the world of reality—and also the great structuring event of reality, the Oedipus complex. "Possibility is the most weighty of categories," wrote Kierkegaard (1935, p. 16), in that it refers to what could have been. But for Foucault, "there is no culture in the world where everything is permitted. And it has long been acknowledged that man's existence begins not with freedom, but with limits and the boundary which cannot be traversed" (Foucault, 1972, p. 578).

At every stage of life the individual is called upon to undertake a working through, a task destined to be repeated endlessly; some might simply call this the developmental process. After the great changes of childhood we have touched on comes adolescence. The theme of the adolescent who leaves his parents antedates even the parable of the Prodigal Son, which tells the story from the parents' perspective; André Gide's version stresses the child's *need* to move away. The Return can only be fraught with temptation, the Siren's song beckoning one to destruction. It is paralyzing, as in the story of Lot, a return via incest to the primary narcissism, to the uterus, to illusion and utopia.

Change is a constant of life, occurring until the individual gradually loses his ability to recathect, which is perhaps the reason for the lack of "elasticity of the mental processes" mentioned by Freud (1905a, p. 264).

For me, mourning and psychoanalytic therapy are inextricably intertwined. In every culture, meditation—whether religious or philosophical—is characterized by seclusion, retreat, a withdrawal from the external world, and occurs only when the habitual context or setting has been temporarily abandoned. Likewise psychoanalysis, which can begin only after one's image of self in a state of well-being has been relinquished. As we know, Freud embarked upon his self-analysis after having lost his father and when far from the reassuring presence of Wilhelm Fliess. His first cases, reported in *Studies on Hysteria* (Freud, 1895d), involved subjects who were undergoing mourning in his presence. "Chimney sweeping" has become the prototype of the internal cleansing by exteriorization and the expression of feelings in the silent presence of the Other: in a word, psychoanalytic treatment.

"Irma's sufferings are satisfactorily explained by her widowhood . . . a state which I cannot alter," we read in Freud's *The Interpretation of Dreams* (1900a, p. 119). Or, in *Studies on Hysteria* (Freud, 1895d, p. 305): "I do not doubt at all that it would be easier for fate than for me to remove your suffering, but you will be convinced that much will be gained if we succeed in transforming your hysterical misery into everyday unhappiness, against which you will be better able to defend yourself with a restored nervous system." Modest changes, perhaps, but changes nonetheless, brought about by psychoanalytic treatment and mourning.

But if the changes are so limited, some might ask, where is there hope? Let us recall Freud's statement that nothing can be relinquished without the hope of "restoration." It is hope that enables us to accept renunciation, to accept the pain of mourning: when we accept this, the mourning can be accomplished in the sense of a working through. In psychoanalysis, the presence of the Other is the pledge of hope.

When I say that there is a close connection between psychoanalysis and the work of mourning, I do not mean to imply that the overriding characteristic of therapy is grief or sadness. On the contrary, because mourning is a release, there is a discharge of blocked energy thanks to the psychoanalytic work, the working through. "These are the tears of mortal suffering," as Virgil wrote, "which touch man's heart" (Virgil, *Aeneid*, 462). The analysand's mourning touches the capacity for identification in the analyst, who listens, who participates; the mourning of the one stirs memories, resonances, in the other. The presence and absence of the analyst follow the rhythmic pattern set

by the endings and beginnings of sessions, the separations imposed by the analytic situation. Harmony,
the fruit of analysis, will be achieved at the price of
a mourning never to be completely finished and the
renunciation of the last traces of omnipotence. The
analysand can then accept himself and learn to understand his own demons. To experience limits is to
experience evil, an evil of which the analysand wishes
to rid himself but which constantly resurfaces, the
repetition compulsion recognized as a "diabolical
streak." The demons are not external, they inhabit
our inner world. Limits can only be moved, never
removed. This in contrast to omnipotence, which is
the total and utopian absence of prohibition, the unity
of Two unhindered by the presence of a Third in a
world without mourning, alpha point, Thalassa, the
refusal of transition from the pleasure principle to the
reality principle, from the primary process to the secondary process, rejection of elaboration and mourning and, ultimately, loss of all possibility of feeling
pleasure.

Psychoanalysis presents us with a fundamental alternative: either wish fulfillment or the work of
mourning. During therapy, the work of mourning,
made possible by the presence of the analyst, predominates. Once this work is accomplished, hope
slowly arises, and the analysand is able to experience
in greater harmony the newly reconciled inner imagos
which have replaced his former conflicts and inner
struggles. To reach that stage, loss had to be accepted
and certain neurotic aspects of the self renounced that
were at the root of those conflicts.

The analysis unfolds "in abstinence" in that all instinctual gratification must be given up in the analytic

situation. Analysis also calls for a certain isolation, a certain solitude: the analysand cuts himself off from the outside world and his normal environment and communicates in one form or another the depression—or fury, which comes to the same thing—caused by this seclusion.

The analyst adapts himself to the analysand and to his rate of working through. Leaving behind his own world and the relative harmony he has managed to achieve, he enters into the world of the Other to participate in the Other's inner journey, which requires constant self-questioning and all the risks this entails. The analyst's ability to forget, to give up his own wish and even knowledge (Bion, 1967), is called into play.

The analysand's mourning causes the analyst to relive his own. He must give up his theoretical models and framework as well as personal ideas in order to meet the Other on his own ground, sometimes even coming up against the very limits of psychoanalytic theory. He must also overcome his temptation to function on behalf of the Other and, the journey ended, must accept his own death in an intense relationship. Our resistances to change, to mourning, our defenses against depression, are put harshly to the test.

Unearthing memories, the memories of dead parents, of losses, can be compared to the process of repression followed by the lifting of repression: bad experiences that were buried, encapsulated, encysted, are dug up so that suppression can give way to true mourning.

"I had wanted to take the elevator down to the basement, but inside there was a dead body. I immediately closed the door in a state of panic. When

I opened it again, the body was gone and instead I saw a broom, a bucket and a few dusting rags the cleaning woman had left behind. . . . The elevator climbed up a few feet and I was no longer able to get in." Once the problem had been outlined—the anal mechanisms, the "chimney sweeping" of Anna O., the cleansing—the psychoanalysis was conceived here as anal mastery, later replaced in therapy by the image of the evacuation of the dead.

I would now like to touch upon several points I shall discuss at greater length presently. The first of these is the silence of many psychoanalytic writings regarding the problem of death—this despite its absolutely central position in the internal structure of life. This silence is all the more puzzling in that death weighs so heavily in the work of Freud, not only in the first part, marked so by his father's death, but in the second part as well. It can be felt in Freud's special relationship with his doctor, described both in Max Schur's book (1972) and in his own writings: "What released the spirit of enquiry in man was not the intellectual enigma, and not every death, but the conflict of feeling at the death of loved yet alien and hated persons. Of this conflict of feeling, psychology was the first offspring" (Freud, 1915b, pp. 293–294). In saying that death is "what released the spirit of enquiry in man," or that "of this conflict of feeling, psychology was the first offspring," is Freud not giving unique and privileged importance to this enigma that encompasses and even transcends the enigma of origin? Is he not saying that this enigma lies at the very source of human culture, from the Neanderthal who painted the bones of his dead to the statues in

Greek burial grounds to Hellenic tragedies? And is not the coincidence of conflicting feelings Freud evokes in this context not also the coincidence of the knowledge of the dead person's disappearance and the knowledge of his survival in the created object (present in ancestor worship, the laws handed down by Moses, etc.)? Thanks to creativity, knowledge of death coincides with knowledge of immortality, absence with restoration, destruction with reparation—the two fundamental seasons of human existence. In a single stroke, these two seasons create the split: the symbolization of the absent one and the creation of his presence, making possible the creation of the replica, the transitional space, the re-creation of the transitional object at a cultural level in the face of the knowledge of the threat of death. "Emergences, resurgences," in Michaux's words (1972), or in one of Richard Wagner's letters: "What is art besides the recognition of our helplessness?" (Wagner, 1971, p. 21).

How strange are the lines of force leading from birth (with the separation from the mother and the ways of overcoming this separation through, for example, the transitional object) to the final separation and the creation of the surviving object! They are always conditional upon the loss, the potential absence, and depression that stalk us, upon the required "work" of maintenance and restoration, that the void may be filled in, the absence overcome, the threat averted.

Eudaemonia, or happiness, is an inner feeling of contentment. It is the harmonious outcome of this movement, not the expulsion of one's demons or the attempt to destroy them. "Man's attitude is determined by his demon": I return again to Heraclitus, but this time to affirm that demons and their assimilation through the work of mourning are at the very heart of all human development, psychoanalytic or cultural.

I would like also to emphasize the importance of a clear conceptual distinction between (1) psychic pain and depression, depression being a response characterized by the feeling of powerlessness *(Hilflosigkeit)* to restore a satisfying internal situation (see Joffe and Sandler, 1965; Sandler and Joffe, 1965); (2) psychic pain and depression on the one hand, and guilt on the other, guilt being characterized by a feeling of anxiety in the face of the superego; and (3) psychic pain and depression on the one hand and depressive anxiety on the other, depressive anxiety being the fear (future-related) of damaging the object and thereby incurring separation from it, with the threatening consequences for the individual that this implies.

I do not ignore the existence of a continuum between depression and the whole range of affective states reflected in the various classifications. Nor do I ignore the possibility of a secondary erotization of the depressive feeling and its value as a defense against more serious disorders such as depersonalization. (The latter, in my view, is the ultimate expression of denial in depressive clinical pictures—"This is not happening to me".) The erotized sadness of sweet nostalgia or the "long moments" of boredom (in German the word for boredom is *Langeweile,* literally "long moment") lead to a multiform quest for consolation: masturbation, hidden erotism, drugs, violence—phenomena all too familiar to require further elaboration. Boredom involves feelings of futility, insignificance, uselessness, emptiness, worthlessness, and lack of interest testifying to the fragility of the relationship with the outside world; as such, it could signal the next-to-last step before the final break with reality we call psychosis. The structure of nostalgia includes both awareness of the loss and recathexis of the pleasant memories—tinged with pain because redolent of disappearance or loss. One of my patients suffered from a veritable "yearning for mud"; he would lie in it, striving for the primal sensation of being encompassed, as if by a mother. He associated this dirty, depreciated substance with prostitutes ("I don't deserve anything better"). But warm mud with its heavy smell brought him contentment at the price of self-contempt.

We now come to the problem of the depressive structure, masochistically eroticized or otherwise. I shall confine my study to individuals tending to live in a depressive state, and shall examine these depressive structures through considering the characteristics of their "imagoic" world—to use the term first used in psychoanalysis by the Swiss writer Carl Spitteler (1906), who emphasized the painful distance separating the idealized imago from the imperfections of the real object.

The imagoic world, composed of the precipitates of the child's gradual separation from his mother, can not be harmonious if the separation occurred painfully and left scars. The separation can be disrupted by the death-reparation instinct brought to light by the Kleinian school. It can also be damaged, during the process involving the constitution of the child's inner world and narcissistic supplies, by a maternal attitude which either stifles the child's desire for independence or, at the other extreme, is not sufficiently "holding" or encompassing (themes addressed by Winnicott, Mahler, and others).

The depressive personality is incapable, it seems to me, of freeing himself from the problem of loss, whereas in other types of neurosis various defense mechanisms are mobilized to keep it under control and to check the harmful inner states it can engender. In neurotic patients, therefore, the depressive affect emerges only at times of change, often precipitated by a decisive event: the result is structural "decomposition," "crisis"—whatever term one chooses to give it.[3] Whatever the case, in neurotics depression remains the *signal of a loss* (often a loss of well-being through a financial setback, the loss of an external object, illness, and so on). People with depressive *structures*, on the other hand, are chronically shackled with the unresolved problem of *constant* loss, the deep-seated conviction that they are losers doomed to disappointment.

The alternative between narcissism and the object relation which grew out of a certain interpretation of Kohut (1971) is in my view contestable. I believe oral avidity and the narcissistic wound to be two aspects of a single process: the process of not receiving enough, of not having had one's fill, of being lacking, disappointed, a loser. This attitude stems from the feeling of having bitten the object and dreaded its

---

[3] The metapsychological position of the precipitating event is not clear, and calls for more thorough investigation.

retaliation, of being unsatiated and not having enough inside to feel replete, of having spit up or vomited out the object, or having encysted and immobilized it, as described in a remarkable text by Torok (1968) [see Abraham and Torok (1972) also].

It is thus that depressives (subjects with depressive structures) make desperate attempts to compel the object to provide them vital narcissistic supplies. Their unconscious thoughts are filled with fantasies about devouring individuals or parts of individuals. The depressive's attempt to *incorporate* the object is what sets him apart from the neurotic of the obsessional type, who wants to *possess* the object (*besitzen*—to sit on it); the depressive is more interested in incorporating, biting, and if necessary destroying the object than in retaining it. If he eventually realizes that he cannot be one with the object, that his dreams of fusion either with a single person or a group of persons are impossible since he enters a vicious circle of changes seen as disappointments and separations seen as wounds—if, in other words, he realizes that paradise is indeed lost—then the trauma of his representational-affective birth will be relived with the feeling of *Hilflosigkeit* (helplessness, rage, resignation, despair) and the depressive—the person with a predisposition to depression—becomes the depressed —the person actually in its grip.

Within this context, the fantasy of omnipotence strikes me as a defense through which the subject hopes to be able, once and for all, to fill the void. The fantasy is linked to an absolute denial of the transition from the pleasure principle to the reality principle, from a world without limits to internal and external worlds that are limited. In other words, it is not Kohut's predetermined "developmental line," but the return to a regressive fantasy.

The rage and hostility directed against frustrating objects will be transformed into hostility against the self, the ego. The introjection whereby the ambivalent love object was devoured and remains within the body has a sexual connotation for depressives, whose sexuality has a decidedly oral bent. Because of its sadistic nature, the introjection is perceived as dangerous and harmful. So the act of contrition follows: the last stage in the guilt-atonement-forgiveness sequence so movingly described by Rado (1927).

The assimilation of the introjects and imagos into the superego–ego ideal system (and even into the ego system) brings us to the problem of guilt. Once the introjection is consummated, the superego sadistically attacks the ego, which has already been altered by the introjection (the point, in fact, of the entire exercise was to provide the ego narcissistic supplies). The ego, under assault from the superego, dissolves in self-reproach aimed at destroying the introjected object, though in fact it is intended also to placate the superego and win its forgiveness. In these situations, suicide is a way of blackmailing the cruel superego. As Grunberger (1966) suggests, suicide, which is always cloaked in an "inner radiance," can be a desire to join a dead person, an erotized identification with death—as in Shakespeare's "if I must die, I will encounter darkness as a bride and hug it in mine arms" (*Measure for Measure*, III, i)—or an oceanic longing to return to the Mother and primary narcissism. Alternatively, it can represent the image of the ultimate orgasm, in which the subject at last becomes one with the primary object (*Urobjekt*), in

XXXPREFACE

which the omega point coincides with the alpha point, the end with the beginning, in a fantasy of eternal fusion.

Were I not afraid of overloading this introduction, I might have raised a number of other points along these lines. I decided, for instance, against broaching the relationship between depression and somatic illness (Marty, 1968), even though the problem frequently arises in the practice of psychoanalysis, because as yet it remains an enigma. I also refrained from addressing the meaning of depression in the withdrawal-rest position (Engel, 1962).

In closing, I want to say a few words about Nausikaa, a frail and touching young woman who went into analysis because, as she put it, she "could no longer put up with her own bad temper." Her situation had recently deteriorated: she no longer found any meaning in life, and her meager satisfactions were drawn from her masochism and from a kind of tyranny or vengeance wreaked upon family and friends. Her marriage seemed to be falling apart, her child brought her nothing but anxiety, and she had quarreled with her parents, could not bear her job, and had made herself hateful to her employer and her colleagues. Yet she refused to admit to depression, insisting she could overcome it with a little "good will."

The early part of the analysis was marked by a honeymoon of long duration. I was the savior, the almighty. All my attempts to interpret an underlying aggressivity were disdainfully and condescendingly denied and, even though she always found fault in what I said, I succeeded in disturbing neither her admiration for me nor her obstinate denial of any real problems. She had locked herself into a desperate hope.

Nonetheless, her reliving of this paradise lost in the early analytic period enabled her eventually to experience the disappointment she sensed in her parents, as well as her own bitter resentment. She then tried to reconstitute her omnipotence; during this period she found all my interpretations wounding and humiliating and found me disappointing, indifferent, incapable of understanding her—in short, totally alien. During this same difficult period she sorely tried my patience with her constant attempts to draw me into a sadomasochistic relationship.    Another disappointment rekindled that of having been excited by and excluded from the primal scene. It was then that the hate, rage, and violence linked to that fundamental disappointment could come out. There was no longer any trace of her earlier, somewhat literary "spleen" and philosophic disillusionment, nor of her self-satisfied complacency. She was then able to confront the primal scene, simultaneously sadomasochistic and disappointing, and all the aggression-filled identifications it aroused.

This was the turning point in the analysis; the follow-up requires little elaboration. What remained for her, after having had the courage to face up to her depression, was to overcome it. Nausikaa, in her fantasies the daughter of a king, was at last able to welcome Ulysses and his shipwrecked companions, for she chose a profession where her understanding of the disappointment of others was put to use. Her psychoanalysis did not have a romantic "happy ending"; it marked the start of a new beginning, the change from "depressive misery" to a life worth living. By confronting the frightening ocean of life, Nausikaa taught me a great deal.

I have attempted in the foregoing to sketch my psychoanalytic approach to the depressed, and especially the depressive. It is based on the integration of ideas from many sources into what I hope forms a synthesis, neither too eclectic nor too syncretic, but a coherent flow of ideas between myself and others.

# Acknowledgment

The author wishes to acknowledge gratefully the funding received from the Ministère des Affaires Culturelles in Paris for the English-speaking edition of the present work. The preparation of the original French version was made possible within the framework of the Department of Psychiatry, Medical School, University of Geneva, Geneva, Switzerland. The author is particularly indebted to Dr. Litza Hynal-Guttières for her unsparing help and advice; to Ms. Marie-Christine Beck, Ms. Dora Heer and Ms. Maud Struchen for their help in drawing up the bibliography and for their secretarial work; to Dr. Archie Hooton and Mr. Philippe Kocher for their many advices: I would also like to express my sincere thanks to the publisher, International Universities Press.

Grateful acknowledgement is also made for permission to reproduce material from the following:

K. Abraham, A short study of the development of the Libido, In: *Selected Papers of Karl Abraham*, published by The Hogarth Press Ltd., London.

K. Abraham, Notes on the psycho-analytical investigation and treatment of manic-depressive insanity, In: *Selected Papers of Karl Abraham*, published by the Hogarth Press Ltd., London.

M. Balint, New beginning and the paranoid and depressive syndromes, In: *Primary Love and Psycho-Analytic Techniques*, published by the Hogarth Press Ltd., London; permission given by Mrs. Enid Balint.

T. Benedek, Toward the biology of the depressive constellation, In: *J. Amer. Psychoanal. Assn.*, published by International Universities Press, New York.

E. Bibring, The Mechanism of Depression, In: *Affective Disorders*, ed. P. Greenacre, published by International Universities Press, New York.

J. Bowlby, Self reliance and some conditions that promote it, In: *The Making and Breaking of Affectional Bonds*, published by Tavistock Publications Ltd., London.

J. Brener & S. Freud, *Studies on Hysteria*, translated and edited by James Strachey, with the collaboration of Anna Freud, assisted by Alix Strachey and Alan Tyson. Published in the United States of America by Basic Books, Inc., by arrangement with the Hogarth Press, Ltd.

O. Fenichel, Identification, In: *Collected Papers*, published by W.W. Norton & Co. Inc., New York.

O. Fenichel, Depression and Mania, In: *The Psychoanalytic Theory of Neurosis*, published by W.W. Norton & Co. Inc., New York.

S. Freud, *An Outline of Psycho-Analysis*, published by The Hogarth Press Ltd., London, and W.W. Norton & Co., Inc., New York.

S. Freud, *The Standard Edition of the Complete Psychological Works of Sigmund Freud*, translated and edited by James Strachey, published by The Hogarth Press Ltd., London; permission given by Sigmund Freud Copyrights Ltd., The Institute of Psycho-Analysis and The Hogarth Press Ltd., London.

B. Grunberger, *Narcissism*, published by International Universities Press, New York.

E. Jones, *The Life and Work of Sigmund Freud*, vol. I, published by Basic Books, Inc., Publishers, New York.

M. Klein, A contribution to the psychogenesis of manic-depressive states, In: *Contributions to Psycho-Analysis 1921-1945*, published by The Free Press, New York; permission given by The Melanie Klein Trust and The Hogarth Press Ltd., London, and The Free Press, New York.

M. Klein, Love, guilt, and reparation, In: *The Writings of Melanie Klein;* permission given by the Melanie Klein Trust, The Hogarth Press, Ltd., London and The Free Press, New York.

M. Klein, Mourning and its relation to manic-depressive states, In: *Contributions to Psycho-Analysis 1921-1945*, published by The Free Press, New York; permission given by The Melanie Klein Trust and The Hogarth Press Ltd., London, and The Free Press, New York.

M. S. Mahler, Notes on the development of basic moods: the depressive affect, In: *Psychoanalysis, a General Psychology*, ed. Loewenstein, published by International Universities Press, New York.

M. S. Mahler, *On Human Symbiosis and the Vicissitudes of Individuation*, vol. I, published by International Universities Press, New York.

M. Schur, *Freud Living and Dying*, (letter to Fliess, Oct. 4, 1899), published by International Universities Press, New York.

D. W. Winnicott, *The theory of the parent-infant relationship*, permission given by the Author's Literary Estate and The Hogarth Press Ltd., London, International Universities Press, New York, and the International Journal of Psycho-Analysis, London.

A.H.

# Chapter 1

## Introduction

> A clash of doctrines is not a disaster—it is an opportunity.
> —*Alfred North Whitehead*

Despair and depression are as old as humanity. From the Book of Job to Gerard de Nerval's "black sun of melancholy," from St. Augustine to Nestroy, we find it described in literature and in every form of artistic expression. According to Aristotle (Problemata 30, 1), Plato and Socrates were of "melancholy temperament," an early suggestion of the connection between melancholia and creativity. Up until the nineteenth century, melancholia was often considered the distinguishing mark of genius. Later, the spleen of English dandyism, the *Wehmut* and *Heimweh* of German romanticism, the nostalgia of the French romantics,

1

were in fact nothing other than slight depressions endowed with cultural value. Walther von der Vogelweide spoke of it *(Wehmut)* and Ronsard wrote: "I can not tear out this mood whose slave I be."

The "sweetest melancholy" of the Shakespearean period became the *Sorge* of Goethe (is it too far-fetched to think here of Winnicott's "concern"?), the spleen of Pope, and, later, the *malheur du monde* of Baudelaire and Verlaine, the *Weltunglück* of Trakl. "Nausea," a literary expression current at the end of the eighteenth century and the beginning of the nineteenth was revived in our own day by Sartre and is another cultural variation of the eternal melancholia. Goethe, in *Dichtung und Wahrheit,* speaks of "the greatest ill, the gravest sickness: life is seen as a nauseating burden."

But let us leave aside the history of melancholia. Qualified authors have studied it in depth (e.g., Fischer-Homberger, 1968), although some have raised the question of whether the continuity lies in the problem itself (Wyrsch, 1965) or merely in its verbal expression (Starobinski, 1960).

It was around 50 A.D. that Aretea of Cappadocia, in the tradition of the Hippocratic writings, set down a description of the melancholic symptoms similar to ours: despondency, fixed ideas, diminution of mental capacities, anxiety, superstition, sudden changes of mood.

"Creative suffering" has been described by writers of remarkable introspection. St. John of the Cross, the Spanish mystic, attempted to differentiate melancholia from "the true dark night of the soul": the one who traverses the "dark night" can find consolation only in constant preoccupation with God (in sublimation!) and should follow the directives of his spiritual advisor. (Today we might suggest that he should go into analysis; the special relationship with one's confessor was a foreshadowing of transference.)

Hamlet appears to tread the border between obsession and depression. The link between the two states, here illuminated by genius, had to wait more than three centuries for Karl Abraham to work out its scientific formulation, just as the fundamental truth contained in the Oedipus myth had to await Freud.

During the Restoration "men of action" made the term "melancholy" a pejorative and used it to belittle intellectuals.

Melancholia has fascinated figurative artists, Michelangelo and Dürer prominent among them (Dürer's *Melancholia* is reputed to have been inspired by a description of Aristotle). For centuries, depression was considered the preeminent mark of genius in artists, testifying to their ability to penetrate the very depths of the soul and to attain creative contemplation. Ronsard believed that boredom and melancholia were the price he had to pay for his creativity:

> As for me, dear Grévin, if my unworthy name
> Boasts some modest honor, too costly is its fame
> . . . . .
> Of Permessa's draining waves having tasted
> I am weary, sad and wasted
> . . . . .
> Fierce, forelorn, mistrusting and melancholy
> . . . . . [Pierre de Ronsard, 1938, p. 921]

With these scattered historical allusions I have attempted to show that despair, like a subterranean river, courses uninterrupted through human history even if not always visible, rising to the surface now and then under different forms and with different manifestations. The suggestion is often made—though no scientific data is offered in its support—that depression is more widespread during certain historical periods, our own among them.

We have in passing touched upon the problem of despair in its existential, historical, and sociological aspects, but what *specifically* can psychoanalysis teach us about it? What is the value of psychoanalytic studies establishing the link between depression and man's capacity to internalize, between the experience of infantile sexuality and later limitations on pleasure? What is the value of elucidating or dwelling upon one's fantasied self-image, instincts in general, disappointing experiences, change and loss?

Despair is not melancholia, though it may sometimes lead to it. It is a concomitant of helplessness, with us from infancy to the end of our days, acting as the driving force behind mental development. Its importance was clearly brought out by Melanie Klein.

Writers and artists frequently served as Freud's guides in the study of despair and may serve us in a similar capacity even today. Indeed, it would be unthinkable to discuss the subject without reference to Kierkegaard. As a result of deep personal introspection, he was able in his *The Sickness Unto Death* (1849) to give a remarkable phenomenological description of despair and to apprehend certain of the dynamic forces underpinning it. He emphasizes the role of guilt and the problem of the nonintegration of Evil, as well as the positive function of despair as a source of personal maturation; the depressive position of the Kleinians may in fact be viewed as germinally present in this work of genius.

I shall attempt to relate these dynamic forces to certain central formulations of Freudian theory. It is obvious that only taken as a whole can provide us a picture of the lines of force leading to despair and flowing from it: "We have no way of conveying knowledge of a complicated set of simultaneous events except by describing them successively; and thus it happens that all our accounts are at fault to begin with owing to one-sided simplification and must wait till they can be supplemented, built on to, and so set right" (Freud, 1940a, p. 205).

In each of the chapters to follow we shall examine one facet of this whole, hoping that the thoughts and ideas which have filtered through our psychoanalytic experience will provide some insight into the meaning of despair, its roots both in human history and in each one of us. I feel justified in this hope because psychoanalysis and despair are intertwined in so many ways. Frequently it is despair that leads the subject to psychoanalytic treatment, which then becomes in a manner of speaking the *scene* of despair, whose shadow, moreover, is present throughout the therapy.

But are there not still deeper connections between the two, including the notions of inner change, loss, and transformation? Can despair, as part of a general problem of change whose paradigm is mourning, increase our understanding of human development in general and psychoanalytic treatment in particular? In other words, can it help us better understand the metapsychology of the process of treatment and of change? Going even farther, can we apprehend in despair something specifically human, something that plays a central role in the cultural process itself and—without venturing out of the psychoanalytic experience into the domain of philosophy—teach us more about human nature and culture?

My point of departure, then, is the depressive affect, a feeling related to the notion of change. It seems to me that if anxiety is the signal of danger, the depressive affect is a signal of *change* in a *negative* sense; that is to say, it is a signal of *loss*. Everything flowing from loss—introjection, working through, sublimation—is triggered by the depressive affect. Its first appearance, whether during the depressive position of Melanie Klein or at the time of Mahler's separation-individuation, is linked to the awareness of a change—such as weaning or separation—or directly to the problem of aggression as defined by Melanie Klein. External changes demand internal ones. This is the meaning of mourning: that adjustment is necessary, from the very moment we're born. Changes that occur during psychoanalysis likewise give rise to depression. Thus, in a way, therapy becomes a reliving of the separations experienced from our earliest moments. Through therapy, we come to appreciate the importance Melanie Klein attaches to the depressive position.

Depressive feelings of abandonment or emptiness are related to narcissism (Grunberger, Kernberg, Kohut). But in my opinion, narcissism plays its predominant role in conjunction with aggression. There is no pure narcissism outside libidinal-objective and aggressive contexts, and to my mind this is the most important objection that can be raised against Kohut. The need to focus my study compels me to ignore or in any case push to the periphery certain subjects, including "depressive equivalents" (addictions, anorexia, etc.) and defenses against depression (especially mania).

Throughout my survey of depression I have tried to situate the thoughts of the authors I cite in their original context so as to do them justice to the fullest extent possible. As to organization, the subject will be treated both synchronically, as it appears to me today, and diachronically, separating out the historical strands of its formulation in psychoanalytic theory. In this regard, it is perhaps superfluous to mention that any undertaking of this type must of necessity be selective; for this I take full responsibility. My choices reflect my personal thoughts and predilections based on my own training and clinical experience.

The more personal Part I, reflecting my own views, will be followed by the exclusively historical Part II, which traces the historical development of psychoanalytic thought on depression. The whole, I hope, will occasion many questions regarding the universal phenomenon of depression, its origins and its resolution through therapy and the creative process—questions, in short, that might give us a better understanding of these depressives we all are.

Freud "did not merely reduce the rich and profuse polysemia of symptoms and symbols . . . he discovered something more unknown and more useful: the functioning of the dream, mourning, treatment, creation" (Anzieu, 1975, p. 749).

The bibliographic study of so vast a subject shows the existence of several distinct psychoanalytic languages, various authors expressing themselves through different metaphors and formulations though addressing the same clinical phenomena. Further diversity arises from the choice of patients studied: thus, the depressives treated by Edith Jacobson are borderline cases quite different from, say, Pasche's subjects suffering from inferiority depressions. I am convinced that the different metaphors reflect differences in knowledge or perception, and also, perhaps, in the level reached in probing the inner worlds of the depressives being dealt with. I have tried to avoid the facile eclecticism of merely juxtaposing these thoughts: these metaphors touch upon multiple dimensions, and it is the author's task to forge a synthesis. The pluralism—linguistic and otherwise—of the psychoanalytic world is readily apparent in the professional literature: This fact, hopefully, will incite to tolerance, and I invite the reader's forbearance if the metaphors I use in either part of the work do not coincide with his own. Indeed, we have left far behind the era when the psychoanalytic vocabulary was the work of a single man, Sigmund Freud (though even then, it should be noted, certain minor variations in language were introduced by authors such as Federn and Tausk in their attempts to shed light on areas more or less neglected by Freud). In the absence today of any such unimpeachable authority, that single language has given way to many dialects. In any event, in conveying what various authors reported from the inner worlds of depressives (often translating it, *nolens volens*, into our own language), I have endeavored to remain faithful to their meaning.

If the present work can lay claim to any originality, I would hope that it is in its concentration on the

processes linked to the depressive *affect* (as encountered in analytic practice) and in its treatment of depressive illness as only one of the possible outcomes
of these processes, another being cultural creativity.

# Part I

# Chapter 2

# The Depressive Affect

> Many are those who find life not bit-
> ter, but very empty.
>
> —*Seneca*

The depressive affect belongs to man's repertory of responses. Like anxiety, depression or the depressive feeling is a universal subjective experience of human development, one of the ways in which man attempts to overcome his conflicts, frustration, disappoint-ments, and losses. Again like anxiety, depression is at once an affective experience with general psycho-logical significance and the principal symptom, char-

13

acteristic and well-defined, of a serious regressive clinical picture.[1]

Compared to anxiety, the elaboration of which is central to the theory of affectivity, depression has been rather neglected in psychoanalytic theory. As early as 1911, Karl Abraham wrote:

> Whereas states of morbid anxiety have been dealt with in detail in the literature of psycho-analysis, depressive states have hitherto received less attention. [And yet, as he stressed:] the affect of depression is as widely spread among all forms of neuroses and psychoses as is that of anxiety. . . . Anxiety and depression are related to each other in the same way as are fear and grief. We fear a coming evil; we grieve over one that has occurred. [Abraham, 1911b, p. 137]

For Bibring,

> anxiety and depression represent diametrically opposed basic ego responses. Anxiety as a reaction to (external or internal) danger indicates the ego's desire to survive. The ego, challenged by the danger, mobilizes the signal of anxiety and prepares for fight or flight. In depression, the opposite takes place, the ego is paralyzed because it finds itself incapable to meet the "danger." [Bibring, 1953, pp. 34–35]

Abraham attempted in his writings (1911b, 1924)

---

[1] Anxiety and depression in my view have a particular dignity, both affects having a specific neurophysiological foundation (they are the two affects which can be treated pharmacologically). Anxiety and mourning—the latter being the paradigm of the depressive affect—can in a way be said to belong to man's basic biophysiological apparatus.

to approach and interpret depressive illness by studying patients suffering from severe depressions. In 1895 Freud described what he called melancholia as "a psychical inhibition accompanied by instinctual impoverishment and pain that this should be so" (1950a, p. 107). If we add to this the role of the superego and the loss of instinctual life, we have our current definition, likewise anticipated by Freud in the same work: "Melancholia consists in mourning over loss of libido" (p. 103). We should of course bear in mind that Freud often uses the term melancholia where we would speak of depression (Strachey, 1966, p. 192).

It was Abraham who first advanced the hypothesis later developed by Edith Jacobson (1946, 1953), namely, that *disappointment* at an oedipal level reinforces and revives in a regressive fashion unresolved pregenital conflicts which in turn trigger recurrent depressive response, subsequent disappointments and losses. Rado (1927) saw analogies between the infant's experience and the attitude of the depressed person's ego to his own superego. As we know, Melanie Klein and her school postulated a universal infantile depressive position whose general characteristics would determine the depressive response in adulthood. Indeed, there is a consensus concerning the role of infantile experience in the predisposition to depression. Authors as far apart as Abraham, Jacobson, Rado, and Spitz have underlined the similarities between the depressive illness of the adult and the affective responses of the infant, even if Spitz (Spitz and Wolf, 1946) clearly distinguishes what he calls anaclitic depression from adult depression, a condition in which the role of the superego is stressed. Other authors—Bowlby (1946), Rank (1949), Mahler (1968), Rochlin (1965)—emphasize the significance of early disruptions leading ultimately to a deficit. One might speak here of a prehistory of depressive vulnerability—Therese Benedek's lack of "confident expectation," Erikson's lack of "basic trust." An entire literature exists on the subject of "deprivation," introduced by Bowlby (1952; see also Nacht and Racamier, 1959). Rado (1927) also attributed to the very earliest stages this need for narcissistic support, this need for love as a narcissistic confirmation, this clinging to the partner as if to merge. Abraham (1911b) showed the role of aggression and ambivalence: the depressive realizes that something "paralyzes his capacity to love," the something being his ambivalence and the latent aggressive tendencies within him. According to Freud and Abraham, the withdrawal from the external world and real objects characteristic of depressive illness implies complete internalizations forcing depressive patients to turn their unmastered aggression against themselves (following their identification with devalued and aggressed objects).

In all the various ways of approaching the subject, predisposition to manifest depression is seen to follow an early vulnerability related to processes of *identification* and to the problem of *aggression*. The literature of psychoanalysis is virtually unanimous on this point, though the terminology varies from author to author. In Abraham's classification of mental illnesses according to libidinal level (1924), depression is situated at the level of orality; more specifically, it is structured around oral narcissistic problems.

It is possible that predisposition to depression grows out of the inability to pass gradually through the developmental stages, a passage requiring the relinquishment of objects or aspects of the object. There is an inability to make the progressive transition from the pleasure principle to the reality principle, with all that this implies in terms of renunciation and loss. The inability to recathect, to detach oneself from infantile ideas—omnipotence most especially—is perhaps one way of defining depressive vulnerability. Moreover, this might also explain why events or crises (the nature of which remains to be defined in psychoanalytic theory) trigger depression at times of major *changes:* adolescence, marriage, first child, "midlife crisis," retirement, changes of residence, city, country, etc.

Melanie Klein almost never used the term "narcissism," yet the theme is not absent from her work: it can be interpreted as the acquisition of a basic security through a metabolism of introjection and projection in which aggression (the death wish) plays an important role. Kohut's study (1971) on the consolidation of basic narcissism neglects the role of the aggressive drive and the conflicts that can arise between the libido and aggression. This is astonishing when one thinks that as early as 1926 Ernest Jones (1926) wrote: "There is every reason to think that the concept of the superego is a nodal point where we may expect all the obscure problems of Oedipus complex and narcissism on the one hand, and hate and sadism on the other, to meet" (p. 188).

According to Edith Jacobson (1946), the depressive's superego is formed following a disappointment relating to the parental imagos, which revives the introjections of the pregenital period. Another formulation is that the disappointing oedipal imagos pushed the child either to pregenitality or toward a negative Oedipus complex extremely difficult to analyze. In Kleinian terms, the latter would involve introjection of the parents as damaged or destroyed by the child's aggressiveness, which in turn was probably born of disappointment. Jacobson, then, seems to attribute depression to the child's feelings of guilt and responsibility for his parents' deficiencies. Melanie Klein (1934, 1940) suggests that the child, like the adult, completes the process of mourning and overcomes depression upon successful introjection of a predominantly good object. Other authors, such as Rochlin (1965), believe the child incapable of this; depressive vulnerability arises from the fact that the work of mourning cannot be brought to a successful conclusion. The failure of this experience will leave scars, a sort of infirmity in a part of the ego.

"Mourning has a very distinct psychic task to perform, namely, to detach the memories and expectations of the survivors from the dead" (Freud, 1912–1913, p. 65). In "Inhibitions, Symptoms and Anxiety" (1926d, p. 87), Freud distinguishes between anxiety triggered by the danger of losing object (for example) and the sadness or grief triggered by the actual object loss.[2] In our elaborations, we must bear in mind the ubiquity of anxiety and depression and the fact that they are inherently neither normal nor pathological, but may equally well be either.

[2] In the same work he mentions the anxiety experienced upon encountering strangers: "the situation of the infant when he is presented with a stranger instead of his mother. He will exhibit the anxiety which we have attributed to the danger of loss of object. But his anxiety is undoubtedly more complicated than this and merits a more thorough discussion" (p. 169).

Depression, then, refers to the past, anxiety to the future. In the second Freudian topography, anxiety signals a danger which threatens (from the present toward the future), while depression, or sadness, is triggered by the perception of having been diminished in relation to something, the feeling of *inadequacy* arising from the gap between the image of what we were and had, or what we wanted to be and have, compared to what we have become or have lost. This thought can also be understood as the expression of a *fait accompli*.[3] The feeling of *fait accompli*, that nothing can be done ("ruined forever," as one of my patients put it), comes out very clearly in what is perhaps the first case of depression Freud cites as such, in Letter 102 to Wilhelm Fliess (January 16, 1899):

> One patient (whom I cured with the help of the fantasy key) was continually plunged into despair by the gloomy conviction that she was useless, good for nothing, etc. I always thought that in early childhood she must have seen her mother in a similar state, in an attack of real melancholia. That was in conformity with the earlier theory, but in two years there was no confirmation of it. It now turns out that at the age of fourteen she discovered an *atresia hymenalis* in herself and *despaired* of ever being able to function fully as a woman, etc. [1899, p. 273; italics mine]

These images, ideas, notions center on the depres-

---

[3] To be wounded, hurt, is different from being anxious or depressed, even though a wound can call to mind the narcissistic wounds experienced as definitive, irreparable, thus triggering the depressive affect.

sive affect: the past, *loss* (often in relation to an *ideal image*), and the problem of *traumatism*,[4] that is, of a memory representing this loss. From the standpoint of the affective organization of memory, we might note the difference between anxiety, where the image of the past is evoked as a future possibility (for example, castration anxiety), and depression, where the loss is experienced as definitive.

Margaret Mahler (1966) was able to observe elational and depressive responses to experiences of gratification and frustration in children at extremely early ages. These responses can also function as a signal, like Freud's anxiety signal; while their role is not comparable to the central role of anxiety, it is certainly analogous to that in other affective states; "One cannot, after all, help suspecting that the reason why the affect of anxiety occupies a unique position in the economy of the mind has something to do with the essential nature of danger. . . ." (Freud, 1926d, p. 150).[5]

Mahler has amply demonstrated that there is al-

---

[4] "Traumatic," according to Freud (1926d, Appendix), is that which keeps alive or reawakens the feeling of *Hilflosigkeit*.

[5] Certain notions formulated by various post-Freudians should be clarified, namely, the depressive position, depressive anxiety, and depression. It seems to me that depressive *anxiety*, as formulated in Klein's *Envy and Gratitude* (1957), contains a *doubt* concerning the good object and the fear that the unleashing of bad instincts—the death instinct—will destroy it. *Depression*, on the other hand, implies loss, the conviction of a *fait accompli*, and a feeling of *powerlessness*. The *depressive position*, or as Winnicott would later call it, "the stage of concern," is reached when the child becomes aware for the first time, and settles in when the subject feels helpless, having lost the good object with the feeling of having killed it (mourning).

ways an instinctual conflict present in infantile depressions. In her view, this fundamental conflict is similar in all depressive states: frustration gives rise to rage and to hostile (aggressive) attempts to procure the desired gratification. If the ego is not capable, for internal or external reasons, of reaching its goal, this aggression is turned against the image of self. What follows is a loss of self-esteem, which is the expression of the narcissistic conflict, that is, a conflict between the ideal or wishful self-image and the deflated self-image—the self which has been unable to live up to its ideal (J. de Saussure, 1971). The nature of the affect will depend on the intensity of the hostility and, obviously, on the gravity and duration of the frustration and disappointment.

My intention is not to delve deeply into narcissistic problems and disorders, but rather to focus on their depressive underpinnings. As Kohut proposed in 1971, we can consider narcissism as a developmental line, the approach to the oedipal problem giving rise in certain cases to a depressive affect connected to a narcissistic disorder. Freud (1914c) relates the formation of the ego ideal to man's inability to "give up the satisfaction he once enjoyed." While the need to focus our study prevents us from considering the narcissistic aspect of depression in relation to the ego ideal, the reader interested in pursuing this dimension can profitably turn to the brilliant report of Chasseguet-Smirgel (1973).

Pierre Luquet (1973) distinguishes two different levels of ego ideal: an archaic and dangerous level linked to the imagoic system and conditioning the ego's equilibrium, and a level orienting narcissism and playing a role in the representation of the "I" and its aspirations (the ideal of the I). Disturbances of the first level result in illnesses of ideality (depression, character neuroses, etc.) while those of the second define illness of "an-ideality" (scleroticizing and operatory illnesses).[6]

Abraham (1916, 1924) highlighted the importance of the oral zone for understanding the depressive constellation; the mechanism of introjection was first brought out by Freud (1917e). Rado (1927) described the child's hunger sequence, his immense craving for gratifications. In a like manner, the depressive depends on the oral-narcissistic gratification provided by an external object—the "external narcissistic supplies" Fenichel (1945) spoke of.

But the depressive has no monopoly on this "narcissistic object" (to use Kohut's term). Bowlby stresses the persistence of a certain independence in the relations of "normal" persons, and indeed, the ideal of total autonomy devoid of any need for an external object, functioning in a state of perfect narcissistic autarky, does not have much reality. Nonetheless, while it is true that everyone depends on the libidinal *and* narcissistic gratifications provided by the Other, in the depressive there is an excessive dependence on narcissistic provision of love, attention, and affection to maintain his self-esteem. ("Compliments are my life's blood," a patient of mine once said.) The narcissistic pathology of depressives, scarcely touched upon here, has been dealt with in depth in recent works devoted to narcissism (Grunberger, 1971; Ko-

[6] If I understand Luquet correctly, this "I" corresponds to what other writers call the "self," the individual's representational system.

hut, 1971; Kernberg, 1975). Glover (1955) describes two depressives in whom oral constructions represented a defensive reaction against the oedipal situation, both cases touched off by the trauma of circumcision following the birth of a rival brother.

The grossly magnified image of the Other and his omnipotence, coupled with the sense of one's own narcissistic lack, is intimately related to the issue of dependence. Indeed, such felt inadequacy necessarily implies dependence on the Other. The notion of one's lack, one's worthlessness (the all-powerful object is dead), is related to the "ideal ego" of Lagache and the "grandiose self" of Kohut. Flournoy (1975) speaks of the "vector of emptiness."

Raymond de Saussure (1934) emphasized the importance of analyzing the ego state, the narcissistic dimension of inferiority feelings. In one of my patients, whose chronic depression was exacerbated by her anxieties about aging, the wishful self-image involved the recollection of a childhood without problems, where everything was good, where she was the best, in harmony with her environment and those around her. The transition to adulthood was experienced as the beginning of inadequacy. Problems emerged; she was no longer ideal. Nor was she able any longer to maintain her feeling of conforming to her ideal, and she suffered chronically a sense of having failed.

Disappointment is often linked as well to a gap between the ideal image of the world, the image one expects and looks forward to (it will be like this or that), and the reality of the facts (the world as it is): the "rude awakening" implied in the Spanish *desengaño*.

With the relinquishment of real and/or fantasized aspects of objects (the result of the intrapsychic weaving together of experience and fantasy, as brought out in Freud's work), the experience of self changes; the loss of the object brings about a change in how one experiences oneself, for instance, in the transition from one level of well-being to another in childhood development, or during changes in the cultural environment or changes occurring in analysis. Joffe and Sandler (1965) believe that loss of the sense of well-being has a greater influence on affect than loss of self-esteem. In their view, loss of the sense of well-being is compensated by the acquisition of new modes of well-being; this diminishes the feeling of dependence on the all-powerful mother and involves a certain pleasure, thus affecting the representations of the self. In other words, acquisitions (introjections) of good aspects may make it possible for one to compensate for the pain of loss or abandonment. Joffe and Sandler's "loss of sense of well-being" and Jacobson's "self-regard" (1971) refer to the same clinical fact, a point also made by Winnicott (1971).

Rado uses the phenomena of love and self-esteem as the starting point for his "The Problem of Melancholia" (1927). Persons with a predisposition to depression have an intense need for narcissistic gratification. Since their sense of self-worth hinges on constant reassurance of love, support, and encouragement rather than on real values or achievements, it may be shaken by the most innocuous remark. These subjects struggle to attract love and support, hence their aggressiveness in response to a threat of withdrawal of love and their feeling that the loss of the object is the supreme injustice. Their first reaction is indignant rebellion; if this fails to achieve its goal, they try to move or touch the object by expiation—this is one of Rado's original interpretations of the phase of remorse and self-punishment that follows loss. In analysis we often encounter subjects locked in a masochistic position who attempt, through self-sabotage and resistance to change, to move the object (the mother or the analyst) and who are incapable of moving beyond this situation for fear of losing all power over the object. Self-accusations can likewise be maneuvers aimed at extorting gratification or satisfying dependency needs. For Rado (1927), depression is a "great despairing cry for love"; the inability to go through mourning often stems from the inability to be vulnerable, to feel oneself in a situation of weakness or supplication. In melancholia, the object whose pardon the subject is seeking is the superego, an agency rooted in identification with the parents. As for the sequence guilt-atonement-forgiveness, Rado proposes another determinant in earliest infancy: the chain hunger-rage-gratification: the child's hunger upon awakening, his impotent rage in the absence of his mother (kicking and screaming followed by exhaustion), and finally the reappearance of the mother and the "oral narcissistic bliss" while being fed at the breast. With the child's development and the emergence of the superego, the sensual relationship with the parents is repressed and becomes unconscious; repressed guilt connected with genitality gives way to conscious guilt linked to aggression. The sequence guilt-atonement-forgiveness will depend on the preceding series hunger-rage-gratification. Thus the hunger situation will become the deepest fixation point for the subsequent model: "the situation of threatened loss of love." In other words, the satisfaction of being at the mother's breast and receiving her care fulfills the infantile need for security. Rado postulates an "alimentary orgasm" here that becomes the prototype of the future genital climate, the fulfillment of desires for an emerging object relationship and the narcissistic satisfactions that attend it.

Insofar as depression follows loss, disappointment, and other painful but inevitable hardships, the depressive experience may be said to be one of the necessary preconditions for optimal maturation (Zetzel, 1970). In the last analysis, what is involved is a sense of loss of self-esteem following experiences of powerlessness that recall similar situations of the child's fundamental powerlessness; hence the need described by Helene Deutsch (1929) for a "protector-companion." Fenichel (1945) speaks of a sort of mystical union with the all-powerful object, the subject seeking to become "companion" to the lost object, to share his food, to become his substance even as the object becomes the subject's. In the same context Modell (1963) evokes "object hunger" as an attempt to avoid even minimal losses and disappointments. Although Greenson (1959) asserts that the prototype of depression occurs later in psychological development than that of primary anxiety, I would argue that the two affects are bound together from earliest infancy and that any attempt to reconstitute them remains fraught with as yet unverifiable hypotheses. What Anny Katan (1972) calls distress[7] is a mixture

[7] In an article alluding to a correspondence with Anna Freud, Anny Katan suggests using "distress" instead of "separation anxiety."

of anxiety and depression that likewise occurs in adulthood. This distress in relation to the traumatic situation is precipitated by separations: in the course of analysis, parting from the analyst at the end of a session frequently triggers anxiety, depression, rage, attempts to move the analyst to pity—in short, a mixed reaction to a traumatic situation. It is hardly surprising that Freud (1926d) had great difficulty, even as late as 1926, drawing clear lines between depression, anxiety, and pain; we experience similar difficulties in concrete clinical situations where the precise distinctions of our conceptual framework frequently prove rather difficult to apply.

What we can say is that the ego changes in the depressive affect include a breakdown in self-esteem and feelings of primary helplessness experienced as a narcissistic wound (Bibring, 1953). The subjective feeling of powerlessness that is present in the traumatic experience has clear depressive implications (Gitelson, 1958). For persons with low depressive vulnerability this type of reaction is temporary and reversible; the outcome will also depend, needless to say, on the importance of the traumatic experience. At one extreme is the experience of well-being and at the other that of panic, with varying degrees of dissonance, pain, and despair marked by reproaches and unsatisfied expectations in between. In my view there is a continuity in the semantic range expressing the affects, a vocabulary whose referents in underlying unconscious forces we shall attempt to delimit: pain, suffering, grief, affliction, desolation, torment, sorrow, sadness, and then also boredom, fatigue, lassitude, morosity, spleen, languor, nostalgia, emptiness, disgust, despair, melancholia. Sadness and pain do not imply a conflict as complicated or as tinged with aggression as does depression.

The communicative aspect of depression implies an entire infraverbal communication, a call for help, for consolation, but at the same time a refusal of help, an insistence on showing oneself inconsolable. The latter stance is often part of the masochistic position and sometimes proves difficult to break out of. Certain psychoanalysts, Imre Hermann (1943) for example, have stressed the communicative aspect of the affects in general.

Hope—the confident cathexis of an image of self and its future potentialities—is the opposite of depression: it is the feeling that the hurt is not definitive, that reparation is possible, that there is no *fait accompli*. In "Inhibitions, Symptoms and Anxiety" Freud (1926d), describes the infant who "cannot as yet distinguish between temporary absence and permanent loss. As soon as he misses his mother he behaves as if he were never going to see her again; and repeated consolatory experiences to the contrary are necessary before he learns that her disappearance is usually followed by her reappearance" (p. 169). This will serve as a description of the birth of hope.

We do not know how the so-called constitutional factor operates. Is it really at the level of increased oral erotism (Abraham, 1924; Ribble, 1943; Fries and Woolf, 1953a, b; Burton and Derbyshire, 1958), or is there a kind of constitutional reaction in neonates, certain of them withdrawing more readily (into sleep-retreat) when confronted with difficulties (e.g., first contact with the breast) while others cry and struggle? It is possible that these reactional modes depend partially on an inborn constitutional *anlage*, which would then have to receive various reinforcements to fully develop. That the affects have some connection with biology seems plausible given their survival function (e.g., the infant's protest upon being left alone, which then dies down after a period of acute agitation) and their existence in animals. In man they are obviously linked to language and distortions of language and in the animal to forms of social communication. Moreover, depression in animals follows a concrete loss, while in man it can follow the loss of an internalized object.

This is where the theory of the object's metabolization comes in, involving the relation with the primal object and its various aspects: separation from the primal object, narcissistic supplies, the imprint of the primal object organized in the ego ideal, the subsequent vicissitudes of this ego ideal, and, naturally, the consequences relating to objects of triangulation.

I have approached one aspect of this whole via the opposed but related feelings of powerlessness and omnipotence, another through introjection. What remains are various theoretical problems regarding narcissism, problems meriting an entire work in themselves.

If the affect of anxiety functions biologically as an alarm signal preparatory to a struggle, depression should be seen as part of the equipment designed to insure the relation with the mother: depressive affect, insofar as it emerges following the acute anxiety phase and in the event of definitive loss, makes decathexis possible. This process, as described by Bowlby (1961a), occurs in three stages: the first is protest (separation anxiety); the second comprises emotions ranging from sadness to despair (depression); the third is detachment, making survival possible in the event of permanent loss. Following Freud, we might speculate that the biological significance of depression is withdrawal following a loss. According to Charles Rycroft (1968), "This kind of neurotic depression needs to be distinguished from apathy, which is analogous to putting the car in neutral, a procedure which can be life-saving in situations of long-continued frustration and deprivation in which the retention of feeling would lead to impotent rage and exhaustion. . . ." Ralph Greenson (1949) points out that in Japanese prison camps the survival rate was higher for American POWs who remained apathetic than for those who rebelled and continued to hope.

If psychoanalysis is the study of "lack," depression can be considered as a particular way of living this lack. Given that the phallus is the desired object, one must accept the fact that one does not of necessity possess it (fear of the possibility of castration). A renunciation is required in the oedipal triangle, as one of the parents and, ultimately, the idea of intrusion in the couple must be set aside. The lack, then, the "need to renounce," is a human task closely bound up with the oedipal constellation; the depressive affect emerges if this task is accompanied by a painful sense of definitive renunciation, by disillusionment experienced as a wound. The "lack" refers to the problem of castration, but through introjection and fantasy it can also be experienced as a void, a lack of structuration of psychic space, something hollow and absent. An absence of spatial structuration leads to lack of structuration in the psychic agencies, and to what Edith Jacobson (1953) describes as a blurred boundary between the superego–ego ideal on the one hand and the ego on the other. It is not only the lack, then, but a nostalgia for an impossible incest (as well as the temptation to parricide that links depression to the Oedipus complex.

As for the cognitive functions in depression, the accent must be placed on the absence or abolition of mental representations, the self-image, and satisfying external stimuli. In the theory of affect, the tension discharge aspect takes precedence over the communicative. And yet our task as psychoanalysts consists first and foremost of receiving, reflecting, and working through the affective communication of the Other, what can be summarized in the term *countertransference*. We are daily confronted with depressive affect communicated to us. I consider this a crucial aspect of the psychoanalyst's experience, one which must be understood theoretically. I will attempt to approach the depressive phenomenon from this standpoint, in the hope of adding my stone to the edifice of a psychoanalytic theory of affect. While André Green's theoretical construction (1970) is admirable, I would like to take an opposite tack and begin with elementary affects such as anxiety and depression. The depressive affect, as already mentioned, relates to a negative change or loss—of a loved object, of cathexis of the self, of capacities of the self. It is here that the acts resulting in loss of the superego's love or the love of the superego–ego ideal system must be situated. According to Federn (1952), cathexis of the ego is experienced as "ego feeling," and the libidinal component carrying the ego's consciousness is responsible for the ability to develop a sense of reality by distinguishing internal processes from those of the external world. The affect can be understood as a feeling of the ego, either elation or resignation. The depressive affect is linked to detachment from object representations and thus to the metapsychological problem of cathexis and decathexis.

Depression is not only a nosological entity. In the final analysis, this affective state seems related less to a structure than to a *change* of structure—a change experienced through tensions between the ego ideal and the superego and giving rise to disappointment.

Psychoanalysts, as Balint (1961) remarked, see a relatively small number of patients and hence have not taken an interest in diagnostics and nosology. While it is true that our method does not compel us to address these concerns, this does not mean that we are oblivious to the nosological problem or that of the psychic structure related to it. The depressive affect, like anxiety, is triggered in clearly defined circumstances: it always coincides with a real or imagined loss (including loss of self-esteem arising from the gap between the ego ideal and the ego) experienced as final and therefore involving an element of resignation. If we accept this basic definition, we will find ourselves confronted with a continuous series of depressive forms ranging from anaclitic depression to internalized depression, depending on the defenses and restorative processes set in motion, the extent of the regression, and the force of the underlying aggression (some would say the force of the death instinct).[8]

---

[8] Anaclitic depression as defined by Spitz and Wolf (1946) occurs when the infant is deprived of his mother (the anaclitic object). Spitz believed that "the dynamic structure of anaclitic depression is fundamentally different from depression in the

The nosological site of depression is uncertain: Freud initially classed it among the psychoses, under the heading "melancholia." But very early on, in 1895 to be precise, he put the affect of melancholia in the same category as mourning, "that is, longing for something that is lost. Thus in melancholia there is probably a question of a loss—a loss in the subject's instinctual life" (1950a, p. 103). He added that *"melancholia consists in mourning over loss of libido."* Freud thus quickly realized that depression is not always psychotic. In the same draft he contrasted anxiety and depressive affect, noting that "any neurosis easily takes on a melancholic stamp. Thus, whereas potent individuals easily acquire anxiety neuroses, impotent ones incline to melancholia" (p. 107).

As noted previously, uncertainty as to the depressive affect's nosological position stems from the fact that it follows a change in structure—it does not matter whether this change is hysterical or obsessional, or even if it tends toward psychosis. In other words, depression is the sequel to neurotic structural decomposition in any form. It is here that we should evoke, with Green (1967), the death instinct or deathly narcissism.

One of my patients sees herself as "a machine for

adult" because of the absence of a superego at that age. To distinguish between them, Blatt (1974) called depressions in the adult "introjective depressions" to reflect the idea that the adult becomes depressed in relation to an introject. But the difference is perhaps not so clear-cut. What are called "reactional" depressions are often nothing but depressions caused by the loss of an anaclitic object in a regressed adult; the same can be said of prolonged or pathological mourning. We should not lose sight of the importance, particularly in depressives, of the anaclitic (oral-narcissistic) object.

doing evil." If she were to undergo a significant regression, this machine could be expelled and replaced by Tausk's "influencing machine"—the fantasy of paranoia. But she managed to keep herself from slipping into psychotic alienation, albeit at the price of depression.

Although Abraham (1924) and a number of authors after him (e.g., Fenichel, 1945) argued the existence of an exclusive link between depression and the obsessional character, today this viewpoint has few adherents. At the same time, a decline in the great hysteric syndromes has been noted in our day, accompanied by a rise in depressive syndromes. Should we attribute this situation to sociocultural changes, for instance to the fact that hysterics are less tolerated today and hence receive less gratification than previously?

Neurotic depressions are distinguished from melancholia, which is characterized by a disintegration in drives and assaults on the ego by the ego ideal. Certain writers, such as Klauber (1967), continue to suspect that even neurotic depressions have an underlying layer of melancholia (on this point, see also Barande, 1975).

In my opinion the depressive affect, like anxiety, can be found in all structurations. It seems to me that it is linked less to a particular structuration than to structural changes (decompositions, crises, etc.). In this I see an analogy with anxiety, which by definition would be eliminated in stabilized neurotic structures. Similarly, the depressive affect appears not in a stable, rigid, neurotic structure but at times of changes in this structure. By contrast, what we call "depressive characteropathy" or "chronic neurotic depression" can be considered a structure (by analogy with the anxiety neurosis).

I shall not further elaborate these ideas. The point I wish to make is that depression occurs over a very wide spectrum, ranging from so-called normal depression (whose paradigm is mourning) to psychotic states (melancholia in the true sense of the word). The psychoanalytic study of depressive fragility encompasses the depressive affect as a ubiquitous phenomenon as well as the increasingly extreme forms of this fragility—neurotic, borderline, and psychotic. A considerable number of patients classified as cases of chronic depressive evolution or chronic neurotic depression are situated somewhere on the fringes of the borderline states (Bergeret, 1975) between neurosis and psychosis, and overlap part of what we presently call narcissistic neuroses (Kohut, 1971), a category encompassing certain character disorders.

# Chapter 3

# Childhood

The child reacts to loss with a feeling of being helpless and defenseless. Later he feels implicated in the loss, indeed responsible for it; he then takes this loss upon himself by asking what he did to cause it, first with guilt, and then with an interest that may lead him to a working through by the ego.

Béla Grunberger (1965) emphasizes the fact that "instincts as such arise only with frustration, that is, from narcissistic injury" (p. 222). This injury, or wound, is linked to the loss of the absolute primary narcissism that Grunberger compares to the prenatal state where every need—except in cases of specific pathological disturbance—is immediately satisfied, thus implying the nonmanifestation of instinctual drives. Primary narcissism corresponds to a phase where the child's sense of self is "one of omnipotence and elation, without body and hence without ego; he is immaterial, boundless, timeless, omnipotent. . . ." (p. 221). But the child must switch from this totally narcissistic system to that of the object world, which entails instinctual frustrations and tensions. He must "integrate his body, his drives, his ego as his own, to invest them with narcissistic libido" (p. 222). For Grunberger, the ego is primitively represented by the body, which must be integrated along with the instincts into the continuum of the self. This process will be experienced as a narcissistic injury, which can be aggravated by the hazards of the developmental process but which in any case will constitute for each individual an open wound —precisely what analysis attempts to bind. At the time of this dialectical evolution of narcissism and instinctual conflicts, the subject needs to identify himself with his parents taken together (the narcissistic triad). The phallus thus becomes the symbol of narcissistic integrity, while its absence—castration—is implied by the instinctual significance of unisexuality.

Thus, the fundamental conflict is defined by the narcissistic wound arising from the integration of the ego with the instincts. There is a tendency in every human being to seek to recover the *state of lost elation*. From this desire is formed the ego ideal, comparison with which is a perpetual trauma for the ego. This metapsychological speculation poses the problem of identification in a psychoanalytic context: we shall see the importance of the experience of identification for human development presently.

Margaret Mahler's observations (1966) concerning

the very young have confirmed the suppositions of Bibring (1953) and the problems he raised.

> In our studies [Mahler writes] we came across un-mistakable evidence for the belief that a basic mood [that is, an individually characteristic affective re-sponsiveness] is established during the separation-individuation process. . . . a loss in fantasy—that is to say, *intrapsychic conflict* of a particular type or con-stellation . . . is the genetic cause for the occurrence of depression as an affect, as a proclivity toward a basic mood. [p. 156]

Concerning the first subphase, differentiation, Mah-ler (1966) emphasizes that "the momentum of libi-dinal responsiveness is greatly augmented . . . by the 'dialogue' with the mother. . . . *Elation* seems to be the phase-specific characteristic or basic mood during the second subphase of individuation (the 'practicing' period)" (p. 158). During the following subphase, "rapprochement," a significant lack of acceptance and of "emotional understanding" by the mother would diminish the child's self-esteem, would lead to am-bivalence and to "especially aggressive repetitive coercion" (p. 161) of the parents. The result would be "a turning of aggression against the self" (p. 167) and a "concomitant deficit in neutralized aggression which . . . create[s] the libido-economic basis for the depressive mood" (p. 166-7).

> Through maturation of the ego apparatuses—and fa-cilitated by the flux of developmental energy (Kris, 1955)—a relatively rapid, yet orderly process of sep-aration-individuation takes place in the second year of life. By the eighteenth month, the junior toddler seems to be at the height of the process of dealing

with his continuously experienced physical separateness from his mother. This coincides with his cognitive and perceptual achievement of the permanence of objects, in Piaget's sense (1936). This is the time when his sensorimotor intelligence starts to develop with true representational intelligence, and when the important process of internalization, in Hartmann's sense (1939)—very gradually, through ego identification—begins. [Mahler, 1968, p. 21]

I have quoted Mahler extensively because her work supports with great clarity my idea that "basic depression" is the result of a conflict tinged with aggression caused by a lack of comprehension and acceptance on the part of the mother, thus undermining the child's self-esteem. Early signs appear even before the child learns to talk; note that Mahler observed the mood of "elation" at an earlier stage than depressive responses.

Growth implies the gradual evolution of the normal state of what Mahler calls human symbiosis and what Imre Hermann and Alice and Michael Balint call dual union. The process is slower in the psychological and emotional spheres than in the physical. The transition from the infant to the small child capable of locomotion, through the progressive development of the separation-individuation process, is facilitated on the one hand by the autonomous development of the ego and on the other by various kinds of mechanisms of identification. This process of growing up physically, of developing to become independent, this "growing away" (Winnicott, 1960; Sandler et al., 1963; Sandler and Joffe, 1965; Zetzel, 1970) implies a mourning process that will continue throughout life. And each new step toward more independent functioning involves a new threat of object loss, a pattern repeated at each successive stage. Mourning is never extinguished, it can always be reactivated; at each new phase of life, new derivatives testify to the fact that the early processes are still and always at work (Erikson, 1968). It can be said that one is simultaneously fully "in" the world yet basically separated "from" it.

In his address on the occasion of the Tavistock Clinic Jubilee, Bowlby (1970) concluded that one never becomes independent, but remains dependent either within the couple or in relation to the internal image. Mahler (1972) formulates the same thought in a different context: "Hence he is *at first absolutely*, and remains later on—even 'unto the grave'—*relatively* dependent on a mother" (p. 333).

Another important aspect of this process was described by Winnicott (1957a): "That which is wanted, expected, thought up, is weighed against what is supplied, against what is dependent for its existence on the will and wish of another person. . . . Even the best external reality is disappointing because it is not also imaginary."

Two issues here are of interest: (1) the problem of mourning and depression in childhood; and (2) the problem of the infantile factors which create a depressive disposition in the adult. Of the questions confronting us, one is whether the child is capable of working through losses psychologically, that is, whether he is capable of the mourning which would allow equilibrium to be restored. If not, the question arises whether losses experienced in childhood become particularly harmful as a result of this early incapacity. Some authors question the very possibility of depression in childhood.

Anna Freud (1966), in order to examine this question, offered the following observation: "If by 'mourning' we understand not the various manifestations of anxiety, distress, and malfunction which accompany object loss in the earliest phases, but the painful, gradual process of detaching libido from an internal image, this, of course, cannot be expected to occur before object constancy (phase 3) has been established (p. 67). She thus does not deny the possibility of mourning in childhood, but stresses the developmental conditions which must be met before it can take place: the child must be capable of reality testing and must have reached the stage of object constancy. The more closely the ego capacities of the child in the areas specified approximate those of the adult, the more closely the length and quality of the child's inner work of mourning will approximate those of which the adult is capable. In any event, the child's mourning can have only a very limited duration. Furman (1964a, b) asserts that in addition to the prerequisite of object constancy the child must have acquired the concept of death before being capable of mourning. In his view, however, children can understand the meaning of death and conceive of its irreversible nature from the age of two and a half or three.

Bowlby (1960) not only believes the child capable of mourning, he sees no fundamental difference between the responses of a six-month-old child and those of an adult. Both follow the same sequence: protest-despair-detachment. One could object that from the vantage point of an outside observer, the analogies between child and adult, and even between the higher animals and man, can be carried quite far. Nonetheless, it is doubtful that the child, not having the same degree of ego differentiation as the adult, could have the same capacities for working through. Moreover, it is only Bowlby's third phase—detachment (the sulking child)—that is specifically human, animals being capable of experiencing separation anxiety and even despair. But detachment implies psychic *work* of a symbolic order, *through time*; it involves internally going beyond images belonging to the former solution and seeking a new solution with all the vicissitudes entailed by the persistence of images and their continuity (that is, memory and the cathexis of mnemonic images).

Many authors (e.g., McConville, Boag, and Purohit, 1972) have stressed the similarity in the grieving process observed in children the same age, irrespective of differences in life experience, intelligence level, and personality. Rochlin (1967), using play therapy with children who had recently observed a death in their entourage, showed that even the "normal subjects" had a system of working through that led to the denial of death, regardless of the importance of the deceased person in their lives. Rochlin concluded that children know more about death than would be supposed from tests (such as those of Maria Nagy) concerning the conscious aspects of their thought, but that denial keeps this awareness from manifesting itself.

In his article on fetishism, Freud (1927e) had already shown how the knowledge and denial of death can coexist in the child in a kind of splitting of the ego. This idea was taken up by Wolfenstein in 1973.

Maria Nagy (1948) classified the results of her interviews with 378 children on the subject of death as follows: (1) Until the age of five, death is not definitive for the child; it is either thought of as a departure or sleep, or is accepted, but as a temporary thing. (2) Between five and nine, the child personifies death: the deceased mother, ghosts, skeleton figures reappear during the night; death is on the *outside* and is not a general phenomenon. (3) As of nine or ten, the child knows that death is inevitable and final.

Rochlin (1959) speaks of the "loss complex"; in fact, although the child can suffer a brief period of sadness, he is not capable, in Rochlin's view, of sustaining the complicated work involved in a mourning process comparable to that of the adult, with the need to detach hundreds of threads through memories. But even if the child cannot perform this task in the same nuanced way as the adult, he is capable of certain internal work whose results would be manifest in a change of behavior after the mourning or, for example, when he is reunited with the person from whom he was separated.

For children, death is undoubtedly first and foremost separation and solitude, a point confirmed by the observations of Raimbault (1975). Death may also be perceived as a return to the mother's womb in relation to oedipal desires, and may thus arouse the fear of retaliation for aggressive wishes (Anthony, 1940). Mahler (1961) believes that starting from the second half of the first year the child becomes capable of mobilizing enough memories of "confident expectation" in order to feel the "languishing" which precedes the affect of sadness "filtered by the ego." From that time on there would be, as Bowlby believes, increased possibilities for mourning, albeit a mourning briefer than that of the adult. Rie (1966) has postulated that in the child it is more a question of grief than of depression. Sandler and Joffe (1965) express a similar thought: they describe *reactions* focused on a central depressive affective state.[1]

In *The Words*, Sartre (1964) describes his fear of death at the age of five and his indifference concerning the death of another:

> I saw death. At the age of five: it was watching me; in the evenings, it prowled on the balcony: it pressed its nose to the window; I used to see it but I did not dare to say anything. . . . Burials did not worry me nor did tombs; about this time, my grandmother Sartre fell ill and died. . . . I took pains to show an exemplary attitude, but I felt nothing. Not even when we followed the hearse to the cemetery. Death was conspicuous by its absence: to pass away was not to die, and the transformation of that old woman into a tombstone did not displease me. [pp. 60–61]

Helene Deutsch (1937) explains this indifference to the death of a loved one by the child's inability to carry out the work of mourning.

Nagera (1970) observes that the grieving process undertaken by the child—in contrast to that of the adult—is often blocked for internal reasons, leading for example to the idealization of the lost parent and to difficulties with the surviving parent. But it seems to me Nagera is using as his point of reference an ideal image of mourning in the adult which doesn't necessarily hold true. How many times have we not seen nostalgia for the past, or for the lost spouse and

[1] The conclusions of Schilder and Wechsler (1935) on children's attitudes toward death coincide with those of Anthony and Nagy.

for a shared life, linger well beyond the "normal" period? How often does mourning really attain this theoretical perfection? Still, there is no doubt that the mourning process can be carried out more intensely and effectively in a differentiated psyche like the adult's, though in my view it is a question of degree. In any event, I agree with the essence of Nagera's thesis: that the child's capacity to tolerate acute difficulties is more limited and that his aptitude for performing an increasingly complete mourning grows in accordance with his ability in the area of reality testing (according to Anna Freud, starting with the beginning of the second year).

It is thus not surprising that the child's depression is not as complex as depressive illness in the adult, who with his more highly differentiated mental apparatus keeps within him the precipitates of countless object relations. Rie (1966) contends that depression can not even exist before adolescence, since the child does not have the stable self-representation which in his view is a prerequisite for the loss of self-esteem that is a central criterion of depression. But self-representation can be seen as a "developmental line"—to use Anna Freud's expression (1965)—starting with the differentiation of self and object. This point coincides with Spitz's "eight-month anxiety" or "stranger anxiety" and brings with it the possibility of depression. Needless to say, the process of separation-individuation, the mirror stage, will further differentiate the representation of self, which at the beginning is embryonic rather than rich and complete.

Adolescence is considered a period of mourning (A. Freud, 1958; Lampl–de Groot, 1960; Jacobson, 1961). The adolescent is absorbed by his "develop-

mental task" of abandoning what his parents represented for him at the object and narcissistic levels; the
intensity of the mourning to be carried out is such
that he is closed upon himself. Guilt feelings vis-à-vis
the superego are aroused by his "daring" to acquire
an independence hitherto not permitted; he is also
seized by feelings of anger against the ego for not
being omnipotent, for not having "arranged everything" smoothly, and for running up against difficulties that might incur aggression and revenge. This
fear pushes him to see himself as a victim. Adolescence is then the second period of mourning, following that of the separation-individuation process. Then
the security-giving symbiotic aspects of the mother
were given up; this time, it is total objects that are
relinquished.[2]

How is the adult's depressive susceptibility constituted during childhood? Abraham (1924) proposes the
notion of a "primal" or "primary" depression, the
forerunner of Melanie Klein's "depressive position"
(1934, 1940). For Abraham there is a predisposition
to disappointment, hopelessness, and feelings of
helplessness *(Hilflosigkeit)*, that is rooted in disappointments occurring before oedipal wishes were
mastered, certain events of pregenital development
thus determining the manner in which the oedipal
conflict is experienced. Jacobson (1946) stresses the
role of early disappointments in giving rise to the
expectation of subsequent disappointments—the
"abandonism" of Germaine Guex (1950) is a similar
notion. Kleinian theory provides an explanation within

---

[2] Wolfenstein (1973) maintains that the adolescent hyperca-
thects the lost libidinal objects.

the logic inherent in her system: work requirements arising from the life instinct, the death instinct, and the struggle between them lead to the depressive position; the individual's depressive vulnerability will depend on the extent to which the depressive position can be worked through.

Finally, depressive susceptibility is connected to the stabilization of the sense of self-esteem and the ability to maintain good object relations; the problem can certainly be seen from the standpoint of the development of narcissism as Kohut (1971) conceptualized it (though I do not agree with all the details of his propositions) or according to the views of Grunberger (1971). We shall return to this presently, but for the moment let us simply underscore the link, in Melanie Klein, between envy and destructive fantasies, and between aggression and the ability to overcome the depressive position through a spiraling repetitive dynamism. By the same token, Jacobson's link between the quality of mothering and disappointments, and between the disappointing parents ("bad" parents, we could say) and the importance for subsequent development of the introjection of these bad parents, should also be stressed. Many authors (Rochlin, 1959; Mahler, 1961; Nagera, 1970) emphasize the importance of infantile losses.

For Melges and Bowlby (1969), a lack of hope characterizes both depression and what they call sociopathy. In their view, the inability to pursue goals arises from traumas of separation and a lack of basic trust caused by inadequate maternal care. I would say that the resulting rage cannot be channeled into constructive activity because of the deficiency in the functioning of the ego and the ego ideal; the rage remains violence, tempered no doubt by a certain element of appeal, but an appeal without hope. The archaic superego is not appeased by the feeling of being able to reach goals, the prototype of which is the mother's love and approval. The archaic superego in conjunction with these ideals tortures the ego to the point of despair. Only the ego ideal, together with the ego's ability to fantasize and orient itself in the direction of reality, can transform the violence into positive activity, and this by working through losses and replacing a void with a plenitude linked to self-esteem.

# Chapter 4

# Some Reflections Concerning Helplessness

According to Bibring (1953), the feeling of *Hilflosigkeit*, or helplessness, is common to all depressive states. The helplessness of the child (Freud) and the distress arising from the anxiety of separation probably describe the same difficult-to-define but fundamental phenomenon. For Anny Katan (1972), it is the depletion of primary narcissism that causes the child's distress. As Lidz expressed it (1968),

> Neonates possess an omnipotence they will never again possess. They but raise their voices and their needs are served. It is an omnipotence of helplessness; but they are fed, cleaned, cuddled, and kept comfortable. The feelings of undisturbed nirvana-like calm remain dimly within a person, and may serve as a retrogressive goal toward which individuals

strive to return as they grow from it into a more de-
manding and disturbing world. All ill persons have
a tendency to regress in order to regain care and protection. [p. 121]

Laplanche and Pontalis, in their *The Language of
Psycho-Analysis* (1967, p. 190), write that helplessness,
"as a corollary of the total dependence of the human
infant on its mother, . . . implies the mother's *omnipotence*. It thus has a decisive influence on the structuring of the psyche—a process which is destined to
come about entirely on the basis of the relationship
with the other person." The ego reacts to the frustration of oral drives (and the accompanying tactile
and olfactory satisfactions) by sinking into helplessness—in contrast to its later reaction when the more
developed infantile sexual instincts are frustrated.
This "infantile distress" or fundamental helplessness
and powerlessness will wound him in the image then
being formed, the image of his self, his narcissism.
Later will come the mechanisms designed to assure
the necessary narcissistic supplies—symbols such as
social status, fashionable dress, any of a variety of
material things deemed "normal," or else a relationship, perhaps symbiotic, based on the need to receive
the *constant approval* of the other. One of my patients,
for example, broke off his relationships the minute
his partner ceased, even temporarily, to provide him
the approval he sought.

Schmale (1972a) distinguishes two types of depressive affect, helplessness and hopelessness, the first
relating to separation and the loss of gratification, the
second to the feeling of castration, the sense that one
can never be accepted by the desired partner. This

introduces, in my opinion, the feeling of being castrated or diminished as a *fait accompli* in the oedipal constellation.[1] Helplessness is an affect accompanying loss of ego autonomy and involves feelings of being resourceless, deprived, abandoned, "dropped" (Schmale, 1972b). Hopelessness, by contrast, is a feeling of frustration and futility arising from the sense of being incapable of procuring gratifications. The two affects are thus closely related except that the subject blames the object for the first and holds himself responsible for the second. Each time the object fails to provide the hoped-for gratification, the subject experiences helplessness along with the painful awareness of his own dependence on the other. Furthermore, he attributes the object's "frustrating" quality to his own shortcomings, so guilt is mixed in with the other feelings. As for hopelessness, Abraham (1924) defines it as the ego's feeling of unfitness to live a fulfilled love because of its ambivalence (linked to a fixation at the anal stage or to a partial regression to the oral stage).[2]

---

[1] It is difficult to formulate a precise theory, at this level, of the "later" imagos; Luquet (1962) shed perceptive light on the problem of precocious identifications.

[2] *The American Heritage Dictionary of the English Language* defines the noun "despair" as "utter lack of hope, that which destroys all hope," and the verb "to despair" as "to lose all hope, to be overcome by a sense of futility or defeat." In its usage notes, the dictionary states: "despair and hopelessness stress the utter absence of hope and often imply a sense of powerlessness or resignation." In German, *"die Verzweiflung"* puts the accent more on the obsessional doubt (Zweifel), on the ego's inability to decide, to *assume*. The French noun "désespoir" and verb "désespérer" are close to their English counterparts (note of the translator).

Despair sets in when the ego feels cornered and powerless, with no chance of escape. This can occur either in the face of a severe and sadistic superego (at the anal level) or when confronted with a megalomaniacal ego ideal. The first blocks the ego and reduces its capacities to nothingness, as in obsessional neurosis (this was the case with Kierkegaard), while the second, even more regressive and impossible to satisfy, paralyzes the ego by setting a standard it cannot begin to approach.

Abandonment can give rise to an affect of powerlessness, distress, helplessness, the feeling of being rejected because worthless. Hence the narcissistic wound. Apathy and boredom, through decathexis of the stimuli, are the result. The infant, though helpless, is not conscious of depending on his mother until he begins to conceive of himself as different, separate from her. Helplessness is thus related to separation, and through it to loss and depression. Hope, by contrast, requires more, even at a cognitive level: object constancy and at the same time a clear consciousness of a self capable of procuring gratification, sexual and otherwise. This sense of hope will be sorely tested during the oedipal period, mastery of which will depend on an internal reorganization based on a confident image of self as able to procure satisfactions. Equally important for overcoming the oedipal conflict is the child's fantasy of not being crushed or powerless compared to the parent of the same sex, even though he must accept partial defeat vis-à-vis this parent. The possibility exists of an inner harmony between the introject which followed this defeat and the child's confidence in his own abilities, and therein lies the hope.

In my experience, the inferiority feelings with which Pasche (1963) is concerned frequently occur in subjects who were "spoiled" or overly gratified by the mother, with whom they lived in a strong dual union. These individuals remain extremely dependent on the mother, with a feeling of being "incomparable" to her, in a relationship that is played out essentially between "superior" and "inferior." It is this sense of inferiority which gives them a feeling of impotence and helplessness which will only increase as time goes on, owing to their lower level of activity and competitiveness.

The feeling of helplessness in the adult undergoing analysis resembles that of the child vis-à-vis his parents. Freud (1926d) attributed helplessness to the infantile condition, to the "helplessness of the newborn baby" (p. 252). One could say that the feeling triggering depression evokes an infantile situation which has not been mastered and never can be: it is the way of experiencing a situation, or (better yet) the image or fantasy evoked by the reality, that gives rise to the depressive affect.

The word "impotence" has a double meaning: it harks back to the totally powerless, helpless infant and by extension to anyone who is helpless and without resources in the face of a situation, and it refers as well to the adult male who is incapable of making use of his sex organ. Impotence, when seen as definitive, engenders the depressive affect.

The feeling of physical weakness, through the memories of helplessness it reawakens, can also trigger a depressive response, an internal movement which sometimes reaches the point of giving up

(Schmale and Engel, 1967). There is a double relationship between illness and helplessness: a bereavement can make us feel powerless, and can also make us ill (as in the case of Anna O. and other hysterical patients of Freud).

From the psychoanalytic standpoint, is there a reactional depression where a reality too difficult for a given ego to bear acts as a trauma? Remember Anna Freud (1967) defined trauma as the distance between the stimulus and the ego's actual capacities. The trauma leads to the feeling of distress and its spatial metaphor, *emptiness:* to be helpless, without force, without content, under threat of death; to feel constrained without hope or, in the words of one of my patients, that one is "dying small deaths." This emptiness has the dimension of a lack, a break, a gap (which will perhaps be filled, as we shall see presently, by the work of creation and culture). Helplessness is what Lacan (1966, p. xi) called the "want-to-be," the deficiency, the subject's condition of existence cut off from his maternal complement (the gap between the "want-to-be" and the maternal complement: the gaping wound).

Lack, flaw, emptiness, and also loss of the object: just so many fundamental dimensions of a man's life. This experience can be fit into a structural vision centered on an oedipal notion, castration, or into a genetic-dynamic continuity, separation and object loss given the status of an evolutionary stage (genetic, or sometimes even epigenetic). These are the two possible ways of approaching this problem, ways which lead to basically different positions concerning the most fundamental questions of psychoanalytic theory, that is, the epistemology of our science. Each of us must settle the debate according to his own personal tastes and inner convictions. I merely wanted to show that there are articulations possible between a vision of the dynamic evolution of the self and objects, and what this reveals and signifies in the continuity of the individual's experience in relation to the fundamental dimensions of human existence.

The study of depression highlights two notions: that of fantasy, the infantile situation evoked by association, and that of trauma, in cases where reality is too overwhelming. Sandor Ferenczi, in his "Confusion of Tongues Between Adults and the Child" (1933), reports the words of profoundly regressed patients: "Help me! Quick! Don't let me perish helplessly!" (p. 157). This must be understood as a reliving of the feeling of helplessness in the transference, a very important moment in analysis, as Balint (1968) also brought out. Freud made the link between *Hilflosigkeit* and the traumatic situation in the appendix to "Inhibitions, Symptoms and Anxiety," a text extremely rich in its conceptual allusions to trauma, anxiety, pain, and mourning. We must stress the fact that the feeling of helplessness is the reliving of the infantile situation vis-à-vis the parents, and not an exceptional situation of extreme privation; this implies that every one of us is capable of a depressive reaction.

The tendency of certain American authors to draw a parallel between helplessness and anxiety does not strike me as convincing. Anxiety is, among other things, a danger signal, while the feeling of helplessness emerges during situations evoking a specific danger, that is, a specific danger *as it was experienced in childhood* with all the feelings of helplessness and powerlessness it engendered at that time. One thus finds in depression both a general character (everyone was a child once) and a specific character (the fantasized characteristics of each situation).

Darwin (1872) emphasized the feeling of helplessness in grief. Freud, as we have already mentioned, characterized the fundamental condition of the child as helplessness. The depressive affect stirs the memory of this childhood fragility: to be helpless, lost. In "Inhibitions, Symptoms and Anxiety" Freud conceptualized a feeling of passive distress *(Hilflosigkeit)* in the face of a tension (for instance, during birth) and a feeling of more active distress, envisaging the possibility of losing the maternal object. This last can be related to separation anxiety, or, in the case of a *fait accompli,* to depressive affect.

Helplessness can result from the feeling of being prisoner of a family situation, of one's parents, with no possibility of escape, with a mourning that must be accomplished in relation to other possibilities expressed in the family romance. I was able to see, in one of my patients, the importance of the moment when the depressive realizes that he cannot bear the slightest frustration. In this case, he had reacted to the loss of his mother as the supreme injustice, and all the losses and changes that had occurred since then had been assimilated to that experience; the one tranquil corner of his life was his idealization of his mother in a kind of cult, encompassing the mother's entire side of the family; certain aspects of the cult were sublimated on a religious level. During a psychoanalytic session, the analysand succeeded in working through the realization that losses can be accepted, that they can even in part be replaced, and that denial is not the only way to overcome them.

What Freud (1926d) described as characteristic of the traumatic situation—the ego's feeling of helplessness in the face of danger—applies as well to situations that trigger the depression: these reactions occur during disturbances in the homeostasis that are experienced as losses of "good states" or of the objects which brought about these states. Attempts at hallucinatory compensation can provide only very temporary results and are doomed to failure. Herein lies the deeper meaning of helplessness. This is also why generalized helplessness leads to a generalized object loss and to an excessive susceptibility to object loss. In this context, the feeling of helplessness ultimately becomes traumatism.

Freud (1919h) evokes the feeling of helplessness arising from the "constant repetition of the same thing": "So, for instance, when, caught in a mist perhaps, one has lost one's way in a mountain forest, every attempt to find the marked or familiar path may bring one back again and again to the same spot . . . or one may wander about in a dark, strange room, . . . and collide time after time with the same piece of furniture" (p. 237). Discovery of the previously unconscious repetition phenomenon, the repetition compulsion, constitutes a narcissistic injury and is undoubtedly felt by the depressive patient as a situation of fundamental powerlessness—the experience of being unable to overcome the "infantile distress" (Hilflosigkeit) and of always falling into the situation of the helpless child. Addressing the phenomenon of the double in "The 'Uncanny,' " Freud (1919h) speaks of the constant "repetition of the same thing" and notes that for depressives this repetition is *unheimlich*, uncanny, depression-generating (like the destiny neurosis). According to Strachey (1955, p. 22), Freud's phrase "constant repetition," which he used again in *Beyond the Pleasure Principle* written the same year, is an echo from Nietzsche. "All these considerations prepare us for the discovery that whatever reminds us of this inner 'compulsion to repeat' is perceived as uncanny" (1920g, p. 238).

Freud (1919h) invokes "die Hilflosigkeit mancher Traumzustände" ("the helplessness experienced in certain dream states"). Here again one finds the repetition compulsion (traumatic dreams). According to Freudian theory as expressed in *Beyond the Pleasure Principle*, the dream is supposed to master the traumatic stimulus retrospectively by creating once again the anxiety that was the cause of the traumatic neurosis. Freud saw a contradiction here with wish fulfillment, but the ideas appear more easily reconcilable if one thinks of Melanie Klein's notion of reparation or of Franz Alexander's corrective emotional experience (which implies, for me, acting out one's fantasy).

In the 1920s, after the study of obsessional neurosis and melancholia, the disruptive factor in Freud's system became what he called the "death compulsion," or a "demonic factor" (1920g). Freud emphasized the phenomenon of repetition characteristic of all instinctual drives; it was in the irrational aspects of these drives that he sought to situate the demonic and find a link with his earlier ideas: the (sexual) instinct of the first formulations, disquieting for the conscience and the censoring agency, became in this later way of looking at things the instinct implying repetition.

The manifestations of the tendency to repeat, as observed in the early activities of the child's psychological life and in the experiences of psychoanalytic treatment, present an instinctual character of the highest degree and, when they run counter to the pleasure principle, a "demonic character" as well. Does not the curiosity of uncovering a demonic neurosis (Freud, 1923d) flow directly from these reflections? Nor is this phenomenon limited to neurotics: what psychoanalysis revealed in the transference phenomena with neurotics can also be observed in the lives of normal persons.[3] Indeed, certain persons give the impression of being pursued by fate or by a demonic trait in their destiny, but in fact these life patterns are undoubtedly in large measure self-imposed and determined by infantile influences. This is *Schicksalszwang*, the destiny compulsion (Freud, 1920g), that would later be called the fate neurosis.[4]

The demonic force in man may arise from complicity with the *fear of death* or, more probably, with the *death instinct*. Freud (1919h) shows that the experience uncanniness is experienced most intensely in relation to death and to dead bodies. "The demonological theory of those dark times has won in the end against all the somatic views of the period of 'exact' science. . . . In our eyes, the demons are bad

---

[3] Freud (1920g) calls these cases "nicht neurotisch" since "such persons have never shown signs of a neurotic conflict resulting in symptoms" (p. 158).

[4] According to Laplanche and Pontalis (1967, p. 161), "The subject appears to be the victim of these chains of events, as though they were willed by some external fate, but psycho-analysis teaches that their origin is to be found in the unconscious and, more specifically, in the compulsion to repeat."

and reprehensible wishes, derivatives of instinctual impulses that have been repudiated and repressed *(Triebregungen)*" (Freud, 1923d, p. 72).

In conclusion, one could say that Freud used the demonic image either in the sense of *Wiederholungsz-wang*, repetition compulsion, or in the sense of the repressed instinctual drive—sexual, aggressive, or death-directed. We could assume a link between what is repressed (sexual or otherwise) and the repetition compulsion: what is repressed remains dynamically active, beyond the control of consciousness and the ego and hence unknown (like the "uncanny"). This is injurious to the ego and its cathexis, that is, to the individual's narcissism.

These forces are experienced as demonic in certain structures which Mahler (1968) describes as follows:

> The internal psychotic reality dominated by the aggression-saturated proprioceptive-enteroceptive bodily sensations seems to be experienced as if the body were powered by more or less demoniacal, ego-alien mechanical forces (the introject), and whatever object libido is available is in turn vested in inanimate objects or quasi-animate machineries. Dedifferentiation and aggression-saturated inner percepts give rise to the delusion of the "influencing machine." [p. 96]

According to Imre Hermann (1943), all this symbolizes the destructuring forces inherent in drives, in sexuality, in aggression. All drives are destabilizing, especially since their gratification entails conflict. They all contain within them a pair of forces ever ready to trigger a vortex-like discharge, an affective maelstrom. Defenses against drives would act precisely to maintain the ego at the farthest possible point from the center of attraction, at the very edge of the abyss where the entire topography risks destruction (a "death vector" such as this, characteristic of every instinct, would correspond to the Freudian death instinct, at least as a destructuring force). The German adjectival pair *heimlich/unheimlich* corresponds roughly to the English opposites *cosy (in the sense of warm, comfortable)/eerie (strange, frightening)* or *uncanny* (as *unheimlich* in Freud's original text is usually translated into English). Etymologically, the stem "heim-" is cognate with English "home" and if speakers of English are to grasp the associative impact of the original, this relationship should be borne in mind. For Hermann—and, in a certain measure, for Freud also—*heimlich* signifies clinging to the *home* and more basically to the *mother* (Hermann, 1943; Freud, 1919h).

As Winnicott (1960) wrote:

> In psychoanalysis as we know it there is no *trauma* that is outside the individual's *omnipotence*. Everything eventually comes under ego control, and thus becomes related to secondary processes. . . . In infancy, however, good and bad things happen to the infant that are quite outside the infant's range. In fact infancy is the period in which the capacity for gathering external factors into the area of the infant's omnipotence is in process of formation. The ego support of the maternal care enables the infant to live and develop in spite of his being not yet able to control, or to feel responsible for, what is good and bad in the environment. . . . The paradox is that what is good and bad in the infant's environment is not in fact a projection, but in spite of this it is necessary, if the individual infant is to develop healthily, that everything shall seem to him to be a projection. Here we

find omnipotence and the pleasure principle in operation, as they certainly are in earliest infancy; and
to this observation we can add that the recognition
of a true "not-me" is a matter of the intellect; it belongs to extreme sophistication and to the maturity
of the individual. [pp. 585–586; italics mine]

Abraham (1911b) laid stress on the connection between depression and the sense of (narcissistic) inadequacy: "It may be noted that in this case the
preponderating attitude of hatred, the feeling of incapacity to love and the association of depression with
feelings of inadequacy were clearly to be seen" (p.
153).

With this overview of helplessness and brief consideration of the repetition compulsion and the death
instinct, we have come back to the importance of the
*heim* in *unheimlich* of the familiar (home) in the un-
familiar (unhomelike), in short, to the mother and to
narcissism. The links of this chain are only parts of
a whole, made up of fantasies and a multitude of
maturative experiences, among them analysis. The
link between fundamental powerlessness and the reconstruction of the lost object is in my view best expressed not by a psychoanalyst but by an
anthropologist, Claude Levi-Strauss (1955):

> The visitor camping with the Indians in the bush for
> the first time, is filled with anguish and pity at the
> sight of human beings so totally bereft; some relent-
> less cataclysm seems to have crushed them against
> the ground in a hostile land, leaving them naked and
> shivering beside their flickering fires. He gropes his
> way through the scrub, taking care not to knock
> against the hands, arms or chests that he glimpses as

warm reflections in the glow of the flames. But the wretchedness is shot through with whispers and chuckles. The couples embrace as if seeking to recapture a *lost unity,* and their caresses continue uninterrupted as he goes by. He can sense in all of them an immense kindness, a profoundly carefree attitude, a naive and charming animal satisfaction, and—binding these various feelings together—something which might be called the most truthful and moving expression of human love. [p. 293; italics mine]

# Chapter 5

# Loss and Mourning

> What is this life? A frenzy, an illusion.
> A shadow, a delirium, a fiction. The
> greatest good is but little, and this life
> is but a dream, and dreams are only
> dreams.
>
> —Calderon, *Life Is a Dream*

Any change is capable of triggering a depressive reaction. But while we are all subject from birth to continual change,[1] we do not all suffer continually from

[1] Some people believe that the stress inherent in contemporary
society is due first and foremost to an accelerating rate of change
and loss of stability in our surroundings and semiotic environment. Toffler (1973) used the term "ephemerization" for the
phenomenon of nonpermanence, that is, the fleeting, transitory,
and ephemeral nature of situations in postindustrial society.
Given this, it is more and more difficult for individuals to an-
ticipate events, to foresee the consequences of their acts and,
especially, the value that will be attached to them, the reactions
of other people and institutions.

depression. We must then assume that there is an individual sensitivity to changes and a greater or lesser capacity to take them in stride.[2] *Trauma* stems from the distance or gap between the event and the individual's inner capacity to react to the event through internal readjustment. It is thus a relative matter, and an event, no matter how cataclysmic, does not become traumatic unless it exceeds the ego's capacity for readjustment or for mourning. "It seems to me that by childhood I had already given up hope of ever having harmony or real satisfaction," one of my patients said, and he added that his life consisted of isolated moments of pleasure—a very specific pleasure of only partial value—with which he consoled himself. An apparent resignation in the face of a sense of definitive loss was at the root of his depressive affect.

Early separations are particularly traumatizing because of the small child's inability, given his immaturity, to accomplish mourning (Bowlby, 1960, 1961a; Rochlin, 1965). His compelling need for the object does not allow him the time to introject and recover an object temporarily or irreversibly lost. "In its place," writes Joyce McDougall (1972),

> will be created massive denials, displacements and distortions of the identificatory process, a disavowal of the world of the living, with all the danger this implies in terms of aggression turned against the self and, ultimately, a deadly suicidal trajectory. To this

[2] The sense of "remaining oneself" makes it possible for the individual not to feel himself threatened by changes to his very identity. ("Everything changes, nothing remains"—Heraclitus, quoted by Plato in *Cratylus*.)

> suppression of the vital ties to the outside world is
> added the risk of an internal object impoverishment
> and, consequently, a lack of interest in the life of the
> imagination. [p. 182]

A further crucial consequence is the child's diminished ability to cathect objects—for fear of losing them
and because of his incapacity to mourn—since the
other can not represent a valid content: hence boredom and the death of curiosity. The child attempts
to conserve the lost object by hypercathecting it, at
the same time that his self-reproaches and guilt feelings (for having caused its loss) block the mourning
process. Upon reaching adulthood, he continues his
search for the lost parent, reacting with rage rather
than grief. Thus, repeated disappointments throughout his life will enable him to perpetuate the presence
of the lost parent, even while such disappointments
constitute defiance and revenge against this parent
(and against the analyst in transference: the defiant
"No one can help me!").

Freud tells us in "Creative Writers and Day-dreaming" (1908e): "Actually, we can never give anything
up; we only exchange one thing for another. What
appears to be a renunciation is really the formation
of a substitute or surrogate" (p. 145). Likewise for
Helene Deutsch (1965): "Probably the inner rejection
of painful experience is always active, especially in
childhood. One might assume that the very general
tendency to 'unmotivated' depressions is the subsequent expression of emotional reactions which were
once withheld and have since remained in latent read-
iness for discharge" (p. 236). Eissler (1971) has observed that the ability to mourn diminishes as of the

seventh decade, indicating that mourning may require an elasticity in the psychic apparatus which exists neither at the beginning nor at the end of life. The capacity for mourning is therefore vulnerable. In adolescence, on the other hand, mourning for real, living parents can make possible the mourning of a loved one who died during one's childhood.

Successful completion of the mourning process makes possible the recathexis by the libido of new objects apt to provide gratification (Freud, 1917e). Its success from the economic standpoint depends on the ego's capacity for reality testing. Mourning is different from melancholia, which involves an impoverishment of the ego and a diminution of self-esteem: "In mourning," writes Freud (1917e), "it is the world which has become poor and empty; in melancholia, it is the ego itself" (p. 246). Mourning is the pain experienced following the real loss of a loved person or some abstraction, such as country, liberty, an ideal, etc. It is characterized by profound despondency, cessation of interest in the outside world, temporary loss of the ability to love, and inhibition of activity. Although it can lead to grave departures from an individual's normal attitude toward life, it cannot be considered a necessarily pathological condition. Normally, after a relatively brief period, the libido and the aggression tied to the lost object are gradually detached from it; the ego once again becomes free and the inhibition declines. Mourning continues until a substitute object is found. In pathological conditions, depression and melancholia can follow an object loss, with the external narcissistic modification caused by this loss being partially or completely denied. The basic structure of depression always involves a loss, but when one speaks of loss, one speaks of disappointment and, in part, the *denial* of this disappointment.

In a case cited by Eissler (1955), amnesia served the dual function "not only of denying that she had suffered a trauma, but also of experiencing the world as one in which no trauma can occur" (p. 77). In severe cases of depressive regression such as this, we sometimes have the impression that the denial reinforces repression. Denial and mourning are both sustained by a desire for withdrawal in the face of reality stimuli. As epitomized in sleep, withdrawal may in fact be a physiological "prototype" of denial.

A premonitory fantasy (Freud, 1941c) may serve to protect the ego from becoming aware of mourning for a long-lost object. Stein (1953) attributes a defensive character to these fantasies: by anticipating the loss of the object, they make it possible to endure the loss with less suffering and to deny the narcissistic wound. For Lagache (1956), "The work of mourning is a task of disengagement: it is accomplished when no confusion remains between the deceased and the survivor. That is why this task is so difficult and takes a pathological form in cases where . . . the personality had never freed itself from the mother, either internally or externally" (p. 74).

The process of separation-individuation, weaning, or "growing away" is related to the differentiation of self- and object representations (among other factors) and gives rise to an internal image—a specifically human attribute. During the first short separations, the infant makes a start at the work of mourning which will prepare him for completing a normal mourning process later on—breaking him in, so to speak. If he does not acquire this capacity, as in the case cited by Lagache, he will never be able to develop the "courage" or the inner capacity for facing separations and so will go through life expecting repeated object losses—depression through hopelessness. One of my patients said: "Whenever I get something, I always expect that it can't last." This attitude might have been interpreted as an expression of insatiability, a kind of greed, but in fact it was a verbalized expectation of rejection. This patient could not conceive of an ongoing state of satisfaction, of an agreeable state that lasts *for some time.* The discontinuity of agreeable states—though part of the human condition—affects certain individuals so profoundly that under the influence of external circumstances they develop the feeling that object loss is imminent (in the case of this particular patient, her mother had alternated between the extremes of wooing or charming her and brutally thwarting her). One can say that the passive acceptance of the inevitability of loss, doubtless accompanied by a sort of masochistic enjoyment, is part of the depressive constellation. Since the depressive affect is retroactive, while anxiety is anticipatory, this *acceptance* of the fact that every satisfaction inevitably leads to loss of the object that made it possible, that all pleasure leads to unpleasure, is likewise retroactive: "It has always been like that." This sort of disillusionment, this despair by lack of hope, this resignation, seems an element common to all depressive conditions and states of boredom; since "it was *always* so," any object that might bring satisfaction will automatically be denigrated.

Freud (1926d) raised the problem of trauma, using *separation* anxiety as the prototype of anxiety. Given the importance of the primal scene, from which the child is excluded, and the concomitant sexual excitation, one can ask if this excitation related to exclusion from the primal scene does not itself constitute, at the human level,[3] the fundamental trauma. Similarly, at the time of the separation from the mother, the child is left to his instinctual drives; the moment of excitation would correspond at the human or sexual level to the separation at the vital level. Abandonment would be a loss of a particular kind, solitude a way of living this abandonment. The work of Guex (1950) emphasized this theme. Research on sensory deprivation has scientifically confirmed what we already knew intuitively: reactions to solitude are relatively universal, man being a *zoon politikon* (a social animal), as Aristotle long ago noted.

Freud went through periods of depression when he finished an important work. After completing *The Interpretation of Dreams*, he wrote in a letter to Wilhelm Fliess (October 4, 1899):

> You describe very aptly the painful feeling of parting with something that has been your very own. It must have been that which made this work so distasteful to me. . . . In my case it must have been even more painful because what separated itself was not ideational possessions but my very own feelings. There is still a long way to the book on hysteria. At times like these no desire to work stirs in me. [Schur, 1972, p. 198]

References to separation anxiety, the role of object

---

[3] Laplanche (1970) distinguishes between the specifically human level and the vital level.

loss in depression, and perhaps even to the mechanism of post-partum depression are all present in this passage.

This is not to deny the existence of an illness of mourning per se. There is no doubt that in certain instances all the material becomes focused on the "trauma" of a real death, or rather on the experience of a death. Maria Torok (1968) described this phenomenon in a work in which she studied the vicissitudes of reactions to object loss leading either to incorporation or introjection. With Nicolas Abraham (Abraham and Torok, 1975) she attempted to delimit the notion of the "inclusion" apt to reconcile "the negation of reality and the negation of the nature of a loss, both narcissistic and libidinal." Nevertheless, classic working through based on the material of mourning is not the sine qua non of the depressive state. The conflict between the ego ideal and the actual ego state (the self) can be experienced in relation to other events; the resulting tension can trigger a depression without the precipitating event being the significant experience of a death. On the other hand, feelings of helplessness and a loss of belief in a previously maintained image of self are *always* present in depression. In midlife, for example, the decline in sexual potency and the idea of one's own death as foreseeable and possible, as having a present reality, represent a blow to "narcissistic omnipotence" and a loss of potency in the true sense of the word. The great moments of crisis—adolescence, midlife, the onset of illness—are always linked to change (Marmor, 1974).

The comparison between being "in love" and the return to the normal state "after love" is likewise part of the midlife crisis. From Freud's perspective, love is a psychotic experience based on overestimation of the object; the aftermath, the return to reality, can be likened to an unpleasant awakening. This aspect of love has to date been little studied. Without doubt "the state of being in love" (see David, 1971), an exceptional state by virtue of its intensity, encourages the establishment of a durable bond; but feelings of love in real life, the actual formation of the couple, pass through changes of cathexis, loss of illusions, renewals.

Loss also calls to mind "the loss of self," one's own death, which is one of the central anxieties of regressed depressive subjects. Discussing serious somatic illnesses, Engel (1962) describes the specific reaction of giving up in response to a loss of health; this he compares to depression, and it may well determine the patient's fate.

Narcissistic disturbances can reside not only in a *loss* of cathexis, but also in the impossibility of cathecting or, better yet, in *loss of the capacity* to cathect. This process gives rise to a feeling of emptiness, or boredom. Nonacknowledgement of this state can lead to a feeling of "depletion," of collapse and intrusion into the subject's inner world: the subject loses his cohesiveness,[4] and a feeling of discontinuity emerges as a source of depression.

In his *Three Essays* (1905d), Freud outlines his concept of neurosis based on the notions of drives and defenses against drives. Later he would take a greater interest in the *object* of the drive and various aspects

[4] The importance of the notion of cohesiveness—the cohesion of the inner world—was evoked by J. de Saussure (1972).

related to it, for example, *dissatisfaction* with the object or *loss* of the object—which led him to rework the notions of mourning, melancholia, and the collective experience (1917e, 1921c).

Bowlby (1970) finds the term "attachment" frequently preferable to "dependence" or "need for dependence": indeed, "dependency" refers to a functional notion (akin to the primary processes), that is, to the individual's need for others to assure his existence. "Attachment," on the other hand, involves only the description of a form of behavior related to desire (on the order of the secondary processes). According to Bowlby, the use of the word "dependence" for a behavior serving to maintain proximity leads to confusion. The object of attachment is someone who has the individual's confidence and who provides a security base necessary for him to act. The need for an attachment figure is not the exclusive province of the child or adolescent, but is equally important for the adult. The adult's need has been minimized, probably for sociocultural reasons, although we find in the notion of genitality the image of a stable relation which could be seen in terms of attachment instead of dependency. More thought should be given to differentiating the tie between the subject and its libidinal object, between attachment to the object and dependence on it. Certain authors present the problem of the genital object relation without according any importance to attachment, as if there were a danger of confusing attachment to the object, the wish to maintain the tie and dependency. In my opinion, if we speak of dependence we must examine its connection with guilt: often, the maintenance of guilt expresses a desire to maintain the dependency (Rado, 1927).

Bowlby (1970) characterizes the functioning of the healthy personality in the following manner:

> Essential ingredients are a capacity to rely trustingly on others when occasion demands it and to know on whom it is appropriate to rely. A healthily functioning person is thus capable of exchanging roles when the situation changes. At one time he is providing a secure base from which his companion or companions can operate; at another he is glad to rely on one or another of his companions to provide him with just such a base in return. . . . It must be borne constantly in mind that many of the most intense human emotions arise during the formation, the maintenance, the disruption and the renewal of those relationships in which one partner is providing a secure base for the other, or in which they alternate roles. Whereas the unchallenged maintenance of such relationships is experienced as a source of security, threat of loss gives rise to anxiety and often to anger, and actual loss to the turmoil of feeling that is grief. [pp. 105–106]

We find here the Freudian notion of a "loss of object" at the base of all depression. We should emphasize that the source of security can be an outside person or an inner state providing a narcissistic security which can be lost. These inner states, in my view, are "internal objects," in other words, precipitates of former identifications which when taken inside insure the subject's smooth narcissistic functioning. Depressives often need an outside person and relationships that are either anaclitic in nature or striving toward union, whence the high vulnerability to loss. This could be explained by a defect in the metabolization of the introjects, related to a basic insecurity caused by the early loss of the person providing the basic security; indeed, we find in the backgrounds of numerous depressives the real loss of the mother through death, or a prolonged absence (as during hospitalization).[5] To make up for this "basic flaw" in the introject, the depressive seeks relationships involving an exaggerated idealization of the object—be it person, party, or religious sect—and a strong "clinging" element. The depressive affect is triggered by the loss of something that provides basic security and well-being, a loss that the subject feels threatening to himself. When the inner conflict becomes too great, the subject can give up and let himself go: he then enters the constellation of despair.

A good illustration of the depressive's desperate quest for unity occurred in a sequence of analysis. After an interpretation in which I showed him that we were two distinct people, he said:

> Psychoanalysis has taken everything away from me. I have never reached this degree of isolation before. There's no way out of the problem. I feel nowhere. To enter, to leave, that's my whole life. What's the use?. . . . You are you, and I am me. I'm speaking to you, but you aren't me. I don't know if you can even understand. . . . This new relationship I'm thinking of implies that I separate from you. What's the use of talking about it? Nothing will change, and soon I'll have to leave here all the same. . . . I am

[5] According to Levi et al. (1966), many more separations are found in the lives of suicidal patients and those who have attempted suicide than in the lives of the control group.

alone, it's only now that I realize it. It makes me want to cry. I belong to no one and no one belongs to me. I can think of nothing but that discovery. . . . I'm looking for someone, *anyone*, with whom to form one. Which explains my brief crushes, then my sudden disinterest, these flames, these passions who take me for someone, and then, always disappointment. . . .

In this perspective, the bad mother is the one who for one reason or another did not make possible the acquisition (through introjection) of sufficient narcissistic supplies. She is not the same as the bad mother who, along with the good mother, is part of every child's imagos, the one who represents a restricting principle needed for the transition from the pleasure principle to the reality principle, for setting out the limits of self, and for the working out, through mourning, of the mature personality. Disappointment is a cardinal moment of depression (Klauber, 1967; Jacobson, 1971). Disappointing objects from the past are grafted onto present objects, which results in feelings of aggression and hatred, as well as in the fear that disappointments will repeat themselves. Sometimes the fear that earlier disappointments were caused by one's own unworthiness leads the subject to idealize his objects. But concealed behind this façade are two images which exist simultaneously: an image of the ideal, omnipotent self and an image of the degraded self (Klauber, 1967). Separation or loss of object triggers anxiety, while the narcissistic wound triggers the depressive affect—this last being born of disappointment in the mother, who was vested with the power to provide vital narcissistic supplies. The loss is experienced as the loss of a preinstinctual au-

tarkic state, a *lost paradise* (Grunberger, 1971). Sometimes the desire to restore past pleasure coexists with
the refusal to accept the *fait accompli* of having lost the
narcissistic union with the mother. One of my patients had very little interest in the possibility of having an agreeable life in the present; what she wanted
was to reestablish a good relationship with her
mother, stressing this old frustration and living only
in the past.

The presence of aggression during mourning can
be explained by the individual's feeling that he has
been attacked through the loss he has undergone.
Another possibility is that the aggression results from
disintegration of the drives under the impact of the
loss and the changes occurring in the libidinal cathexes. In any event, the aggression is often turned
against the self. For Engel (1962), the role of aggression in depression has been exaggerated, but, as we
have mentioned, his article is based on observations
of depressive reactions during serious illness; it is
possible that under such circumstances self-directed
aggression would be less apparent.

Under the rubric of "depressive position" or other
formulations expressing the same concept, Melanie
Klein and other authors, whose viewpoints do not
always coincide with hers (including Winnicott, Balint, Benedek, Zetzel, and Sandler), emphasized a
stage belonging to a developmental line leading to
the oedipal situation (the individual's most important
acquisition at the level of socialization and indeed
humanization). From reading these authors it becomes clear that the acceptance of separations and
frustration and the relinquishment of omnipotence
are finally *firmly* established only later, through the

renunciation, in the course of sexual development, of the oedipal desires conceptualized in the introjection of the superego. Thus, the forerunners of the superego and the Oedipus complex have a contribution to make in the organization of the personality. There is also, at the oedipal level, the loss of certain possibilities imagined until then, leading to a fundamental reorganization and change of structure. In neurosis, depression and anxiety are thus linked to the dynamism of this neurotic oedipal structure.

If the mourning connected with the renunciation of oedipal wishes is not accomplished, as in hysteria, depression is likely to ensue. In the obsessive, mourning is linked in addition to parricide, encompassing oedipal renunciation or oedipal murder and guilt; in either case depression may result. Obviously, the oedipal reorganization and the way in which the complex is resolved will depend on how the period preceding the oedipal phase was experienced, just as the refusal to mourn—nostalgia—leads to narcissistic and depressive vulnerability.

# Chapter 6

# Death and Immortality

> Well, death's the end of it all
> —*Romeo and Juliet* III, iii

Faced with a particularly destructive war, the crumbling of the Austro-Hungarian empire, the cumulative effect of the loss of many loved ones, and the discovery of his own cancer, it is not surprising that Freud was to turn his attention to the theme of death, which cast its shadow over all his works as of 1915, or that it was shortly thereafter that he developed his concept of the death instinct. In Max Schur's perspective (1972), Freud's work may be seen as (among other things) an attempt, constantly reworked and rethought, to overcome the dread of death.

Human existence is inseparable from death as the ultimate loss. Its inevitability, and the knowledge of this loss of the self have been at the heart of all man's efforts at cultural creation since the dawn of time. We shall come back to this idea in another chapter.

The ineffable, unfathomable experience of death has spawned analogies, myths, poetic images, fantasies—all attempts to apprehend a phenomenon that represents the greatest Evil and from which there is no escape. The image of death as a nuptial celebration expresses the triumph of the narcissistic libido, disguising the tragic event as something joyous, even erotic:

> If I must die, I will encounter darkness as
> a bride, and hug it in mine arms.
> [*Measure for Measure*, III, i]

The image of a narcissistic elation in death—the idea of destroying the bad in oneself while retaining the good, the immortal soul, of casting off the shackles of the body in order to float freely, unimpeded—all this plays a role in certain suicidal ideas and death wishes.

Death as aggression (unconscious, and also a victory over the conscience, in the sense of the superego) has always fascinated man.

Death has been likened to sleep: witness Socrates in Plato's *Apology* and Shakespeare in *Hamlet* (III, i): "To die, to sleep; to sleep, perchance to dream, ay there's the rub. . . ." The child struggles against sleep for fear of the loss it involves, and accepts it only thanks to the transitional object, something symbolizing the permanence of the Other. In certain phases of life, on the other hand, man seeks refuge in sleep as well as in death. One finds the same ambivalence toward these two phenomena, as if one sought to recover, in the powerlessness of sleep, the helplessness and omnipotence of infancy.

Death is also castration, loss of pleasure, *aphanisis* (Jones, 1927), absence. Hanna Segal, in her "Fear of Death" (1958), shows that old age and death may be experienced as persecution and punishment.

The links between love and death are innumerable. A Hungarian proverb compares "to love" with "to die a little," just as "to die" in Elizabethan English carried as a second meaning "to make love"—perhaps allusions to the diminution of the conscious level during intercourse.

In a letter to Wilhelm Fliess dated October 3, 1897 (Letter 70), Freud (1897b) refers to his own death wishes directed against his younger brother and to the feelings of guilt they engendered.

Freud writes at length in *The Interpretation of Dreams* (1900a) about the death of beloved relatives, the death wish, and the child's difficulty in conceiving of death: "Being dead means, for the child, who has been spared the sight of the suffering that precedes death, much the same as being gone, and ceasing to annoy the survivors" (p. 254). According to Freud, a small girl could distinguish between *fort sein* (to be away) and *tot sein* (to be dead) around the age of four. A frequent source of dreams is the hostility between brothers and sisters, and death wishes between siblings and against parents. He interprets the dream *non vixit* as elucidating the guilt of the survivor (1900a, p. 421). Through a recollection of Goethe, Freud (1917b) interprets the act of throwing objects out the window as the wish to expel something *(hinausbefördern, fortschaffen)*, a symbolic act whereby the child wishes to be rid of the intruder, the younger brother, a death wish arising from sibling rivalry and jealousy. In his "Thoughts for the Times on War and Death," Freud (1915b, p. 293) suggests that the hating relationship with the object is older than the loving one.

According to Freud (1915b), our unconscious is "inaccessible to the idea of our own death" (p. 299). It is as if we could not die a natural death, but could only be killed, by the law of Talion or by guilt. Death exists only for the Other: *he* can die. But this death gives rise to feelings of guilt.

At the time of a separation or death, one's inner well-being and sense of continuity are called into question. Self-confidence and adequate narcissistic supplies depend on a general confidence that the world will be defendable in itself and that the individual will be neither party nor prey to the external destructiveness of the Other. The death of loved ones engenders feelings of abandonment and guilt. At times it is experienced as a fundamental limitation: the limitation of our own existence. The denial of this limitation—the most painful of denials because perhaps the most fundamental—is the feeling of immortality.

In the interfoliated 1904 edition of *The Psychopathology of Everyday Life* we find the following remark, reproduced in the *Standard Edition* (Freud, 1901b, p. 260): "My own superstition has its roots in suppressed ambition (immortality) and in my case takes the place of anxiety about death which springs from the normal uncertainty of life. . . ." Freud comes back to this subject in his work on Jensen's Gradiva (1907a), where the immortality of Zoe is equated with that of the unconscious without mystical or religious con-

notation—in a way, it is the immortality of the principle of the unconscious discovered by science. His
"Great is Diana of the Ephesians" (1911f) also shows
the continuity of history, again as a kind of immortality revealed by science. The Three Fates of "The
Theme of the Three Caskets" (1913f) look on "inex-
orably" and supervise "the regular order of nature";
the third of the three feminine figures in the life of
man is Mother Earth, "the silent goddess of Death."
Freud writes in *The Ego and the Id* (1923b), "We know
that the fear of death makes its appearance under two
conditions (which, moreover, are entirely analogous
to the other situations in which anxiety develops),
namely, as a reaction to an external danger and as an
internal process, as for instance in melancholia"
(p. 58).

Our mortality may be viewed as the symbol of a
personal failure. What we call "the wisdom of old
age" is perhaps nothing more than the acceptance of
failures and limits, from the vantage point of a balance
sheet which can no longer be altered. Similarly, the
situation of old people with respect to the ego ideal
is different from that of the young: the more or less
definitive nature of their accomplishments leads them
either to acquire a certain distance (wisdom) or to sink
into depression, while for the young there is still the
escape route into the future.

The confrontation with death gives rise first to
dread, then it calls into play defense mechanisms such
as denial and isolation; if defenses such as magical
thinking (of the "bargaining-with-fate" type) do not
succeed, depression sets in, which can lead to acceptance and hope. Once again, depression has been
able to pave the way for a later harmony.

Between the confrontation with death and the denial of death falls the work of psychoanalysis: the working through of the self-image and the mourning for the loss of an aspect of one's own nonlimitation (omnipotence). One of my patients, after a painful session during which he confronted his limits, the resulting narcissistic wounds, and mourning, said with a sigh of relief, "Finally, I can live, in the meantime. . . ."

For Max Stern (1972), "Mastering the fear of death represents an important moment in the development of the individual's maturity; failure to do so is an element in the etiology of neuroses. The examination of clinical cases demonstrates that the in-depth study of the fear of death is an essential condition for a successful conclusion to analysis" (p. 901).

# Chapter 7

# Mourning and the Psychoanalytic Process

> If experience should show—not to me, but to others after me, who think as I do—that we have been mistaken, we will give up our expectations. Take my attempt for what it is. A psychologist who does not deceive himself about the difficulty of finding one's bearings in this world, makes an endeavour to assess the development of man, in the light of the small portion of knowledge he has gained through a study of the mental processes of individuals during their development from child to adult.
> —Freud, *The Future of an Illusion*

From the beginning, the history of psychoanalysis has

been intertwined with mourning. Anna O., the patient with whom the talking cure originated in 1881, had just lost her father, for whom she had been caring when her "hysterical" condition worsened. Similarly, most of the patients described in Freud's *Studies on Hysteria* (1895d) had succumbed to their illnesses following a bereavement. Using these cases as a starting point, Freud developed the theory of neuroses, but did not embark upon the study of the mourning process until much later, in "Mourning and Melancholia" (1917e), and then in "Inhibitions, Symptoms and Anxiety" (1926d).

In his letter to Binswanger of April 11–12, 1929, Freud wrote: "We know that the acute grief we feel after such a loss will come to an end, but we shall remain inconsolable, and never find a substitute. Everything that comes to take its place, even if it were to fill it completely, nevertheless remains something different. And this is really as it should be. It is the only way of perpetuating the love which we do not wish to renounce" (Schur, 1972, p. 421).

Fenichel (1945) compared mourning to a device whose very duration is aimed at protecting us from being overwhelmed by the violence of the affective shock; it enables us to live through the trauma caused by the object loss in small doses, ideally until the libido is completely detached from the object. In reality, this last is difficult to achieve and the "languishing and wasting away" stage can last for years, long beyond the time generally set aside for mourning. Normally, however, the trauma is defused through the mourning and transformed into a process, just as traumas experienced in earlier stages of life are worked through in analysis (which is what makes analysis a creative process).

A number of synonyms for "mourning" are in current use—"acute grief reaction" (Lindemann, 1944), "normal depression" (Bibring, 1953), "simple depression" (Fenichel, 1945)—although their meanings are not identical. "Acute grief reaction" (Pollock, 1961) refers to the initial reaction to the loss rather than to the entire mourning process. "Depression" indicates an affect rather than a clinical entity (Bibring, 1953). Opinions differ concerning the relationship between mourning and clinical depression. Freud (1917e) clearly distinguished between "mourning" and "melancholia": the loss of self-esteem characteristic of the latter stemmed from the *ambivalence* of the subject's relationship with the object and of the ego's identification with this object; in mourning, by contrast, this relationship ideally would be positive. In "Thoughts for the Times on War and Death" (1915b, p. 293), however, and in *Totem and Taboo* (1912–1913), Freud allows that "our unconscious is . . . just as ambivalent towards those we love" (p. 299). The ambivalence toward lost objects is at the root of pathological mourning (1917e): in cases of obsessional neurosis, for example, self-reproaches express the survivor's guilt feelings, as if he had desired the loss of the loved object.[1] In "Mourning and Melancholia" (1917e), Freud connects the identification with the object to melancholia alone; in *The Ego and the Id* (1923b), however, he remarks: "It may well be that identification

---

[1] Nonetheless, in this case the ambivalence is not accompanied by a libidinal regression of the ego as significant as that seen in cases of melancholia.

is the general condition under which the id will relinquish its objects" (p. 29).

Following Abraham (1924), numerous authors
(Bibring, 1953, in particular) have included the loss
of self-esteem, ambivalence, and identification with
the object as an integral part of mourning as well as
of depression, but at different levels of regression.
Thus for Fenichel (1945), "what is pathognomonic for
depression is the depth and the definite and full character of the regression, which extends beyond the
later anal phase to orality and narcissism. . . ." (p. 396).

Freud describes, in "On Transience" (1916a), the
various stages of development of the libido, its attachment to and then diversion from a succession of
objects, and its reluctance to renounce lost objects
"even when a substitute lies ready to hand" and remarks: "But why it is that this detachment of libido
from its object should be such a painful process is a
mystery to us. . . ." (p. 306).

It could be said that (1) death, through the force of
the ambivalence, is also wish fulfillment, and thus
engenders guilt feelings, with the suffering resulting
from the superego's reproaches to the ego; and (2)
the observation of children (Spitz's anaclitic depressions) and animals (who become depressed when
they lose the person to whom they are attached), in
conjunction with ethnopsychoanalytic and transcultural material, enables us to advance the complementary hypothesis that attachment to the mother and
the painful nature of the loss are biological facts of
great value to the individual's survival.[2] Schneirla

---

[2] This perspective is close to that of the school around Hermann, the Balints, Bak, et al. It also recalls Bowlby, as well as
Schur (who bases himself on Schneirla, 1959, 1965).

(1959, 1965) and Schur (1966) explain one of the profound biological meanings of mourning and depression through the dialectic of approach and withdrawal: detachment from the object releases the libidinal cathexes. According to these authors, withdrawal is related to an altered state of consciousness (introversion, inhibition) classically described in mourning and depression, but which is also found in boredom. The manic individual, on the other hand, seeks stimuli.

In "On Transience," Freud (1916a) describes separation, the mourning it engenders, and the wound inflicted by the ephemeral, perishable nature of things we believed changeless: "But this demand for immortality is a product of our wishes too unmistakable to lay claim to reality" (p. 305). Beyond separation and mourning, he alludes to the narcissistic wound caused by the thwarting of our megalomaniacal desires and to the difficulty we have in accepting this reality. He ends by expressing a hope for reconstruction (Melanie Klein would say "reparation"): "It is to be hoped that the same will be true of the losses caused by the war. When once the mourning is over, it will be found that our high opinion of the riches of civilization has lost nothing from our discovery of their fragility"; and further, "We shall build up again all that war has destroyed, and perhaps on firmer ground and more lastingly than before" (1916a, p. 307).

Edith Jacobson (1971) cites three patients in whom "the predominant feature of their reaction to the early object loss was a stubborn refusal ever to accept the reality of the actual events. They remained doubtful about them, distorted them, or even denied them altogether" (p. 186). In "A Type of Neurotic Hypomaniac Reaction," Lewin (1937) described in the same type of patient the glorification of the lost parent, the unconscious belief the parent was not dead, and a conflict marked by particularly intense ambivalence with the surviving parent. In certain cases, we have encountered denial to the point of hoping —unconsciously or even sometimes consciously—that one day the lost parent will reappear; these fantasies of return are associated with daydreams of the family romance type.

If, after the fashion of Stone (1961) and Meltzer (1967), we were to place ourselves within the context of a theory of treatment, the old notion of mourning would seem to us a dynamic *process* that we should take care not to "petrify."[3]

The psychoanalytic process was compared by Freud (1917e), Rado (1927), Fenichel (1945), and Lewin (1961) to *Trauerarbeit*, the *work* of mourning, and described as an "identity crisis" (Erikson, 1968), a "creative illness" (Ellenberger, 1970), and as a developmental phase bringing about a disruption in the affective equilibrium.[4] During psychoanalytic treatment, the progressive loss of feelings of omnipotence makes it possible to get closer and closer to the reality of the self and to the "reality principle" in general. In a way, this prefigures the image of death in that once death is worked through, it can be partially experienced, or better still, anticipated as a loss.

[3] "The knower petrifies the known: / The subtle dancer turns to stone"—Allen Ginsberg.

[4] In this sense we might speak of Freud's frame of mind at the time of his friendship with Fliess as similar to that of somebody being in analysis.

The time needed for psychoanalysis depends on the mourning to be performed. The child's dependence is such that the mourning process—a secondary (spontaneous or analytic) working through constituting the psychological work necessary to detach the libido from old objects and to release the "libidinal cathexes"—can be performed only in the barest outline. When the libido is detached, precipitates of the object are introjected. "The work of mourning frees the object libido; the elaboration adds to that all the energy released by the countercathexes" (Sauguet, 1969, p. 925).

To describe psychoanalytic treatment as a process of mourning, as the repetition of the successive losses undergone by the child so as to pass from the stage of omnipotence to the stage where the reality principle can be assumed, strikes us as a valid heuristic device. Sauguet (1969) underlines in his report the analogy, or even the identical nature (of the analytic process) with the psychological process of maturation (p. 926). Maturation implies change, and therefore mourning.

In certain severe cases the analysand, above and beyond feeling the loss of an "object," also has the sense of losing the unity or continuity of self; in certain obsessional neuroses, an attempt to maintain this unity is made through rationalizations and self-isolation. Winnicott would speak of a structuration on the mode of a "false self"; within this framework, it would be the loss of the false self, experienced as jeopardy, that would trigger a depressive state. Psychoanalytic therapy implies separation from internal objects, thus stirring the deeply buried memory of the original trauma—separation and exclusion from the primal scene. The interpretation would then be the voice of the Other, the voice of the mother, which could be the "soft voice [*leise* in German] of the intellect" Freud speaks of (1927c, p. 5). This outside voice does not re-create the union with the original object, even if it can re-create the illusion of it. And since it is the voice of the intellect, of comprehension, the voice of the Other, it is neither a sham nor an illusion; it introduces the reality principle, a soothing reality in that it signifies the presence of the Other. Like mourning, the psychoanalytic process consists of relinquishing the old objects and former ideals that are now inadequate. Even more, it consists of relinquishing a megalomaniac image of the self and the acceptance of one's limits. This explains the painful nature of working through. This work is particularly important in depressions: to accept one's limits while taking care that the narcissistic wound that inevitably results from the realization of limits (through disrupting megalomaniacal ideals) does not trigger a new depression. *Durcharbeiten, Traumarbeit, Trauerarbeit* (working through, dream-work, work of mourning): all are terms that contain the notion of work, of *toil*. The goal of this work is renunciation: renunciation of the feeling of omnipotence linked to primary narcissism, renunciation of the vestiges of omnipotence within the subject's personality, and, finally, renunciation of the hope for omnipotence in the Other. We can say that the *transition* from the narcissistic world to a real object world is a work of mourning, and that in this sense psychoanalysis is a working through, a *Durcharbeiten*, a work of loss. Freud (1926d) believed that the work of mourning was likewise triggered by the reality testing that confronts us with loss of the

object. In psychoanalysis we are faced with the problem of continuity and discontinuity: the analyst and
the analysand are not together twenty-four hours out
of twenty-four; the session always comes to an end,
there is always a separation, a loss; there is thus discontinuity in the very continuity of the work, which
explains the frequency—not to say ubiquity—of the
depressive affect during therapy. What is involved,
in fact, is to construct bit by bit the image of the total
object.

Working through is a phenomenon truly analogous
to mourning, with every change requiring the relinquishment of attachment to certain objects, parental
figures or familiar models. Like mourning, working
through implies recognition of the fact that the object
is no longer attainable in its former context; what is
involved in depression is not the loss of an actual
person but of an ambivalently cathected internal object (Freud, 1917e; Abraham, 1911b, 1924).

Mourning becomes essential when external changes
make internal ones necessary, this necessity being
experienced as a "demand" coming from the outside.
That is what takes place in therapy with the working
through of the depressive position.

Analysis sometimes makes it possible to resume a
mourning process which has long been blocked. One
of my patients, just before interrupting analysis to
take a vacation, suddenly began talking of his mother,
who had died when he was nine. The prospect of
mourning the analyst during his vacation enabled him
to undertake the mourning of his mother, whose loss
he had denied until then.

Using material from the study of sixty analyses of
adults who lost one or both parents during childhood,

Fleming (1972) underscored the difficulty these patients had in establishing a therapeutic relationship and entering transference, this resistance serving to ward off the massive anxiety the prospect of separation would cause. The relationship which would later be established, it goes without saying, would be of the symbiotic type.

Impulsiveness can break the continuity of emotional development; it runs the risk of interrupting the psychoanalytic treatment or introducing a discontinuity. Certain severely depressive patients use this means in order to repeat, or re-create, the relationship with the primitive object. While we could perhaps be criticized for being overly influenced by "ocnophilic prejudices," to use Balint's term (1959), we believe it essential to create a supportive environment—what Winnicott (1958) called a "holding environment"—for the reliving of philobatic experiences.

The novelist Philip Roth gives us an example of intersexual victimization in the character of Tarnopol in *Portnoy's Complaint:* a false renunciation of women, a false mourning, not unlike the false mourning of many of our analysands following rationalizations that end up making their lives static and rigid. If psychoanalysis is a process of mourning, acting at the level of object loss works totally at cross purposes with analysis: the patient, reluctant to lose his objects in the analytic process, suddenly tries to recover them in actuality in the outside world. In many cases, we are confronted with aspects of the repetition compulsion: resistance to change, disorganization, depression. The subject struggles to keep from giving up an internal organization because of the loss it implies. Similarly, in cases where the subject persists in expecting the return of the lost object, refusing internally to accept renunciation and loss, this expectation leads to repetition and disappointment.

Depression moreover is not found solely on the side of the analysand. The analyst, too, can feel helpless, depressed, without hope. The complex process of mourning is then precipitated in him, involving perhaps the relinquishment of certain ideals, sometimes disguised as theoretical positions, so as to meet the analysand. Indeed, I sometimes wonder if it is not the analyst's very vulnerability, in the sense of a capacity to lower his defenses so as to approach the Other, that is not the source of his development as an analyst, his ongoing maturation in his listening function. And to understand the reality of the Other—which during the mourning process is experienced as continual change—implies the acceptance of one's own death when the analysis ends.

The borderline cases, the limits of analyzability, bring us face to face with the limits of psychoanalytic theory (as the explanation of mental life and all human behavior) and psychoanalytic practice (as an effective means of helping human beings). For the analyst, the Pygmalion temptation relates to the aggressive connotation of the interpretation: to function in the place of another, to deprive him of a morbid pleasure.

Our reticence in the face of theoretical disruptions, like resistance to life changes, can stem from our fear of losing the security inherent in an inflexible purism. But this is inevitable, and theoretical modifications bring about changes in our practice and vice versa.

The problem of guilt is likewise experienced on both sides, with the analysand trying to make the analyst feel guilty (Jacobson, 1971; Abraham and Torok, 1975) by turning the conflict upside down and by playing the superego vis-à-vis the analyst, who then embodies the ego.

The foregoing remarks on the analytic process can perhaps be criticized as a "depressive notion" of psychoanalysis (or even of the culture). Naturally, the psychoanalytic process cannot be *reduced* to a mourning process, but this mourning process is one of its aspects in a overdetermination which, in my opinion, is worthy of close examination.

Klauber (1967) remarks that the "psychoanalytical process itself—which provokes and then destroys the processes of narcissistic defense—makes it impossible for anyone still deeply in analysis to reach an optimal liberation from all depression."

The object of therapy could very well be the sort of quest for "things past" that Proust sought in his writing. Some years ago, a spirited controversy arose as to whether the goal of analysis was "construction" or "reconstruction." It seems to me that it would be more useful to consider as essential to the psychoanalytic process the subjective recovery of the lost object and the mourning of elements definitively abandoned. Within this perspective, the object cannot be falsehood, but a nucleus of reality—although a reality forever subjective—because anchored in our experience.

# Chapter 8

# Introjection and Identification

> You belong to him and you don't
> know it.
> You are he, even while thinking you
> are yourself.
>
> —*Eugenio Montale*

The term "introjection," coined by Ferenczi (1909),
designates the process whereby "in fantasy, the subject transposes objects and their inherent qualities
from 'outside' to 'inside' himself" (Laplanche and
Pontalis, 1967, p. 229). The definitions of "introjection" and "identification" have been reformulated by
Laplanche and Pontalis in their *The Language of Psychoanalysis*. According to them, incorporation provides the corporal model of introjection, "but it does
not necessarily imply any reference to the body's real
boundaries" (p. 229). They specify that introjection

97

is closely related to identification, "a psychological process whereby the subject assimilates an aspect, property or attribute of the other and is transformed, wholly or partially, after the model the other provides" (p. 205). "In Freud's work, the concept of identification comes little by little to have the central importance which makes it, *not simply one psychical mechanism among others, but the operation itself whereby the human subject is constituted*" (p. 206; italics mine).

Our knowledge in this domain is certainly not complete. Freud, in his *New Introductory Lectures on Psycho-Analysis* (1933a), appeared dissatisfied with the manner in which he had formulated these notions, and spoke of identification *in terms of* attachment to the object, whereas on other occasions he had distinguished *between* identification and object choice. Later, in *Moses and Monotheism* (1939a), he used a clinical example to demonstrate the primordial importance of identification for the development of the individual. A patient became "a faithful copy of his father as he had formed a picture of him in his memory: that is to say, a revival of the identification with his father which in the past he had taken on as a little boy from sexual motives" (p. 80). Identification, with the element of internalization it implies, could be a specifically human acquisition, necessary among other reasons in order to transcend the "sensorimotor" level of intelligence (Piaget, 1936) and to go beyond imitation (see Lincke, 1971).

We have seen that the child's development is influenced by the situation of equilibrium that exists between himself and those around him. The imprints left by the *relationship* with these individuals (rather than imprints of the individuals themselves) are ultimately conceptualized through the mode of *intro-jection*. There are, however, more complex cases where introjection is not the simple "transposition from the outside to the inside" of a fact, relationship, or consequence of this relationship (that is to say, the precipitate of an interpersonal relationship), but where one is confronted with shifting patterns, such as in the projective identification described by the Kleinians. The fate of these introjections is complicated by mechanisms of defense and adaptation, such as idealization, denial, reaction-formation. What can be said is that many aspects of learning undergo modified processes of introjection and identification.[1]

Brierley (1942) differentiated between "introjection," a descriptive term designating a psychological mechanism, and "incorporation," a term referring to the realm of fantasy. This idea was taken up again by Abraham and Torok in their work on metapsychological realities and fantasies (1972): "Incorporation corresponds to a fantasy and introjection to a process: a useful distinction. . . ." (p. 111).

Three interrelated notions can be distinguished: (1) the notion of *imago* or *inner object*, determinative for one of the aspects of the ego's dynamism; according to Freud (1923b), the ego is a precipitate of abandoned object-cathexes (p. 48); (2) *introjection*, which has obvious links with object relations; and (3) *regression*, during psychoanalytic treatment, at the level of old object relations and the introjections linked to them.

---

[1] The notions of identification and introjection are often defined in a contradictory fashion in the literature. We refer the reader to the dictionaries of Laplanche and Pontalis (1967), Moore and Fine (1968), and Rycroft (1968).

Is it necessary to make a distinction between the *inner world* and the *internal world*, as Rapaport (1959) did, the first being a sort of geographic map of the outer world, the second comprising the most important structures of the psychic apparatus? Or is the internal world not an elaboration of the inner world, with extremely close ties between the two? We shall not expand on this subject, or on the relations that exist between identification and sexual identity (Haynal, 1968, 1971, 1975). It should be noted, however, that Luquet (1962) made an exhaustive survey of early identifications and their role in the development of the individual and in therapy.

Freud, in "A Disturbance of Memory on the Acropolis" (1936a), strikingly illustrates the extent to which introjects (inner *imagos*) are part of the ego and influence "autonomous" ego functions such as the investigation of reality: he attributes his doubt concerning the reality of the Acropolis to guilt feelings at having surpassed his father. Although Freud (1933a) described identification in terms of attachment to the object, he distinguished it from object choice. The male child identifies with his father in wanting to resemble him. If he identifies with his mother, it is the father who becomes the coveted object. Freud emphasizes the difference between the narcissistic object choice and the anaclitic object choice. In normal circumstances, we know little about the advantages and disadvantages of these two modes. However, in pathological circumstances (for example, in the event of object loss), an individual making a narcissistic object choice can develop depression (regression to identification), as if he lost not only something he needed, but something he considered part of himself as well. He would then have to dig partially into his own reserves to replace the lost object. Instead of seeking a new object, he vents his aggression (originally directed against the lost object) against himself, becomes depressed, and wants to die. What is the relation between the object choice and the discharge of aggression? It seems that we hate those who frustrate our desires (anaclitic object choice), as well as those who inflict on us narcissistic injuries (narcissistic object choice). From an economic point of view, the libido and aggression attached to the object can be discharged by an anaclitic object choice, while the narcissistic libido and aggression can be discharged through a narcissistic object choice. Only the narcissistic libido is used to cathect the representation of self. Depression reveals the importance of the introjects the subject carries. One of the aspects of internalization that Kohut (1971) called *transmuting internalization* is then lacking: objects strongly retain the stamp of their origin, remaining linked to the introjected person.

Already in 1915, in "Instincts and Their Vicissitudes," Freud mentioned "in so far as the objects" are presented to the ego as sources of pleasure, "the ego takes them into itself," introjects them . . .; and, on the other hand, it expels whatever within itself becomes a cause of unpleasure . . . the mechanism of projection" (1915c, p. 136).

In the chapter devoted to the "internal world" in "An Outline of Psycho-Analysis" (1940a), Freud discusses the role of the superego, showing how identification with the partially abandoned objects of the "external world" introduces them into the "internal world" (pp. 205–206). In "Negation" (1925h, p. 235) "judgement" is described as the continuation of the original processes through which the ego takes objects inside itself or expels them according to the pleasure principle. It could be said that man keeps the memory of his experience inside himself: thus objects of satisfaction leave their mark as good objects and those of nonsatisfaction as bad objects. These internal objects would thus act as a kind of compass (Stierlin, 1970).

Experience and the functioning of the human memory are linked to introjection; indeed, this is perhaps one of its fundamental functions.[2] The concept of introjection, as already stated, was brought to light by Ferenczi (1909), for whom every relationship includes a part of introjection. Relations with the outside world are likewise object relations; they thus have an energy source in the instinctual drive, and an introjection linked to them.[3]

Freud (1941f) described the identificatory object relation as follows: " 'Having' and 'being' in children. Children like expressing an object relation by an iden-

[2] The word for memory in German is *Er-innerung* (taking inside).

[3] Fenichel (1926) wrote: "Following the literature of the subject, we have uncritically adopted the label 'introjection' for the oral incorporation which represents the pathway of identification. But for the sake of clarity it should be mentioned that originally Ferenczi meant something entirely different by 'introjection.' He had in mind the tendency to bring everything that was perceived into relation with the unconscious, to involve real happenings in repressed thought processes, as occurs, for instance, with the day's residues in the course of dream work. Nevertheless, it might be worth investigating whether such processes too do not perhaps take place to the accompaniment of genuine identifications" (p. 105).

tification: 'I am the object.' 'Having' is the later of the two; after loss of the object it relapses into 'being.' Example: the breast. 'The breast is part of me, I am the breast.' Only later: 'I have it'—that is, 'I am not it' " (p. 229).

In his "Outline" (1940a), he demonstrates brilliantly that the object relation with the mother is the source of future narcissistic cathexes.[4] The mother, as the satisfying object for the ego, becomes confused with it at the stage of the symbiotic nondistinction between the ego and the object.

Concerning melancholia, Freud, in *The Ego and the Id* (1923b) advances the hypothesis that a lost object was set up in the ego, and that an object cathexis was thus replaced by an identification. Rosenfeld (1959) emphasizes the intensity of ambivalence in patients with a depressive predisposition. He warns against

---

[4] "A child's first erotic object is the mother's breast that nourishes it; love has its origin in attachment to the satisfied need for nourishment. There is no doubt that, to begin with, the child does not distinguish between the breast and its own body; when the breast has to be separated from the body and shifted to the *'outside'* because the child so often finds it absent, it carries with it as an 'object' a part of the original narcissistic libidinal cathexis. This first object is later completed into the person of the child's mother, who not only nourishes it but also looks after it and thus arouses in it a number of other physical sensations, pleasurable and unpleasurable. By her care of the child's body she becomes its first seducer. In these two relations lies the root of a mother's importance, unique, without parallel, established unalterably for a whole lifetime as the first and strongest love-object and the prototype of all later love relations—for both sexes. . . . And for however long it is fed at the mother's breast, it will always be left with a conviction after it has been weaned that its feeding was too short and too little" (pp. 188–189).

using the term "narcissistic" without first defining it, since the concept is understood to mean a great many different phenomena: egoism and egocentrism, the feeling of superiority, as well as the regression to the oral stage, the introjective process, the withdrawal from the outside into the inner world, the fusion and identification of self with objects, and even certain ego states (see also Van der Waals, 1949).

J. H. Smith (1971) distinguished the nondiscriminatory massive introjections of depression from the more subtle introjections of the mourning process. In his formulation, what distinguishes depression is its demand for "all or nothing" (the "nothing" being denial), while in mourning the approach is more differentiated.

I would like to show through an example how omnipotence on the one hand, and the all-or-nothing alternative on the other, manifest themselves in the first experiences of limitation, the limitation of omnipotence: if one is not all-powerful, one is practically nothing (a little ant).

A patient suddenly expressed the wish to discontinue analysis, which I attributed to negative feelings toward me. "I don't believe it's that," she responded, "I think it's just the opposite. But I feel compelled to take my distance and demolish you. From the minute I realized that the analysis could end, I stopped idealizing you. I didn't do it on purpose. But before, I had a more idealizing feeling toward you. Ever since I thought of the end of analysis, my image of you has changed."

We could say that as soon as she took cognizance of the ephemeral nature of our relationship, the object I represented was devalued for her. She compared me to a man with whom she had been involved who had likewise been depreciated as soon as she realized that the relationship could not last forever.

Another patient refused at all costs to acknowledge the slightest resemblance to her mother. The massive introjection of a mother highly present internally expressed itself in her need to reject her totally. At the same time, this hated internal image defended her against the anxiety of separation, the feeling of solitude, whence her inability to give it up.

Meissner (1972) considers incorporation, introjection, and identification as different forms of internalization corresponding to different stages of psychological development and to different qualities of object relations. Be that as it may, the fusion-confusion of the rudimentary schemas of the self with the representation of the object must be distinguished from the oedipal identification with the sex characteristics of the parent of the same sex (see Sandler, 1960). Depression implies a problem of introjection and identification with the bad object or with something threatening for the organization of the narcissism insofar as the bad object is confused with the self. Going back to Abraham's notion of incorporation, it could be said that the depressive *devours* in introjection and that the object is not taken into account. In melancholia it is the incorporated object that suffers: the incorporation of a highly persecutory (partial) object leads to melancholia, while the introjection of a (total) object leads to the depressive position (normal). The imago (of a broken-up object) retains all its functions in melancholia—the characteristics of these imagos remain unchanged during the assimilation by the ego.

Abraham (1916) used a *digestive* vocabulary: when the object taken inside by the subject remains "indigestible," it is expelled, spewed out, vomited up. In his work of 1916 we find links between depression and anorexia and vomiting, which opened the semantic field all the way to *hypochondria*. The "indigestible" hypochondriacal object can be compared to the melancholic object, the "bad object." Harnik (1932) described the oral expulsion of the object using the image of vomiting: It is after the depreciated narcissistic object is "vomited" that depression occurs (once again, a loss!).

In "Introjection and Transference" (1909), Ferenczi emphasized an aspect of the psychoanalytic process that complements the work of mourning. Stressing the fact that with object loss there is a parallel *recathexis* of the object, he considered transference as a possibility for the libido in search of cathexis to find a satisfactory object, which then becomes, by *displacing* the cathexes, similar to the former libidinal object. Through introjection, the object will enrich or "expand" the subject's ego within the context of the relationship itself without there being object loss. Thus, psychoanalysis, through the introjection of successive images, leads to a maturation of the ego reminiscent of the human being's development outside the analytic situation, during childhood, for example. It should be mentioned that this conception of introjection in the relationship is fundamentally opposed to the various conceptions of introjection that came later.

Freud and Ferenczi thus both saw in the psychic apparatus a tendency to retain old objects, such that any loss implies an introjection-identification. According to Klauber (1975), the characteristic feature (and difficulty) of the psychoanalytic profession lies in the preponderance of identification at the expense of possibilities for direct motor, psychomotor, and expressive responses. Indeed, the psychoanalyst must allow himself to become imbued with the Other's mode of operating before settling on the technique of interpretation to the exclusion of all others.

Clinical experience has confirmed Freud's hypothesis (1917e) that the object relation in melancholia and depression is replaced by identification. For example, all the efforts of one of my patients tended toward obtaining narcissistic confirmation rather than an object relation, that is, a relationship—even a partial one—with an object. Both the child's anaclitic depression and the adult's introjective depression show the same need for the constant presence of a gratifying object; both stem from difficulties in internalizing such an object. In anaclitic depression, the presence of the object and the good state have not been sufficiently internalized; in the adult's introjective depression the gratifying object is no match for the prohibiting and frustrating object, so feelings of helplessness and guilt get the upper hand. According to Kohut (1971), the psychoanalyst's role in such cases should be to confirm the subject's narcissism and self-esteem.

In Chapter III of *The Ego and the Id* (1923b), Freud extends this identification process, no longer confining it solely to melancholia. These regressive identifications seem in large measure to constitute the basis of what we call the individual's "character." "Character" thus grows out of object relations and the identifications that follow. Thus it could be said that the first object relations, the child's relationships with those around him, leave indelible precipitates; this is a human characteristic. The most important of these regressive identifications are the ones stemming from the dissolution of the Oedipus complex which therefore occupy a special position in the formation of the superego, the core of socialization. What we are seeing in depression, in a way, is the derailing of this process. The discovery or resurgence, at the time of the transference neurosis, of turmoil aroused by decisive events or important relations in early life confirms the presence of these precipitates, the taking inside of what was outside, thus introjection and, in part, identification.

One can ask at what point in the phallic and oedipal stage evolution takes over the earlier depression. In one of my patients, an idea of injured femininity was manifest in a fantasy in which she identified herself with feces in the toilet and feared that someone might flush it. Abraham (1924) already made the connection between the oedipal problem and dysphoria:

> I should be inclined to speak of a "primal parathymia" ensuing from the boy's Oedipus complex. We see with impressive clearness how much the child longed to gain his mother as an ally in his struggle against his father, and his disappointment at having his own advances repulsed combined with the violent emotions aroused in him by what he had observed going on in his parents' bedroom. He nursed terrible plans of revenge in his breast, and yet the ambivalence of his feelings prevented his ever putting them into practice. . . . In the years that followed he made repeated attempts to attain a successful object-love; and every failure to do so brought with it a state of mind that was an exact replica of his primal parathymia. [p. 469]

Andrew Peto (1972) called attention to the frequency of disturbances in body image which he relates to the lowering of self-esteem (feelings of inferiority, weakness, impoverishment, helplessness). In his view, the roots of this situation can be traced to the point of juncture between preoedipal and oedipal conflicts. These conflicts, which seem linked to a sense of weak phallic capacity, could perhaps be better understood with reference to Jones's notion of *aphanisis*, the abolition of sexual force. Disturbances in body image sometimes make it possible to isolate the depressive problem in the aim of controlling it. A sort of resignation sets in that stabilizes the decline in self-esteem at a relatively low level.

The "overidealization" of the psychoanalyst, studied by Mahler (1967), can be considered a consequence of these phenomena (idealization of the mother, often definitive). It is very possible that the pregenital fixations emerge in the course of the child's quest for a symbiosis made up of the introjective and projective processes where the images of self and object tend to merge; the child's repeated and unpleasant frustrations with and separations from the love object give rise to fantasies of total incorporation of the gratifying object in the hope of restoring a lost unity.[5] This hope will persist throughout our emotional life. The fusion and the "identity" of pleasure (shared pleasure) in the sexual act likewise give rise to the sense of recovering the original union Plato speaks of; this may be called the "oral aspect" of orgasm. The attempt to seek exclusively within one-

[5] This hypothesis can be understood within the framework of Freud's ego-pleasure (Lust-Ich) (1915c).

self for what is good can play a role in the separation anxiety of later life.

In order to understand others, we need an identification of greater or lesser duration which does not endanger our sense of identity or the boundaries of our ego.

In the union with the mother, the child either becomes part of her (devoured by her and sleeping on her breast) or tries to devour her (in the aggressive act of grabbing the breast) (Lewin, 1950). We thus encounter two attitudes which may enter into contradiction: submission-passivity or aggression-activity (in Lewin: to devour, to be devoured, and, as a third phase, to enter into sleep). Next comes *magical participation* (Szondi's "participation" [1956], Kohut's "idealized parents" [1971], Levy-Bruhl's "mystical participation" [1910]). The magic age is a stage in the formation of the ego to which the ego can later regress (Ferenczi, 1913). At that level, the fusion between images of self and images of objects is possible, without taking into account the real differences that exist between them.

Introjection and projection are thus processes whereby self-images can assume characteristics of object images, and vice versa. These mechanisms are rooted in infantile fantasies of incorporation or ejection, but, as Jacobson (1964) points out, it is important to distinguish between them. The small child's ability at the magic stage to differentiate between outside and inside is limited: the result is constant introjective and projective operations, what Freud called the "ego-pleasure" stage. These processes are attenuated with the acquisition of reality (see "reality testing" in Laplanche and Pontalis, 1967, and Jacobson, 1964).

Gerö (1936) showed how the analysis of pregenital fixations in depressives brings fears of castration to the forefront of the psychoanalytic work and leads to progress at the genital level. He emphasized the masochism found in this type of patient: clinical observation frequently shows symbiotic relationships in a profound masochistic equilibrium between mother and child or with the partner. According to Gero's hypothesis, the oedipal development in these subjects was interrupted prematurely, resulting in fragile object relations characterized by submission and preoedipal narcissistic dependence. It is as if they had expected too much both of the love object and of themselves; the self could thus not be gratified, and the libidinal objects were overestimated and idealized. In other words, the ego ideal was set too high to ever be attained.

Rapaport's conception (1951) whereby the introject is a hypercathected memory does not strike me as sufficient. Introjects in fact are intended partially to lose their character as memory and to be transmuted into identifications and lasting structures.

When the parents are depreciated, the child can no longer accept anything from them: the result is a deficiency in the ego ideal, the failure of the reparation impulse, and the turning of hostility against the self, leading to a destruction of self and the depressive affect.

Rado (1927) was the first to emphasize the dual nature of the introjective process in melancholia. The good object that the ego desires is introjected into the superego, which has the right to become angry at the ego. Meanwhile, the devalued image of the parents is introjected into the ego. Here, then, is the impotence of the ego vainly waiting for something; here, too, is the disappointment of the ego ideal, omnipotent and grand. Jacobson (1971), starting from an idea close to Rado's, formulates a brilliant hypothesis whereby the superego comprises an inflated image of the good and bad parents, while the self constitutes a deflated, depreciated image of the bad parents. She also remarks that representations of the self and the parents are not clearly separated, and that the antagonisms of these introjections could lead to the disintegration of the ego and superego systems.

Fenichel (1945) described melancholic depression as a total and profound regression leading from the anal to the oral stage and to primary narcissism.[6]

---

[6] "It has been stated that depression is a loss of self-esteem, either a complete breakdown of all self-esteem or a partial one intended as a warning against the possibility of a complete one. This formulation must now be supplemented by the statement that the depressed person tries to undo this loss and actually aggravates it by a pathognomonic introjection of the ambivalently loved object. . . . Ambivalence, however, gives this introjection a hostile significance. The wish to force the object to give his consent to the union ends in the attainment of punishment for the violence of this wish. After the introjection, the struggle for forgiveness is continued on a narcissistic basis, the superego now struggling with the ego.

"The depressed patient complains that he is worthless and acts as if he has lost his ego. Objectively he has lost an object. Thus ego and object are somehow equated. The sadism that once referred to the object has now been turned on the ego. . . . By virtue of the introjection, a part of the patient's ego has become the object; as Freud puts it: 'The shadow of the object has fallen on the ego'. . . . 'Regression from object relationship to identification,' 'regression to narcissism,' and 'regression to orality' are terms that mean one and the same thing looked upon from different viewpoints" (Fenichel, 1945, pp. 396-397).

According to Zetzel (1953), the "normal" subject going through a process of mourning is capable of introjecting most of the positive part of the lost object; when this task is accomplished, the mourning comes to an end. If earlier mournings (including weaning) were not carried out satisfactorily, the subject will slip into a more or less manifest depression. While I agree that there are cases where the mourning process does not reach a satisfactory conclusion, I believe this failure is due to events which were not accepted by the ego and the ego ideal, so that the lost object remained as it was, "indigestible," neither accepted nor metabolized, not harmoniously integrated into the personality but rather split, isolated from the rest.

As a final characteristic of depressive introjections, I would like to add to the foregoing the confusion (to which Jacobson called attention) between self- and object representations (or, better yet, a confusion at the level of inner objects), and the deep-seated antagonism between these objects, with the object representations belonging to the ego ideal or superego crushing those of the ego.

# Chapter 9

# A Word about the Superego

No one is without guilt.
—*Eugenio Montale*

For many authors, there is a link between depression and the importance of the superego. Freud, in *The Ego and the Id* (1923b), paid considerable attention to the mode of relationship between ego and superego. In obsessional neurosis the ego revolts against the superego, while in melancholia the ego admits its guilt and submits to punishment. Freud emphasized the sadism, "a pure culture of the death instinct" (p. 53), entrenched in the superego and unleashed against the ego. The severity of the conscience serves to check and control the aggressive tendencies against others, and is said to be involved in the diffusion of instincts after introjection. In melancholia the

114

ego—hated and persecuted by the superego—gives itself up and dies; the superego is a persecutor to the death. We find here an element of resignation which in my opinion plays the determining role in the birth of the depressive affect, and the relentless harassment of the ego by the superego leading to death or despair.

It is obvious that the degree of importance we accord to the death instinct in our conceptions will have an influence on our vision of depression. In depression the death instinct seems to me clinically mediated by problems of the superego, which comes down to stressing the problem of guilt. I have the impression, however, that the death instinct (or aggression, as certain authors prefer) here possesses an almost pre-superego quality, a lesser degree of organization than in the oedipal superego.

The importance of guilt in depression has been greatly emphasized. For Rado (1927), guilt is the last weapon in the struggle to regain the object's love (expiation, reparation, pardon, and reconciliation), whence its connection to obsessional neurosis and masochism.[1] In his study on Segantini, Abraham (1911a) remarks upon "the sadistic impulse finds satisfaction in the contemplation of 'the' child's dead body" (p. 220). In his later works (1911b, 1924), he emphasizes the death wishes directed at younger brothers, reflecting elements of comparison, jealousy, and guilt concerning an infantile "double." The

[1] In contrast to masochism, however, depression lacks the libidinal pleasure of suffering; even if the suffering may sometimes appear masochistic, the context is different, and what actually exists is unpleasure, despair, the desperate quest for expiation.

theme of the double was taken up and developed by Rosolato (1975), but he believes the word should refer first of all to the father, since the taking upon oneself of the deadly intention is a paternal function. The narcissistic axis of the beginning is thus tied to oedipal development: "This positioning of the father soothes the lethal confrontation and, in so doing, orients and releases the potential for a homosexual, strictly narcissistic cathexis which enters into the dynamic composition of the ideals" (pp. 29-30).

For Rochlin (1959), Beres (1966) and Guntrip (1969), guilt and the ego-superego conflict are at the very core of depression. I do not find this formulation entirely satisfying. Although guilt and depression are bound together by a thousand threads, the two affects must be distinguished, and just as there can be depressive affects without guilt—in the child and in certain non-Western cultures (see below)—so too can we find in many neuroses guilt complexes without depression (in obsessional neurosis, for example, where the neurotic, though feeling guilty, is not necessarily depressed). Depression seems to me to stem from a loss relating to the self-image, which may be linked to guilt but is not necessarily.

The subject is controversial. While certain authors are convinced that guilt occupies a central place in the psychoanalytic theory of depression, Jacobson (1971), among others, disagrees. "I realized as early as 1943," she writes, "that the emphasis laid upon the guilt problem as the core of the conflict did not do justice to all the cases" (p. 171; see also Pasche, 1969).

The dichotomy between "classic" neurosis and depression could likewise be interpreted from the standpoint of relations with the superego for the former, and with the ego ideal for the latter (see Grunberger, 1971). For depression to appear, however, the projective system must fail and there can be no possibility of blaming the "interdiction."

Jacobson (1964) examined the superego system in relation to the introjections that comprise it, bringing to the fore an internal dynamic of the superego comparable to the dynamic of the ego and that of "intrasystemic" tensions (Hartmann, 1939). Luquet (1962) rightly points out that "the theory of the imago would facilitate the comprehension of the metapsychology of certain agencies"; he recalls that "the conscious ego ideal, very often forming the representation of self, depends in large measure on the introjection of the object's image of the self. When this mechanism is firmly established, it remains a 'solid armor' against later narcissistic traumas and allows a more flexible adaptation and a more subtle conflict resolution" (p. 125). The deficiency of certain introjections and certain images forming the "ego ideal–superego system" could be at the root of depressive vulnerability.

According to Bion (1965), among others, the superego can sometimes develop *before* the ego and prevent its formation and development. I would say instead that these depressive patients behave as if they saw reality through the eyes of the superego, which distorts their perception. I have had patients of this type who appear to be either severe depressives or character neurotics with a wounded narcissism, or the two simultaneously, that is, borderline character neurotics with depressive and narcissistic problems. I assumed that a significant "identification with the aggressor" formed the basis of their personality, as if their ego had been overrun by precipitates of this identification, leading to (a) nonconsolidation of narcissism due to constant inner disapproval; and (b) a perception of reality from the standpoint of identification with the aggressor, or rather with the censoring agency. They experienced solitude as a punishment ("solitary confinement" as the next worst punishment to death).

For Lewin (1961), the depressive is seeking a narcissistic regression toward the relationship with the maternal breast, but the superego denies him this refuge. For example, the desire to sleep is coupled with the inability to sleep.

*Depression and guilt in non-Western cultures.* A number of researchers (Lin, 1953; Yap, 1958) have stated that depression among the Japanese and Chinese is not accompanied by ideas of guilt or sin as in Judaeo-Christian societies. By contrast, however, the Chinese living in Hong Kong and exposed to Western influences, present a clinical picture of depression similar to that observed among Westerners (Yap, 1965). Venkoba (1966) and Teja, Narang, and Aggarwal (1971) found notions of guilt in only a third to a half of the depressed Indian patients they examined, while Lambo (1956) found no trace of guilt whatsoever among Nigerians.

Mendels (1970) maintains that depression is rare in Africa (as it is claimed to be as well in such other non-Western societies as Java, Haiti, and the Tara Humara Indians of Mexico). Among the explanations given for this fact is that African cultures include the open expression of grief and guilt among their acceptable social models; and that the extended or tribal family protects the individual, while the collective superego (of the tribe) replaces the individual superego. It should be mentioned, however, that these observations have elicited controversy. Recent studies show that depression in Africa is more widespread than previously believed, but that it is difficult to identify because of the predominance of confusional and hypochrondriacal symptoms. For example, Leighton et al. (1963) reported numerous symptoms of depression in the Yoruba of Western Nigeria, and Field (1958) in the Ashanti of Ghana. However, they found neither guilt nor shame. According to these authors, the concept of depression as defined in the West is foreign to Yoruba culture. Kiev (1972) maintains that depressive states are extremely rare in preliterate and preindustrial societies. The findings of Murphy et al. (1967) cited by Kiev show the presence in these cultures of mood changes following a daily pattern, insomnias, awakening in the night, and withdrawal of interest from the social environment. On the other hand, ideas of guilt appear to be absent outside the Judaeo-Christian context, where they seem related to internalized standards of behavior (superego) that are not present in people of other religions or cultural milieus.

This brings us to the question of whether guilt and shame are integral to the notion of depression. In the classical psychoanalytic framework they are. Thus, for Spitz (1965), anaclitic depression does not qualify as a true depression because true depression presupposes structuration of the superego. Nonetheless, we can allow that the adult depression of Western culture is but one particular form, and that depression and an internalized superego are not linked in any necessary fashion. This would support the Kleinian position, which is that the concept of depression is of wider scope than that of the structured oedipal superego.

Ayo Binitié (1975) did not find suicidal tendencies among depressed Africans, and he contends that ideas of suicide as well as of guilt are culturally determined. This might be taken to suggest that suicide is closely related to guilt, and thus to the superego. For Grunberger (1971), however, the wound of being unhappy may push the melancholic to suicide. If this is so, then narcissism may be seen to play a role at least as important as that of the superego.

# Chapter 10

# Defenses against Depression

Despite the wide interest in antidepressive defenses, I shall confine myself to a few brief remarks on the subject, not wishing to further extend the already vast scope of my topic. The antidepressive defense of creativity, however, will be dealt with separately in chapter 12.

The manic defense is the denial of psychic reality through excitation, an attempt to deny inner reality; the manic defense is therefore denial as well as excitation. In pathological states, the suppression of superego factors combined with the fusion of the ego with the ego ideal leads to euphoric or manic states (Kanzer, 1952; see also Khan, 1974).[1] What is not certain, however, is whether in mania we are dealing

---

[1] Freud (1921c) spoke in this context of the fusion of the ego with the superego.

with a defense or a constellation in which several defenses play a role: denial of loss, feverish activity giving rise to a particular body sensation, and the euphoria stemming from total reversal of a situation where the self seen as worthless confronts an omnipotent object, into one where the now omnipotent ego faces the object, which has been reduced to nothingness.

A schizoid organization (Fairbairn, 1940) approaching paranoid or autistic structures is another way in which the personality can struggle against depression; distance vis-à-vis the depressive affect is maintained at the cost of a distance in object relations. Explaining why the depressed person abandons his objects, Bowlby (1963) suggests that an earlier disappointment could have pushed him to decathect them to the point of total detachment, allowing no more than "shadow" object relations, scattered and of feeble intensity (part-object relations). This raises the question of depression's role as a defense against possible later regression, which would be psychosis, paranoia, or autism. I can conceive of certain situations of temporary depersonalization during therapy, such as decathexis of the self-representation, or a sort of denial: "that couldn't have happened to me." Depersonalization can be considered a defense against intolerable affects. In *The Interpretation of Dreams*, Freud (1900a) cited the case of a ten-year-old boy whose father had died suddenly: "I know that my father is dead. What I can't understand, is why he doesn't come to dinner." There is denial here, but only partial denial going hand in hand with a split within the ego (see Freud, 1915b; Moellenhoff, 1939; Sterba, 1948; Wahl, 1958). Denial is related to the impossibility of accepting a bad reality (which in the last analysis means a bad inner state); the defenses are the partially inadequate means of overcoming difficulties.

According to one of the hypotheses of psychoanalysis, depression stems from ambivalence concerning the lost love-object. Kiev (1972, p. 61) notes that this ambivalence is less pronounced in African societies, less centered on a single person, since the presence of numerous "substitute" parent figures lessens the intensity of the ties to the real parents, making their loss less serious, less significant. Further, in such societies rage at the time of loss is more externalized.

Interdisciplinary studies combining ethnology and psychoanalysis have brought to light the importance of the "inhibition of the bite" (Lincke, 1971). In acquiring the ability to get along with others, children, like primates, learn to inhibit intra-species aggressiveness. To establish the good relationship which will become good narcissism, they must learn to come to terms with their aggression; such ideas recall Kleinian formulations regarding the constituent forces of the ego and the ego ideal.

Freud investigated the relation between cultural factors and personality in *The Ego and the Id* (1923b); in particular, he worked out the notion of a tension between what one is and what one would ideally like to be (the ego ideal). This tension between ego and ego ideal expresses itself as guilt. Social sentiments grow out of identifications with others on the basis of a shared ego ideal, that is to say, cultural values. To my mind, this point has direct bearing on the question of "the psychoanalyst's moral philosophy," so fashionable a few years back in French-speaking countries. When one speaks of guilt in depression, is the guilt real or imaginary? For the psychoanalyst, the latter characterization seems more appropriate, at least to neurotic or clinical depression. Here we differ fundamentally from the behaviorists, whose psychotherapy is based on a nonpunitive attitude, a "listening without retaliation," whereas we believe it necessary to enter the internal dialectic of guilt. Thus behaviorism seems to us the last illusion of technological and mechanistic simplification born of belief in the efficacy of manipulation. Psychoanalysis has chosen the more complex position, one that involves identifications (with, among other things, ego-syntonic ideals) and a dialectic of viewpoints that are antagonistic, contradictory, conflictual: a true dialectic of guilt that explains the importance of negative transference.

We could illustrate this thesis through clinical cases in which the technique of nonpunitive listening is simply inadequate, as in the face of dilemmas in which both sides in an ambivalent conflict are held to be guilty. The transference and countertransference difficulties experienced by this type of patient stem from the recourse to denial mechanisms. Indeed, it is not long before the tenuous nature of the patient's relationship with reality becomes apparent: without warning, a virtually delirious nucleus takes shape with a massive denial of reality, and the interpretation is perceived as a reproach for this reluctance or inability to enter into the conventionality of life's reality. Abraham (1911b, 1924), by underscoring the importance of the oral demand in such patients, did not ask himself if their behavior was defensive or not. For

Jacobson (1971), it was. Some of my patients incline me to the same view. One of them, formulating his desire for reassurance in a provocative manner, repeated the classic mechanism described by Guex (1950): putting to the test so as to obtain the expected proof of rejection.

Illness and pain always inflict a narcissistic wound and consequently may generate depression in the absence of an adequate defense. This is why illness is denied. It is possible that discussions which tend to deny the unhealthy nature of certain psychological conditions are fueled by this reluctance to speak of "pathology" and individual deficiencies—hence the spate of simplistic sociogenetic theories that would all too readily place the blame on society.

If depression is a state connected to object loss and attendant reproaches from the primitive superego, *elation* by contrast is a guilt-free fusion with the primitive object combined with *negation* (denial). (Let us note that sleep, as another return to primary narcissism, a state of fusion, may be either permitted or forbidden, depending on the depressed person's superego.)

Denial is the defense mechanism specifically mobilized against reality, and is associated with idealization and omnipotence. In this regard, one may ask what Freud (1924e) meant by the "reality," or the perception of the reality, of castration. If "penis envy" in the woman is denied as a source of depression,[2]

---

[2] Freud (1937c) attributes depression in women to a narcissistic wound linked to castration: A male "refuses to subject himself to a father-substitute, or to feel indebted to him for anything, and consequently, he refuses to accept his recovery from the doctor. No analogous transference can arise from the female's

it is difficult to speak of a perception of reality, since the absence of something can only be perceived in relation to its possible presence. We thus find here a general element of the depressive constellation: *comparison*. This is the constellation specifically making possible the primal jealousy and envy that Kleinians speak of. The woman who suffers from not having a penis thinks she can have one (there is a fantasmatic loss consequent on the comparison of a real situation to a state perceived as "ideal" or "complete"). Denial excludes not merely desire (as in suppression), but the entire constellation.

Humor pokes fun at reality. The affect of sudden hilarity in dreams was studied by Reik (1929), who demonstrated the role of introjection and projection in Jewish jokes by comparing them to manic-depressive mechanisms. Freud (1927d) interpreted humor as a vindictive triumph of narcissism (being ironical about life's miseries); as a mechanism, it involves the displacement of ego cathexis onto the superego, which, looking down at things from a higher plane, comforts the frightened ego as a father might console a small child distressed over a minor worry. A number of psychoanalysts have described the countertransferential temptation to share the analysand's denial in "hypomania" (Lewin, 1932, 1950; Deutsch, 1933). Kris (1938) suggested "that the most comic phenom-

wish for a penis, but it is the source of *outbreaks of severe depression* in her, owing to an internal conviction that the analysis will be of no use and that nothing can be done to help her. And we can only agree that she is right, when we learn that her strongest motive in coming for treatment was the hope that, after all, she might still obtain a male organ, the lack of which was so painful to her" (p. 252; italics mine).

ena seem to be bound up with past conflicts of the ego, that they help it repeat its victory and in doing so once more to overcome half-assimilated fear" (p. 89). It should be possible to confirm this psychoanalytic theory by clinical investigations into laughter and the comic sense in children. When someone falls down in the street, the onlooker's first reaction is to identify with the person who has fallen. Next, realizing that he is in control of his own body, his fears vanish and he feels his superiority. Now he can relax once more, participate in the experience through an innocent release, uncontrolled but socially acceptable: the burst of laughter that is simultaneously pleasure, narcissistic triumph, and an escape valve for aggressive instincts.

Idealization is another defense against narcissistic wounds and is sometimes a component of the denial of reality: one sides with the Other seen as "strong," "complete." All such defensive solutions serve to forestall depression and the working through of mourning.

# Chapter 11

# Boredom

Tears that have no reason
Fall in my sorry heart.
What, there was no treason?
This grief hath no reason.

Nay, the more desolate,
Because I know not why. . . .
　　　—Verlaine, *Romances sans paroles*

All things are full of labor; man cannot utter it: the eye is not satisfied
with seeing, nor the ear filled with
hearing.
　　　—Ecclesiastes 1:8

It would seem that the latest in the age-old succession
of historical and literary forms expressing varying
shades of sorrow and pain is boredom, this inner

emptiness tinged with indifference that is our contemporary version of the eternal melancholia.

Boredom: The *Oxford English Dictionary* defines it as "the feeling of mental weariness and dissatisfaction produced by want of occupation, or by lack of interest in present surroundings or employments," and as "the malady of *ennui,* supposed to be specifically 'French' as 'spleen' was supposed to be English." But ennui, as used in English, has lost the old meaning one finds in French etymological dictionaries, the meaning which conveys the notion of a torment of soul caused by the death or absence of loved ones or the loss of hope. Hence a *loss,* as in depression. Indeed, as a psychic structure boredom is related to depression, against which moreover it is a defense.

Boredom has been attributed to a lowering of stimuli or configurations of stimuli. According to the classical definition, it springs from a discrepancy between the subject and the stimuli of his environment. The subject becomes bored when he experiences his environment as poor in stimuli. This perception can reflect reality, or, as psychoanalytic examination frequently discovers, the problem can lie within the subject, due either to an inability to find stimuli in the outside world, to a rich inner world, or to a tendency to devalue available stimuli. This last occurs more frequently than generally believed.

For instance, young people in the less favored social classes of large cities—the urban poor—can become bored through lack of opportunities or life goals: the available stimuli of their very nature cannot fit the configuration of youthful ideals. This situation can be seen as an example of a depression-generating (or neurosis-generating) reality. Moreover, psychoanalytic examination of depressive patients complaining of boredom frequently reveals that the stimuli received are depreciated by the ego ideal or, in the most advanced cases, by the superego. This would seem to denote an arrested development of the superego–ego ideal system and a lack of flexibility in the ego ideal, which remains megalomaniacal and hence devalues the stimuli. Sociologists have described the raptus of disillusioned adolescents who escape boredom through senseless acts of rage and violence. In psychoanalytic treatment, this phenomenon is seen as the consequence of an extreme state of tension between an immature megalomaniacal ego ideal and the desperate awareness of falling short of this ideal. The rise over the past fifty years in the number of "gang rapes" might well be a function of such "boredom," perhaps reflecting a mechanism whereby the sole possibility of confronting the most massive prohibitions of the superego (murder and incest) is through eroticizing guilt. One of my analysands, raised in an extremely strict and prohibition-filled environment, indulged in perverted sexual activities in public places. Sexual excitation provoked by the fear of being caught was mingled with an aggressive feeling of triumph at the idea that one person—revealed through free association to be his mother—would then learn of it. The feeling of boredom frequently coexists with affective frustration and violence (this last in the sense of destroying the disappointing, frustrating object). It is thus that in clinical experience we often find a kind of alternation between psychopathic structure and depressive states.

What is sometimes expressed in the "family romance" is the feeling that the others—the parents—can provide nothing: the feeling of being superfluous, an unwanted child. Instead of actively seeking satisfactions, the subject can react to this feeling by passively giving up on the fulfillment of his desires; a sort of chronic apathy then sets in. The family romance was probably determined by the relationship with the primitive object—more precisely, by a preponderance of frustration in the relationship with the mother —without this frustration having incited the subject to make demands. Subsequently, aggression was turned against the self and blocked by the archaic superego. In this case, boredom would derive from a poverty of cathexes, either through the absence of identifications or through their psychotic-like blockage. Fromm (1971) attributes chronic boredom to the inability to have a meaningful, that is, goal-oriented, activity. Boredom implies a lack of interest, a distancing oneself, often in relation to oedipal conflict.

Freud (1916d) showed the connection between boredom, thrill seeking, and aggression in discussing Shakespeare's *Richard III:*

> Richard seems to say nothing more than: "I find these idle times tedious, and I want to enjoy myself. As I cannot play the lover on account of my deformity, I will play the villain; I will intrigue, murder and do anything else I please." Such a frivolous motivation could not but stifle any stirring of sympathy in the audience if it were not a screen for something far more serious. . . . When we do so [undertake to understand what lies behind Richard's soliloquy] however, the appearance of frivolity vanishes, the bitterness and minuteness with which Richard has depicted his deformity make their full effect, and we clearly perceive the fellow-feeling which compels our sympathy

even with a villain like him. What the soliloquy thus means is: "Nature has done me a grievous wrong in denying me the beauty of form which wins human love. Life owes me reparation for this, and I will see that I get it. I have a right to be an exception, to disregard the scruples by which others let themselves be held back. I may do wrong myself, since wrong has been done to me." And now we feel that we ourselves might become like Richard, that on a small scale, indeed, we are already like him. Richard is an enormous magnification of something we find in ourselves as well. We all think we have reason to reproach Nature and our destiny for congenital and infantile disadvantages; we all demand reparation for early wounds to our narcissism, our self-love. [pp. 314–15]

André Gide (1951), writing of Paul Valéry in his *Journal* (November 3, 1920), ascribes this sub-depression we call "boredom" to the depreciation of stimuli or "objects": "How could it be surprising if, after having disenchanted the world around him, after having strained his wits to lose interest in so many things, he is bored!" (pp. 685-686).

We could say with Beck (1967) that one of the characteristics of the ego in the depressed person is the constant tendency to underestimate the value of his experiences—with others and with himself—just as another is to underestimate or devalue stimuli and activities proper, and to see the self, in anticipation of the future, as being worthless, without future prospects. These traits are a natural consequence of the discrepancy between the ego and the ego ideal. It goes without saying that situations reflecting the reality, such as an actual lack of possibilities, can trigger reactions of this kind, but the situation of present reality does not explain the inner situation (a statement equally valid for every psychoanalytic reflection on situational phenomena). Without a background making it possible to understand this depression in its developmental dimension, with reference to infantile experience and the unconscious, our explanation cannot, needless to say, be anything but skewed.

I would compare boredom to what Luquet (1973) has called the "illness of an-ideality." The tension between the ego ideal and the ego, caused by the latter's inability to live up to the former's demand, gives rise to a feeling of frustration which in turn triggers a great aggressiveness that cannot be channeled into sublimated goals (the "ego ideal-superego system," as we know, plays a role in activities having such goals).

The feeling of not being as strong as one would like expresses itself in terms of "fatigue," as does the feeling of being less stimulated than one would like. When the subject complains of being tired, he is probably often speaking of a subjective feeling of inadequacy. It seems to me that fatigue and its semantic field encompass a range of depressive states such as neurasthenia. Depression raises the question of psychic forces (psychic energy, asthenia); psychoanalysis and psychoanalytic psychology view these forces from the standpoint of inhibition due to the superego-ego ideal system. What Janet saw as a simple *diminution* of psychic forces becomes, for the psychoanalyst, the *inhibition* of psychic forces in their conflictual dynamism.

Fenichel (1934) brought out very well the connection between boredom and inhibition. Boredom derives from the attempt to push aside instinctual tensions. An analysand, bored from the beginning of analysis, suddenly discovered that he had desires and became depressed. It soon became clear that his periods of boredom were connected to traumatic events and corresponded to the emergence of vague recollections and the desperate effort to quell them. These periods were also associated with voyeurism, with a high degree of guilt-laden curiosity in relation to certain traumatic childhood events, and with a feeling of emptiness that signified hunger. This young man had memories of strong women, physically and otherwise, envied to the point that he wanted to be like them. His sexual contacts with these women involved by preference cunnilingus and fellatio. At these moments he no longer had the feeling of being empty; rather, he felt full. Nor was it mere coincidence that these activities regularly followed food orgies. His fantasy was that these women were full, while he was empty and hungry. Drinking alcohol was associated simultaneously with the feeling of filling oneself and of becoming intoxicated, making possible guilt-free sexual desires. One whole part of the analysis of this young man—who was moreover very gifted—was centered on the problem of boredom. It was only after having analyzed the danger of the instinctual desire concealed beneath the boredom, and the risk of depression were he to let himself go, that we were able to tackle the problem of identification with powerful phallic women. Once he understood that boredom was a defense both against his desires and against the threatening depression that resulted from yielding to his instincts, a large part of his inhibition disappeared and he was able to feel himself more in touch with his desires.

Boredom can thus be explained as an inhibition of the ego through the impoverishment of interests following a failure to mourn and the consequent non-recovery of available energy; alternatively, it may be characterized as a feeling of emptiness, likewise ascribable to the mourning process, with persistent feelings of impoverishment (Greenson, 1953). This feeling of emptiness seems overdetermined and is connected to the utilization of inner excitations either (a) as hypomanic defenses (false agitation, hyperactivity, etc.) temporarily masking depression or (b) as anxiety-producing stimuli, their repetition leading to a sense of despair and the feeling that satisfaction cannot be obtained, thus triggering the depressive affect.

The adolescent is called upon to accomplish the mourning process in order to replace the lost oedipal (and narcissistic) object. Boredom sets in with the feeling that that object is not worth replacing. By contrast, when the adolescent falls in love, he overestimates this new object choice and transfers onto it narcissistic and megalomaniacal ideas; the love-object thus becomes a "narcissistic object" in Kohut's sense.

In another of my analysands, boredom could be understood as painful solitude. He was alone, and this because he felt rejected by the internalized and idealized object; in any event, he could do nothing to recover the lost love of this idealized object, which he believed was destroyed and could never be revived. He felt responsible for this, but denied his guilt and projected it onto others: it was their fault; it was the fault of the forces of evil who always got the upper hand. In his mind, his life had no meaning because he would never be able to recover the approbation of the primitive object.

One wonders if the "apathy" or boredom found in certain drug addicts is a consequence of the drug or a reflection of the preexisting state of mind that led them to drugs in the first place, at least as concerns the so-called minor drugs.

Depressive problems in the retired can likewise take the form of boredom. In this case it reflects the inability to invest in objects not seen as "dependable": the fear that they will turn out to be useless. Franz Alexander (1960), in his *The Western Mind in Transition*, begins his penultimate chapter, entitled "Retirement Neurosis of Malignant Boredom," with the sentence: "The creative utilization of leisure requires life-long preparation." This life-long preparation, far from being merely intellectual, is an intrapsychic constellation in which intellectual curiosity is stripped of its aggressive character experienced as harmful. The aggressive component present in curiosity may then harmonize with the ego, thus becoming ego-syntonic. This modification can serve to counterbalance the loss of professional status and the death of one's peers in old age.

Another form of depression, fashionable during the eighteenth and early nineteenth centuries, is nostalgia, *Heimweh*.[2] The nostalgic object relation—that can

---

[2] *Heimweh* (an expression of Swiss origin dating from the period when Swiss mercenaries were to be found throughout Europe), nostalgia, *desiderium patriae* and *desiderium* for love, all express desires tinged with renunciation. Starobinski (1966) recalls Kant's remark that the nostalgic is less interested in seeing his birthplace again than in recovering the sensations of his childhood. A return *(nostos)* accompanied by sorrow *(algia)* and desire—*nostalgia*. "Nostalgia" is a neologism of relatively recent date—1688—and is credited to Johannes Hofer.

be encountered equally well today—presupposes an idealized object, conceived as very distant and unattainable; the sorrow experienced relates to its inaccessible nature. This sorrow, this longing, creates and maintains the tie with the idealized object, which involves an obvious benefit. Similarly, in the depressive constellation, masochism procures a secondary pleasure that transforms pain into something pleasant (in "classical depression" the depressive constellation is secondarily erotized and transformed into masochistic pleasure). Thus, the subject clings to his nostalgia, which creates and maintains a tie with the idealized object, a tie of erotized refusal. An analysand, ten years after the break with her "first love," was still carefully nurturing all the recollections that brought her closer to this relatively brief episode with someone who had not even been her lover and who from the outset had shown but passing interest in her. But she needed this nostalgic relationship with its safe distance: having lost her father at a very young age, she had maintained throughout her childhood and adolescence an idealized and nostalgic relationship with this perfect father.

It seems to me that this desire to "recapture the past" is different from the "regret for something that is over" in that it implies a repetition compulsion and a working through which can become a source of creativity. "When there is hope in regard to the inside things," writes Winnicott (1957b), "instinctual life is active, and the individual can enjoy using instinctual urges, including aggressive ones, in making good in real life what has been hurt in fantasy. This forms the basis for both play and work" (p. 172). This is not the case with boredom, where hope is absent.

Illusion (see Gressot, 1973) and "ideality illnesses" (Chasseguet-Smirgel, 1973) have received considerable attention. Boredom poses the problem of *disillusionment*. The withdrawal of cathexes from the external world, during a kind of idealization process, has something in common with the narcissistic recathexis of the ego described by Freud (1911c) in psychotic processes. In a changing world requiring frequent recathexes, the object cathexis no longer has a libidinal character but uses the narcissistic libido; one might say that the objects cathected with narcissistic libido become part of the self, idealizations of objects. Disillusionment stems from the realization that the idealized object does not have the omnipotence earlier ascribed to it.

How does the patient communicate his depression? His language varies and is determined by numerous factors, cultural among others. Long before the current linguistic fashion in psychoanalysis, Balint (1959) raised this problem, showing that the subject is dependent on the terms available to him, i.e., on the language he uses, to identify and communicate certain feelings. Balint illustrated his point with the term "thrill" *(Angstlust)*, which conveys a mixture of anxiety and pleasure or excitement, an erotization linked to the ludic anxiety it stirs in us; it has no exact equivalent in French. Lewis (1974) points out that there is no word for "depression," "mourning," or "nostalgia" in the Tahitian language, but that there are some forty different terms there for varying degrees of anger. In certain cultures, depression is expressed through somatic sensations, a mode of communication, like others, interpretable by doctors. According to Balint (1968), patients learn and use the language of their psychoanalyst; they will therefore speak to us of depression. Some subjects are incapable of it, however, because they are not able to feel it (Jacobson, 1971). This reminds me of a patient with an obsessional structure who made impressive strides in analysis, progressing from fatigue to depression. The moment he began to feel depressed, sad, helpless, the actual analytic work could begin.

# Chapter 12

# Creativity, Culture and Civilization

Nothing makes us greater than a great suffering.
    —Alfred de Musset, *La Nuit de Mai*

Man owes his greatest accomplishments to the painful feeling of the incompleteness of his destiny.
    —Mme. de Stael, *De la Litterature*

For Winnicott (1963a), "A mental breakdown is often a 'healthy' sign, in that it implies a capacity of the individual to use an environment that has become available in order to re-establish an existence on a basis that feels real. Naturally, such a device does not by any means always succeed, and it is very puzzling

140

to society to see a compliant and perhaps valuable false self destroy [apparent?] good prospects by a renunciation of every obvious advantage simply for the hidden advantage of gaining a feeling of reality" (p. 225). The environment is important for the depressive; the analysand needs his aggression in order to feel himself, to have a sense of reality that will manifest itself during transference. The sequence goes something like this: to feel oneself = the pleasure of functioning = narcissism = the reality of self-cathexis: *to feel oneself real.* "It is only under conditions of ego adequacy," writes Winnicott (1963b), "that id-drives, whether satisfied or frustrated, become *experiences of the individual*" (p. 241; italics mine), to which we could add: "and a part of reality experienced as such." The analyst's interpretation can be understood as the confrontation between two realities: the reality of the outside world, as represented by the analyst, and the subject's inner reality.

The journey from a closed inner world to a life open to and in contact with the external world can be compared to that of the child, who sets out totally helpless, completely dependent on his mother, and who, through the trauma of separation, passes from the anaclitic situation to the depressive position. Among the terms used for this are "postdepressive working through" (Klein), "libidinal clinging" (Hermann), and "transitional object" or "transitional space" (Winnicott). Róheim (1943) reminds us that the road to culture is a narrow one; our aggressive impulses may easily lead us astray. In a dream fragment of an analysand, the analyst was assigned the role of emptying the coffins representing important childhood imagos. The working through process takes place in psychoanalysis, but also through and within the culture.

The dream has a restorative function. In dreams, as in psychoanalysis, it is the withdrawal connected to suffering and depression that makes possible St. Augustine's "return into yourself."

The libidinal dynamic forces underlying instinctual manifestations in our culture can be brought to light by the analyst. Indeed, it is through the depressive neuroses that these lines of force can best be apprehended, although in elucidating them the psychoanalyst should avoid being drawn into ideologies positing noogenetic or purely sociogenetic neuroses. For Róheim (1943), "In growing up we substitute active for passive object love. We find substitutes for the love objects of infancy but under the veneer of giving love we always retain the desire to receive love, and the loves and triumphs of adult life are really 'Paradise Regained,' the refinding of the infancy situation at another level" (p. 39).[1] In Róheim's conception, civilization is, among other things, a system of institutions erected for the security of man, this creature who at bottom remains a child fearing nothing so much as solitude and darkness. In a sense, this comes down to giving "depression" and "solitude" a central significance, which is what Melanie Klein did in her conceptualization of the aggressive instincts and post-depressive working through. This interpretation in

---

[1] "Civilization originates in delayed infancy and its function is security. It is a huge network of more or less successful attempts to protect mankind against the danger of object loss, the colossal efforts made by a baby who is afraid of being alone in the dark" (Róheim, 1943, p. 100).

no way excludes others: It is obvious that culture is the culmination of many different lines of force, one of which is unquestionably centered on the oedipus complex and its marking the emergence of a third person, thanks to whom the dual relationship with the mother can be superseded. At the root of culture is the incest taboo, as Freud and, more recently, Claude Levi-Strauss have demonstrated. Elaborating his theory on the fundamental importance of the gift, Levi-Strauss (1949) writes that the incest prohibition "is the fundamental step because of which, by which, but above all in which, the transition from nature to culture is accomplished" (p. 2).

Human culture thus began at a collective level, and, more specifically, in the shadow of the tomb.[2] For while the anthropoid apes show signs that can be interpreted as analogous to our depression and mourning, they do not build tombs for their dead: because of their extremely limited capacity for internalization, the capacity for reparation in the Kleinian sense is lacking. The Neanderthal painted the bones of his dead, and it was in these burial grounds that began what was to become illusion, the cultural sphere, or Winnicott's transitional space between ego and environment.

The fact of death brought with it the desire for

---

[2] Róheim (1943, p. 85): "To be alone is the great danger. To obviate it, mankind has invented the psychotic hallucination of a world to come where the dead will be in company with other spirits of the departed and the obsessional neurotic ceremonial of mourning and ancestral cult thereby keeping company with the dead. The countries in which these elements have been developed more than anywhere else are also the cradles of civilization."

reparation. When speaking of the killing of the primal father of the primitive human horde, Freud (1912–1913) goes a step further and names guilt. With death emerges the splitting of the image of existence: on the one hand, there is the image of one who is gone, on the other, the image that continues to be present, either through laws (Freud's example) or, more generally, through culture. Ancestor worship, which involves nonrenunciation of the deceased's image by the superego, is yet another way of preserving this continued presence.

The dramatic action in Greek tragedy, punctuated by the Kommos, the chorus' chant of mourning, is the reenactment of tragic events of the past, of a mourning to be accomplished. Thus, the most profound masterpieces of our culture are bound, through the Kommos, to the cult of the dead.

Creation and creative activity attempt to re-create a unity, a completeness (often bisexual) unmarked by separation or differences (neither sex differences nor castration). Creation is thus a defense against the anxiety of separation from the gratifying maternal protection, a defense against a "lack" and attendant castration anxiety. The representation is a re-presentation, and the creation of the object is, in a way, a re-creation of the lost object. As Picasso remarked to his biographer: "At the beginning of each picture . . . there is someone who works with me. Towards the end I have the impression of having worked without a collaborator" (Muensterberger, 1962, p. 168). First, a preoedipal mother is there so the child will not be helpless, so he can work; then, when the object has been resurrected, he no longer needs help. One of the tasks of culture is to make it possible to go beyond the universal ambivalence, to accept it by expressing it in our creative works.

Kanzer (1953) investigated the effects of the early loss of parents on creativity. Among the many writers who were orphaned in childhood, he lists Baudelaire, the Brontë sisters, Dante, Dumas, Rousseau, Poe, Sand, Tolstoi, Voltaire, and Dostoevsky, whose father was assassinated. In English literature, Byron, Keats, Wordsworth, Coleridge, Swift, and Gibbon were all orphans before the age of fifteen. In French literature, we may note the following: Molière, whose mother died when he was a child, wrote a masterpiece following each of his depressions stemming from marital problems; Racine was orphaned at the age of four and raised by a grandmother; Rousseau's mother died when he was born, and he was left to fend for himself from childhood; Chateaubriand's mother suffered from melancholia; Victor Hugo began to write when his parents separated; Stendhal lost his mother and rebelled against his father; Baudelaire's father died when he was six; and Camus and Sartre both lost their fathers in childhood.

The relationship between the loss of parents and depression, and then between depression and creativity, has been elaborated by Gregory (1966).[3]

[3] Pierre Rentchnick (1975) gives the following list of philosophers, writers, artists, and scholars who were either true orphans (the majority) or abandoned or illegitimate children: Voltaire, Rousseau, Tolstoi, Gandhi, Sartre, Descartes, Erasmus, Pascal, Kierkegaard, Bertrand Russell, Renan, Péguy, Racine, Gabriel Marcel, Francis Bacon, Diderot, Paracelsus, d'Alembert, Schopenhauer, Aristotle, Plato, Camus, Molière, Dickens, the Marquise de Sévigné, Jules Renard, Baudelaire, Victor Hugo, Dostoevski, Maupassant, Marcus Aurelius, Dante, Dumas, Poe, Sand, Keats, Wordsworth, Coleridge, Swift, Gibbon, Drink-

Anzieu (1975) recalls that Joyce, Pascal, and Proust became creative only after the death of their fathers. To what can this be attributed, if not to separation, the need to become independent and to detach oneself? The work of mourning set in motion at the moment of death impels the individual to seize his independence, for henceforth he can rely only on his own resources. Anzieu further stresses the importance of the midlife crisis, as in Freud, Proust, and Joyce.

The biography of Max Weber reveals that his greatest works, including *The Protestant Ethic and the Spirit of Capitalism* (1904–1905), were written following the death of his father in 1897 and a nervous illness which had prevented him from working for several years (1898–1903). It is possible that this crisis corresponded to the relinquishment of an idea of narcissistic omnipotence precipitated by the confrontation with his father's death or the prospect of his own (an idea dear to Kierkegaard and Kafka).

According to legend, the Buddha Siddhartha Gautama was twenty-nine when for the first time he was confronted with the sight of an old and decrepit man. His coachman's explanation that this was the fate of humanity and that all men were doomed to die triggered in him the profound meditation and "identity crisis" that led to his quest for truth. In the legends of the Middle Ages, too, it is the realization of death (the father's death, the plague, etc.) that precipitates

---

water. . . . We could also study the great musicians and artists (Leonardo da Vinci was an illegitimate child; Michelangelo, Rubens, and Puccini were orphans). Pollock (1975) counted 1200 writers "having suffered such a trauma."

the "identity crisis" (Erikson, 1950) and the inner need to work through loss through creativity.

The great Jewish philosopher Martin Buber was raised by his paternal grandparents after the divorce of his parents when he was three; his nostalgia for his mother, for the relationship with the lost object, profoundly marked his philosophy and his theory of the I-Thou relationship.

The impossibility of total satisfaction is rooted in man's very biopsychological condition, in his neoteny (Róheim, 1950, inspired by Bolk, 1926). His need for replacement, which implies the opening of the cultural sphere, is born of this mourning for Paradise Lost. It should be noted that the myth of the lost paradise and the nostalgic longing for a past that was never in reality as it is imagined in retrospect are not confined to ideologies that make a career of looking backward (Rousseauism and the other "noble savage" ideologies). On the contrary, it would seem that the tendency to seek an "era of reference" in the past has been present throughout history, with the model changing according to the culture and the age: for the southern European countries during the Renaissance, for instance, it was ancient Greece; northern Europe during the Reformation looked to Early Christianity; for the Romantics it was the Middle Ages; for Erich Fromm and many others, it was the egalitarian matriarchal society, and so on. The fact of calling attention to this need for support or confirmation from the past should not be taken to imply anything on an axiological level, that is, as concerns the actual validity or truth of this thought. But it may imply something about human nature, in that it is perhaps memory or a solid grounding in the past that makes possible the leap into the unknown, the movement toward the future. (And, as is well known, history will repeat itself for those with no memory of the past; the position of Freud and psychoanalysis in this regard is the same as that of Arnold Toynbee and George Santayana.)

The relationship between the working through of guilt feelings following a death and the creation of the art object is sometimes extraordinarily clear. Proust's *Remembrance of Things Past*, for example, was unquestionably his attempt to overcome feelings of grief and guilt aroused by his mother's death, feelings which in fact had been present in their relationship even during her lifetime, as the work shows.

Grunberger (1965), returning to an idea developed by Ferenczi in *Thalassa* (1924), explains the central place of the Oedipus complex in neurosis by the nostalgia of return to the mother's breast, which he believes gives rise to incestuous desire. Oedipus complex contains narcissistic desire; it straddles thus narcissism and the object relationship. In his essay "The Oedipus Complex and Narcissism," Grunberger (1971) sets forth the hypothesis that the incest prohibition (or "incest barrier," as he calls it) is a protection against narcissistic injury. Thus the child seeking to recover the bliss of prenatal existence through incest can attribute his inability to do so to a parental injunction rather than to his own functional incapacity; guilt arising from oedipal desire is similarly projected onto the external prohibition. In the absence or laxity of such a prohibition, the narcissistic wound is laid bare, as we see both in cases where incest is consummated and in cases, frequent today, where authority is lacking and the child feels inadequate—in all areas, not merely the sexual.

The fear of punishment and internalization of guilt (it matters not whether the transgression was actually committed or merely dreamed of) become entrenched during childhood. The father's role as the sociofamilial protector-repressor obviously reinforces this inner anxiety, born of the fear of death and the insecurity that myths, magic, and religion strive vainly to keep at bay. Love and death are also bound together by the parental interdiction. Fulfilled love gives rise to the anguished expectation of vengeance from the prohibiting parents; it recalls the situation where the child was incapable of fulfilling his desires and where the only attempt to do so was met by rejection, abandonment, and death, as in *Romeo and Juliet*.

Psychoanalysis and civilization have other points of contact as well. Anthropologists have taken great interest in these matters. Margaret Mead (1956) underscored the disorienting effects of rapid cultural change, while Peter Marris (1974) expresses analogous ideas on culture, civilization, and the process of scientific discovery in his *Loss and Change*. Nostalgia for a lost communion expresses itself in many ways in contemporary Western civilization.

One of the main characteristics of contemporary society is the growing isolation of the individual, as attested by the striking number of books on the market today dealing with loneliness. We must, however, make a distinction between isolation and solitude. Isolation, which implies loneliness, has a pejorative connotation of withdrawal from the world and from social life, while solitude can have a positive side entailing even communication. The profession of psychoanalyst, for example, even while necessitating a certain solitude, in no way excludes communication.

The ability or inability to tolerate solitude, to be alone, is a function of the individual organization of the personality, as Winnicott (1958) has shown. Certain individuals, feeling that the "communication" they receive does not meet their needs, decathect it. This situation may be tolerable for exceptional individuals, but it is evident that for the average man it poses considerable problems, and we may well ask whether the increasingly pronounced tendency toward isolation in modern society does not exact of even moderately vulnerable individuals a toll too great to bear. The current fashion in expressions such as "community," "communication," and "meaningful relationship"[1] express the aspiration underlying these apparently scientific concerns.

The road leading from depression to the various forms of addiction is traveled with ever greater frequency. Rado (1933) brought out the parallel between depression and the seeking of artificial narcissistic relationships aimed at counteracting psychological pain.

Depression in certain cultural contexts manifests itself through physical illness: in preliterate societies, it often takes the form of hypochondria (Lambo, 1956; Field, 1958). Hypochrondriacal fantasies (palpitations of the heart, breathing difficulties, etc.) often express a need for support and depressive feelings through a language of the body in which one can read the "return of the repressed" that Freud found in hysteria.

New forms of contact have been initiated with the

telephone, television, and widespread travel, but too often these contacts are either ersatz (as in television) or fleeting and superficial.

In this age of great change and confusion, where a hectic pace and unprecedented stress are creating ever greater needs and vulnerability in the population, some may question the pertinence of our work as analysts and our individual orientation. But it seems to me that our probing into these affective disorders—particularly depressive disorders, which can be seen as paradigms of human existence—provides us a great many insights of general applicability by shedding a harsh, a troubling light on many of the lifestyles we have imposed upon ourselves despite their destructive aspects. Our work brings us face to face with problems relating to the fear of attachment, the anxiety of separation, the fragility of identity, aggression, major splits in feeling (representations and affects), the blind and often harmful attachment to artificially created symbols, undeveloped and poorly understood needs, and the distortion of the body schema. It shows us, with a clarity worthy of the laboratory, insights which, taken together, give the range of most of the adult personalities requiring analysis.

Can the psychoanalyst, working through the individual, make a contribution to our culture in the eudaemonological sense, improving our well-being? If, as is supposed, depression is an important factor underlying violence, can anything be done to transform it into an activity consistent with the ego ideal? Has psychoanalysis provided us any kind of model for a satisfying art of living, in Bertrand Russell's sense? Is it capable of carrying on a maieutic legacy, clarifying human existence through a contribution of its own? (By this I do not mean to suggest a reinterpretation of psychoanalysis from a Heideggerian or other nonanalytic perspective. Without wishing to venture too far into the realm of social psychology, my experience with patients leads me to wonder whether our current generation—depressive, guilt-ridden and constantly in mourning—will not be succeeded by another which, unable to bear the oppressive weight of the superego, will simply cast off its constraints and "get down to action." Civilization is an immense undertaking, and Freud's celebrated cultural pessimism is turning out to be realism; overcoming depression through an activity equally valid for the ego and the ego ideal is difficult to achieve. Freud (1915b) raised this problem in "Thoughts for the Times on War and Death":

> The very emphasis laid on the commandment "Thou shalt not kill" makes it certain that we spring from an endless series of generations of murderers, who had the lust for killing in their blood, as perhaps, we ourselves have to-day. Mankind's ethical strivings, whose strength and significance we need not in the least depreciate, were acquired in the course of man's history; since then they have become, though unfortunately only in a very variable amount, the inherited property of contemporary men. [p. 296]

The problem of aggression, whose importance is underscored in this text, brings us back to reparation and the need for restitution, a source of creativity. These are found in the creative and above all restitutive process of the dream, the "wish fulfillment." If we suppose with Grunberger (1971) that the primary trauma is that dealt to narcissistic "complete-ness"—the "narcissistic trauma" which he defines as the loss of infantile omnipotence—then what would logically follow is the pressing need to repair this fundamentally traumatic situation. Man confronted with his limits can react either by sliding into depression or by mobilizing his vitality in an attempt to go beyond them.[4]

This attempt to transcend one's limits is itself a kind of reparation: it can take several forms, for example, harnessing the drive for mastery or the drive for knowledge. It is of course true that frustration of the instinctual drives can trigger a feeling of limitation, the very opposite of omnipotence. Since it was at the level of infantile sexuality that the child experienced his greatest frustrations, since it was there that his inner needs were in greatest contradiction with the possibility of fulfilling them, it is not surprising that infantile sexuality is the principal source of disturbances in psychic development and of depressive states. It is understood that these major conflicts at the level of sexual drives (in the Freudian sense) will play a role during a second phase in the course of early childhood. The first instance of nonsatisfaction will arise in relation to even more fundamental needs called "oral": separation and the processes that Winnicott described at the level of illusion and disillusionment.

In the course of his development, man has used a

---

[4] In Sartre's *Nausea*, an intellectual engaged in tedious historical work is seized by a kind of nausea, a paralysis, but envisioning a new philosophy, transforms his nausea into creative activity.

variety of techniques to diminish the unpleasant nature of disagreeable experiences ("bad inner states"). The most primitive of these techniques—expulsion—is linked to ego pleasure; another is the transformation implied in the proverb "absence makes the heart grow fonder" (it at any rate embellishes memories); yet another is the restructuration of the inner traces of these bad experiences, which strips them of the connections that made them disagreeable (one of the functions of drugs is to suppress these connections); and finally, there is sublimation, elaboration in another context.

Galenson and Roiphe (1972), according to whom the child's early discovery (between 18 and 19½ months) of anatomical differences and sexual sensations causes disappointment and rage toward the mother, show the sexual problem as an element engendering depressive affect through the image of a limited self (castration at the level of narcissism). Confronted with the painful sense of limitation, loss of omnipotence and omniscience, the individual seeking reparation may turn to art, religion, or science for a certain promise of immortality. Paradisal existence attempts to deny the weight of separation, loss, and death. The idea of an afterlife allows us regression through death, in the continuum of immortality, and a restitution of Paradise Lost after the Resurrection.

# Chapter 13

# Conclusions

> O Melancholy, be not wroth with me
> That I this pen should point to praise
> thee only. . . .
>
> —Nietzsche

It is time to return to the questions we asked ourselves at the outset. Does despair have a meaning? Is it a particular phenomenon, or do we find it in the lives of us all? Since any developmental process is of necessity accompanied by external change and the loss of successive inner states, is not despair a necessary concomitant of human development? Certain of its aspects are brought out through the mourning that takes place during psychoanalysis, when cathexes of the object world and representations of the self are finally relinquished.

I have attempted to investigate the problem of depression using as a starting point the concept of trauma. Some might find this approach obsolete: even the "cumulative trauma" proposed by Masud Khan (1963, 1964) is rarely at the center of clinical considerations. But in my view, ˙trauma conceived as an inadequacy, as the gap between an external event and the subject's capacity to work it through, can be of use to us. In this sense, it is at odds with a balanced mourning process, since the external event (the disappearance of an object) overcome in mourning cannot be overcome during a trauma. Understanding the mourning process gives us some indication as to the unfolding of the psychoanalytic process; it is the gradual working through of something traumatizing, that is, something that could not be overcome earlier. We could use, as an example, the model of the primal scene. The child observes the scene, becomes excited, but is incapable of overcoming or mastering this excitation; inadequacy is inherent in the notion of trauma (A. Freud, 1967). It thus encompasses, as a concept, both the sexual element (or, more generally, the *instinctual* element) and the narcissistic wound, which makes it an important point of junction between narcissism, libido, and aggression.

We have seen the influence of narcissism as the early developmental phases unfold, in the child's helplessness, in the acceptance or nonacceptance of his efforts at individuation (in Mahler's sense of the term), experiences which are the basis of narcissistic vulnerability. For Freud, as we noted, the prototype of castration anxiety is separation anxiety: the child is capable of imagining castration because he has experienced separations. We can say that separation anxiety and the problem of narcissism in its entirety are always in the background of the oedipal situation, lending a particular nuance to trauma and traumatizing events. Freud (1915c, p. 227) described object love as an attempt to restore the ideal primary narcissistic state, a point forcefully developed by Grunberger (1965).

This leads us to the problem of loss and change as depression-generating elements on the basis of a particular narcissistic vulnerability. A loss sets in motion internalization processes, whose particular nature will be brought to light in depression. Fear of change is, in the last analysis, a separation anxiety vis-à-vis particular states or objects. The questions to be asked are how narcissistic vulnerability can lead to massive introjections; why persons suffering from separation anxiety are unable to bear losses; and why the loss of omnipotence probably lies at the root of all these losses.

In conclusion, we have come back to the Oedipus complex that Freud considered the core of all neuroses. It is in the Oedipus complex, too, that the lines of force of narcissism and the object converge, further confirming its pathogenic importance. The upsurge of interest in depressive and narcissistic phenomena in recent years is perhaps related to changing parental roles and their consequences on the younger generation: the decline of the traditional parental protective/repressive function appears to have resulted in less structured—or at any rate differently structured—superegos in their children. The narcissistic wound, springing from helplessness and sexual immaturity, is more open, more exposed, since less repressive oedipal taboos make the child's incapacity and immaturity (experienced as a narcissistic wound) more clearly manifest.

While the liberation of the sexual content has ceased to occupy center stage in contemporary psychoanalysis (Green, 1974), it is now the inner contradictions engendered by the sexual content on the one hand, and the internalized prohibitions and ideals on the other, that determine the perturbations, feelings of insecurity, and depression apt to bring the subject to analysis. Analysis consists in the quest for a better tolerance of tensions, an attempt at integration against dissociative tendencies. Its ultimate aim is to provide a sense of security within the context of the prevailing and inevitable insecurity that is life.

Within this perspective, the most fundamental question of psychoanalysis is not, in my opinion, the "myth of origins," but rather, the "origin of evil," evil here viewed as disruption of inner equilibrium, the source of suffering, uneasiness, anxiety, and psychic pain—in short, what has been termed "frustration."

For Freudians, absence, frustration (Rapaport, 1961), and "lack" (Donnet and Green, 1973) are present in rudimentary form even at the origin of thought itself. The enigma of evil, lack, frustration, imposes on the human psyche a never-ending task. For Melanie Klein, it is related to the "death instinct," the threat against life. According to classical theory, it is prohibition, the appearance of the Law which is responsible for this experience of unpleasure: with the advent of the Oedipus complex, frustration of the instincts predominates. This great event that is the Oedipus complex condenses (in part after the event) all frustrations in order to constitute the human personality, thus presenting itself as a prerequisite of psychological development. The world's great religions brought together the suffering of moral obligation and the obligation of asceticism, of expiation. In so doing, they perhaps expressed the sense that this suffering—as in the case of Oedipus—is bound to the Law.

Freud showed that knowledge and understanding go hand in hand, and that the obstacle, the stumbling block of the problem of evil, can be avoided by understanding. Depression implies a resigned retreat in the face of this obstacle. Analysis encompasses the problem that is at the heart of the depression by attempting to elucidate it, while at the same time combating any tendency toward bitter resignation. If the individual is to be spared the vicious circle arising from a perpetual sense of injustice (the injustice, the "bad" of the Other, or the sense of oneself being "bad") and the resignation and sense of inevitability it entails, human life must be accepted with all its clash of truth and error, good and bad, accepted as such.

It is latent despair and the feeling that one's inner world is crumbling that finally incite the subject to a working through, with all its pain and toil, thus paving the way for a better integration of the inner world and creativity. This work can be accomplished outside of psychoanalysis as well, through the cultural process; success in either is creativity.

Psychoanalysis has shown us that we must live in the shadow of despair. Our demons can be neither expelled nor stifled: they are precious to us as an attribute of human existence. If we learn how to live with them, they will even end up by helping us, in the sense of promoting a psychic equilibrium that might be called a "eudaemonistic moral code." Traces of our losses and despairs, born of the child's primary condition, his helplessness, will accompany us always: in the words of Seneca, "The Fates lead the willing, and drag the unwilling."

# Part II

# Chapter 14

# Freud and Depression

> It was a melancholy mood, and con-
> sequently one most opposed to my
> natural disposition, brought about by
> weariness of the solitude in which a
> few years ago I buried myself, which
> first put into my head this idle thought
> of writing. And then, finding myself
> entirely unprovided and empty of all
> matters, I proposed myself to myself
> for argument and for subject.
>
> —Montaigne

Grief following death is present in Freud's earliest
writings. He laid the groundwork for the theme of
depression as far back as January 1895, the probable
date of his Draft G, where he used the term "melancholia" to designate the conditions we currently

call depressions.[1] And yet it was not Freud but his friend and student Karl Abraham who published in 1912 the first elaboration of this theme.

Freud was himself subject to depression. Jones (1953) speaks of "anxieties" manifesting themselves through the "dread of dying" (Todesangst), attacks of "anxiety about travelling by rail" (Reisefieber). He likewise cites a "violent anxiety attack" at the time Freud separated from Wilhelm Fliess, "extreme changes of mood,"

> alternations of mood between periods of elation, excitement and self-confidence on the one hand, and periods of extreme depression, doubt, and inhibition on the other. In the depressed moods he could neither write nor concentrate his thoughts (except during his professional work). He would spend leisure hours of extreme boredom. . . . Sometimes there were spells where consciousness would be greatly narrowed: states, difficult to describe, with a veil that produced almost a twilight condition of mind (6 December 1897). [pp. 198–99]

"In the remarkable letter of 16 April 1896, Freud mentioned attacks of fear of death. . . . He had recognized that it was neurotic" (Schur, 1972, p. 100). In addition to the psychic disturbances, there was physical discomfort: all his life he was subject to migraines, though they became less frequent in later years. Beginning in 1889, he suffered from heart trouble

---

[1] We shall steer clear of fastidious investigations into the nosological classifications of the time; let us simply remark that depressive states were often grouped together under general headings such as neurasthenia.

(arhythmia), which grew progressively worse until reaching its peak in April 1894. He attributed his cardiac problems to his abuse of nicotine, which Schur (1972) speaks of as his "addiction": "Freud could not overcome his addiction" (p. 364). His correspondence with Abraham confirms the fact that he had attacks of depression which left him feeling apathetic, useless, and incapable of writing. The depressions that followed each publication were temporarily somewhat alleviated by reassurance and praise from his students. We shall not go into detail concerning the "cocaine episode" (Byck and Freud, 1974), even though one could read into it a depressive problem and the hope of escape through drugs.

Anzieu (1975) has "amply demonstrated that it was in order to combat his depressive tendencies that Freud undertook his self-analysis, and that the formulation of psychoanalytic theory, especially in its economic and dynamic aspects, corresponded to the establishment of obsessional defenses against depressive anxiety" (p. 747). Anzieu underscored the "counterphobic and antidepressive" conception of psychoanalysis, thus explaining its limited hold over "the fears of persecution and of disintegration" (p. 748). Be that as it may, it is through Freud's own mental structure that we see the link between the analytic process and depression. Concerning the death of Freud's father, Anzieu writes:

> We have reached a turning point in the inner life of Freud, whose work was to show its effects. The idea of subjecting himself to a systematic self-analysis and of writing a book about dreams grew out of it, and he realized this himself once the dual task was com-

pleted. As he wrote in 1908, in the preface of the second edition of his *The Interpretation of Dreams:* "For me, of course, this book has an additional subjective significance, which I did not understand until after its completion. It reveals itself to me as a piece of my self-analysis, as my reaction to the death of my father. That is, to the most important event, the most poignant loss in a man's life. Once I had realized this, I felt that I could not obliterate the traces of this influence." [p. 234]

"This work of mourning culminated in a creative crisis which began to bear fruit from October 1897 on and which was marked principally by the discovery of the Oedipus complex. Freud was then forty-one years old (Anzieu, 1974, p. 9). The work of mourning triggered by Jakob Freud's death at the end of October 1895 was to lead to *The Interpretation of Dreams,* but it was not until after his break with Jung in 1913 and the death of his brother, Emmanuel Freud, the following year[2] that he addressed the psychic work of mourning per se, in his "Mourning and Melancholia" of 1917. Thus, between the mourning and the working through of this mourning process, over two decades were to pass (1896–1917) and Karl Abraham was to make his theoretical contribution.

Freud's early cases likewise confronted him with the grief of his patients. In "Studies on Hysteria" (1895d), he noted the relationship between the onset of neurotic symptoms and a bereavement of loss.

If the sick person recovers, all these impressions, of

---

[2] Freud's admission of death wishes directed against his son during World War I testifies yet again to his courage in confronting the truth about himself.

course, lose their significance. But if he dies, and the period of mourning sets in, during which the only things that seem to have value are those that relate to the person who has died, these impressions that have not yet been dealt with come into the picture as well; and after a short interval of exhaustion and hysteria, whose seeds were sown during the time of nursing, breaks out. [p. 162]

Two of the young women whose cases he reported had lost their fathers, another her husband. Does this symbolize the loss in an unresolved oedipal situation, "thwarted by its very impossibility"? Whatever the case, the process set in motion by death led to the "talking cure" and the "chimney sweeping"as it emerged in the case of Anna O. (Freud, 1895d).

Anna O. fell ill in 1880, during the illness of her father, for whom she had been caring and who died in 1881. After his death, Anna's condition worsened:

a year had passed since she had been separated from her father and had taken to her bed, and from this time on her condition became clearer and was systematized [p. 32]. . . . The first provoking cause was habitually a fright of some kind, experienced while she was nursing her father. [There was] a particularly terrifying hallucination. While she was nursing her father, she had seen him with a death's head [p. 37]. . . . She began coughing for the first time when once, as she was sitting at her father's bedside, she heard the sound of dance music coming from a neighbouring house, felt a sudden wish to be there, and was overcome with self-reproaches. [p. 40]

The life of Emmy von N. was marked by numerous deaths, including those of her sister, aunt, brother, and finally her husband, who died before her eyes of a heart attack. The illness of Lucie R. was attributed to her forbidden love feelings toward her employer, the husband of her dead friend. Elisabeth von R.'s illness can likewise be traced to the death of her father after the year and a half she devoted to nursing him, and then to the death of her sister.

In *Studies on Hysteria* Freud (1895d) gives a description of "this psychic work" of hysteria, which originates in a "disruption in the dynamic equilibrium of the nervous system, the unequal distribution of a heightened excitation which constitutes the actual psychic side of the affect." This imbalance runs counter to "a tendency in the organism towards the constant maintenance of an intracerebral excitation." Sexuality appears as a disrupting agent, but the dimensions of change and grief also emerge.

In his Draft N, dated May 31, 1897, Freud (1897a) spoke about hostile impulses against parents (a wish that they should die) as an integral part of neuroses:

> They come to light consciously in the form of obsessional ideas. . . . One of the manifestations of grief is then to reproach oneself for their death (*cf.* what are described as "melancholias") or to punish oneself in a hysterical way by putting oneself into their position with an idea of retribution. The identification which takes place here is, as we can see, merely a mode of thinking and does not relieve us of the necessity of looking for the motive. [p. 207]

In this passage we find a connection with oedipal guilt, which is not named. According to Strachey (1957), it is the first "foreshadowing" of the Oedipus complex in Freud's work: "It seems that in sons, the death wish is directed against their father, and in daughters against their mother. . . ." (Freud, 1950a, p. 207). What I would like to emphasize in this text is the link between melancholia, identification, and the oedipal problem. On January 16, 1899, Freud wrote to Fliess (Letter 102), "I have convinced myself that there really is a hysterical melancholia and established what its indications are" (1950a, p. 273).

Irma, one of Freud's celebrated patients (Anna Hammerschlag), was a widow. And Irma's friend, whom Freud (1900a) substituted for her in his dream about the case, was likewise a young widow. In his analysis of the dream, Freud's conclusion concerning his hysterical patient was as follows: "Irma's sufferings are satisfactorily explained by her widowhood . . . a state which I cannot alter" (p. 119). In his article "Psychical (or Mental) Treatment" (1905b), he uses as his starting point the importance of the depressive affect in the case of illness, which brings to mind the reaction of "giving up," the sense of despair that follows a loss of health the patient considers unacceptable, but which has come about nonetheless.

Another hysteric, Dora (1905e), witnessed a number of serious illnesses in her father since her sixth year, including tuberculosis and then, when she was about ten, a detached retina which left his vision permanently impaired. She herself suffered from a respiratory ailment exacerbated by asthmatiform attacks. Moreover, she was depressive, with suicidal ideas. Among the symptoms of the *petite hystérie*, Freud listed somatic and mental signs: dyspnoea, *tussis nervosa*, aphonia, and possibly migraines, "together with depression, hysterical unsociability, and a *taedium vitae* which was probably not entirely genuine" (p. 24). This theme is again present in the paper on Jensen's *Gradiva* (1907a): Norbert Hanold, a young archeologist, had lost both parents in childhood and was chronically depressed. It hardly needs mentioning that archeology, which deals in relics of the past, is symbolic of his attachment to lost objects. His fantasies and dreams and the sites he frequents can be understood as attempts to overcome separation through regression and fusion with the maternal object. Finally, this process leads to restoration of the lost object through the realization that Zoe-Gradiva is really a living person.

During a discussion on suicide which took place at the Vienna Psychoanalytic Society, Freud (1910g) stressed the importance of the comparison between normal states of mourning and melancholia: as he stated already in 1895 "the affect which corresponds to melancholia is that of mourning (p. 232), that is, the bitter regret for the lost object. In melancholia, it could be a loss in the domain of sexual needs. . . . Perhaps one could start from the following idea: melancholia consists in mourning over loss of libido" (Freud, 1950a, p. 101). If we replace "libido" with "object of libido," we arrive at the current definition. Concluding the discussion at this session—one of the last to include the original nucleus of the Vienna Society before the withdrawal of Adler and Stekel—Freud admits that little is known of the fundamental causes of suicide: "is a disappointed libido sufficient to justify it? Or is it the ego's renunciation of life? This last remark foreshadows the death instinct hypothesis he was later to formulate. Freud was unable to resolve this question until he had studied melancholia"

(Jones, 1955, p. 261) and the chronic affect of mourning some five years later, but in the meantime, it is clear that he touched upon many problems with his profound insights. At the same session on suicide, Sadger declared that "no one gives up his life who has not abandoned the hope for love" (Nunberg and Federn, 1967, p. 492), and that "what is true of the suicide of adults is also true for children: suicide is the self-inflicted punishment of the person who kills himself. . . . No one ever kills himself who has never wanted to kill another, or at least wished the death of another" (see Friedman, 1967, pp. 71-87).

Very early on, in "Further Remarks on the Neuro-Psychoses of Defence" (1896b), Freud made the connection between "periodic melancholia" and obsessional neurotic conflicts, a viewpoint he would evoke in his Letter 102 to Wilhelm Fliess. In his Draft G of 1895 (Freud, 1950a) he had attributed the predisposition to melancholia to a low level of tension, stating that all neuroses can present a "melancholic complexion." In this, he seems to establish a kind of bipolarity between anxiety and the melancholic affect and to postulate that either one or the other, anxiety or depression, would appear in accordance with the personality type.

The theme of identification emerged clearly in "Totem and Taboo" (1912–1913). His paper on narcissism and on the "critical agency" in cases of paranoia (1914c) paved the way for "Mourning and Melancholia," which while written in 1915 was not published until 1917. It was Abraham who first underscored the importance of the oral phase in melancholia, but Freud showed considerable interest in the subject already in the fall of 1914, when he wrote the case study of the Wolf Man (1918b); he further refined the concept in *Group Psychology and the Analysis of the Ego* in 1921 and *The Ego and the Id* in 1923. In a text appended to *Three Essays on the Theory of Sexuality* (1905d), Freud spoke of the importance of the cannibalistic oral phase as the prototype of a process which would play an important role in the mechanism of identification. The presence of remorse and guilt in grief is tackled in *Totem and Taboo* (1912–1913). In "The Theme of the Three Caskets" (1913f), Freud takes up man's relationship with the three feminine figures of his destiny: the creator, the companion, and the destroyer.

> We might argue that what is represented here are the three inevitable relations that a man has with a woman—the woman who bears him, the woman who is his mate and the woman who destroys him; or that they are the three forms taken by the figure of the mother in the course of a man's life—the mother herself, the beloved one who is chosen after her pattern, and lastly, the Mother Earth who receives him once more. . . . The silent Goddess of Death who will take him into her arms" [p. 301].

One might ask why Freud placed death on the same level as the mother and the mate, which seems to evoke the fantasy of the infanticidal mother, the image of the bad mother; in any event, this idea was to remain without echo or further comment in Freud's work.

The problem of mourning and melancholia had absorbed Freud's attention for some years. We know that he had spoken of it in January 1914 to Ernest Jones, and then in December of the same year at the

Vienna Psychoanalytic Society (Jones, 1955, pp. 328–329). The first draft of "Mourning and Melancholia" was written in February 1915, then submitted to Karl Abraham, who sent his comments, especially as concerned the oral stage of libidinal development. The final revision was written in March 1915 but published only two years later, in 1917.[3]

"Mourning and Melancholia" represents a curious chapter in the history of psychoanalysis. Apart from a few allusions, Freud did not address the topic until 1914; moreover, it was not he but one of his students, Karl Abraham, who laid the first theoretical framework for the subject, in his paper of 1911. What makes this remarkable is the fact that Freud's cases brought him directly into contact with the problem of loss and mourning, and that his own self-analysis had been triggered by his own mourning at the loss of his father, which led to his writing *The Interpretation of Dreams*. It was as if Freud in his self-analysis had applied himself to understanding the *makeup* of his unconscious rather than the *process* itself, which is, as we have noted, a mourning process. Indeed, I have come to believe that mourning, the depression it generates, and the analytic process are all closely related, which comes down to drawing a link between depression and creativity, a connection which has in fact often been suggested in the history of ideas.

Freud sent a first version of "Mourning and Mel-

---

[3] In the Preface we mentioned two other works written in 1915: "Thoughts for the Times on War and Death" (written in March-April) and "On Transience" (written in November but not published until the following year).

ancholia" to Abraham, who made lengthy comments on it. Freud (1915a) replied as follows:

> Your comments on melancholia are very useful to me, and I unhesitatingly incorporated in my papers those parts of them that I could use. What was most valuable to me was the reference to the oral phase of the libido, and I also mention the link with mourning to which you draw attention. . . . I should like to make only two points: that you do not bring out sufficiently the essential feature of your assumption, that is to say the topical element, the regression of the libido and the abandonment of unconscious object cathexis, but instead put in the foreground sadism and anal eroticism as explanatory factors. Though you are correct in this, you miss the real explanation. Anal eroticism, the castration complex etc. are ubiquitous sources of excitation that are bound to play their part in *every* clinical picture. Sometimes one thing comes of them and sometimes another; it is of course always our duty to find out what has become of them, but the explanation of the disorder can be derived only from its mechanism, seen from the *dynamic, topical* and *economic* aspects. [Letter to Karl Abraham, 4 May 1915]

"Mourning and Melancholia," which we can consider the principal work on the subject, develops the comparison between the nature of melancholia and the normal affect of mourning first sketched out at the Vienna Psychoanalytic Society in 1910. Freud (1917e) warns that the definition of melancholia has fluctuated and that it has taken on various clinical forms "the grouping together of which into a single unity does not seem to be established with certainty" and that "some of these forms suggest somatic rather than psychogenic affections" (p. 243). Melancholia, he writes, is characterized from a psychic point of view by "a profoundly painful dejection, cessation of interest in the outside world, loss of the capacity to love, inhibition of all activity and a lowering of the self-regarding feelings to a degree that finds utterance in self-reproaches and self-revilings, and culminates in a delusional expectation of punishment" (pp. 243–244). Mourning involves the same traits, except as concerns disturbances in feelings of self-esteem. Concerning the work performed by mourning, he writes: "Reality-testing has shown that the loved object no longer exists, and it proceeds to demand that all libido shall be withdrawn from its attachments to that object. This demand arouses understandable opposition," but "normally, respect for reality gains the day" (p. 244). This task is accomplished in the course of a long and gradual process wherein "each single one of the memories and expectations in which the libido is bound to the object is brought up and hypercathected, and the detachment of the libido is accomplished in respect of it" (p. 245). "In one set of cases it is evident that melancholia too may be the reaction to the loss of a loved object. . . . In yet other cases one feels justified in maintaining the belief that a loss of this kind has occurred, but one cannot see clearly what it is that has been lost, . . . he knows *whom* he has lost but not *what* he has lost in him. This would suggest that melancholia is in some way related to an object-loss which is withdrawn from consciousness." The internal work is similar to the work of mourning: in both cases there is inhibition and loss of interest, but in melancholia it "seems puzzling to us because we cannot see what is absorbing him so entirely. The melancholic displays something else besides which is lacking in mourning—an extraordinary diminution in his self-regard, an impoverishment of his ego on a grand scale. In mourning it is the world which has become poor and empty; in melancholia it is the ego itself" (p. 246). This poses the problem of self-denigration in melancholia.

Freud then broaches "the view which the melancholic's disorder affords of the constitution of the human ego" (p. 247) and sheds light on the agency which he distinguishes from the rest of the ego and which he will later call the superego, postulating an identification of the ego with the abandoned object[4]: "Thus the shadow of the object fell upon the ego, and the latter could henceforth be judged by a special agency, as though it were an object, the forsaken object. In this way, an object-loss was transformed into an ego-loss and the conflict between the ego and the loved person into a cleavage between the critical activity of the ego and the ego as altered by identification" (p. 249). The object choice having been effected on a narcissistic basis, there is a regression from narcissistic object-choice to narcissism. As to the ambivalent conflict vis-à-vis the object, after the object loss and its introjection, the hostile part of the ambivalent feelings toward the object will manifest itself in hatred and sadism directed against the ego (and its introjected object) in self-reproaches and self-depreciations. A central part of the work is the description of the process in melancholia whereby an object

---

[4] "We perceive that the self-reproaches are reproaches against a loved object, which have been shifted away from it on to the patient's own ego" (p. 248).

cathexis is replaced by identification. In mania, the ego has recovered from the object loss, thus freeing the anticathexes that melancholia had withdrawn to itself from the ego and bound. This liberation of cathexes which had been bound, combined with a regression of the libido to narcissism, makes mania possible once the work of melancholia has been completed. The mania would thus also represent the ego's attempt to overcome the object loss and free itself from the object that was the cause of its suffering.

The loss of the love object provides an excellent occasion for the ambivalence of love relationships to come to the fore. In this regard, Freud raises the problem of suicide; only sadism can resolve the enigma of suicidal tendencies—the turning back upon oneself of murderous impulses against others. The ego can kill itself only by treating itself as an object. It is here that Freud brings in the concept of anal erotism. The preconditions of melancholia are: object loss, ambivalence, and regression of the libido into the ego.

Freud lists three criteria which distinguish normal grief (mourning) from pathological mourning (melancholia): (1) absence of hatred for the lost object in normal mourning (subject to doubt in view of the following); (2) frequency of identification with the lost object in pathological mourning (he would abandon this criterion in *The Ego and the Id* in 1923); (3) in normal mourning, withdrawal of libido from the object and its displacement onto a new object, as opposed to melancholia, where it is withdrawn into the split-off part of the ego where an identification is established with the disappointing object (here cathexis of the real object is abandoned and ambivalence and hatred of the object comes to the fore; mania erupts when the narcissistic ego triumphs over the scorned object and becomes free of it).

For reasons probably inherent in the material furnished by depressive analysands, the importance of introjection has been studied with particular thoroughness. Freud's work on "Mourning and Melancholia" led directly to *The Ego and the Id* (1923b); in other words, the study of depression opened the way to the study of certain fundamental mechanisms of the human psyche.

In 1923 Freud returned to the investigation of the superego in melancholia. In obsessional neurosis, the ego rebels against the superego; in melancholia, the ego raises no objection, but meekly accepts its guilt and submits to punishment. The destructive element, "a pure culture of the death instinct" (p. 53), has taken root in the superego and turned against the ego. Freud would continue to develop ideas relating to this theme; for example, in his "Fetishism" (1927e) he went back to the problem of the cleavage in the ego:

> In the analysis of two young men I learned that each—one when he was two and the other when he was ten—had failed to take cognizance of the death of his beloved father—had "scotomized" it. . . . It was only one current in their mental life that had not recognized their father's death; there was another current which took full account of the fact. The attitude which fitted in with the wish and the attitude which fitted in with reality existed side by side. [pp. 155–156]

The foregoing briefly surveys what is essential in Freud's contribution to the study of depression. In the next chapter, we shall examine the contributions that followed in his wake.

# Chapter 15

# The Evolution of Ideas on Depression in the Psychoanalytic Literature

> The complexity of philosophy is not in its matter, but in our tangled understanding.
> —Ludwig Wittgenstein, *Philosophical Remarks*

The psychoanalytic works to which I have referred in outlining my personal ideas are those which in my view most clearly bring out the leading thread I wished to follow. I would now like to give these authors who contributed to clarifying the problem of depression their due, briefly summarizing those of their works that have the greatest bearing on the subject and placing them in historical context. In short, I shall now attempt to give a systematic survey of the history of psychoanalytic ideas on depression. The reader may find it useful to refer to the interesting summaries of the subject written by Garma (1947), Rosenfeld (1959), and Mendelson (1974).

Depression ties in with many other problems, and there is no doubt that recent findings in the areas of pregenital development, the mother-child relation-ship, narcissism, and the psychoanalytic experience in general could all find a useful place in these pages. Nonetheless, I shall confine myself to the historically important works dealing with depression per se.

## Early Works

Among the first writings devoted to the subject, those of *A. A. Brill* (1911) and *A. Maeder* (1911) should be mentioned for curiosity's sake. Maeder published a case of "psychogenic depression belonging to melancholic depression" involving a problem of homosexuality: a forty-two-year-old peasant examined at Jung's polyclinic in Zurich was cured in four sessions focused on the homosexual problem, after which he reportedly recovered his confidence and zest for life.

### Karl Abraham

Karl Abraham's 1911 study on Giovanni Segantini, an Italian painter who died in Switzerland in 1899, stresses the close connection between the artist's creative powers and his depressive tendencies. Abraham believes the event which most profoundly marked Segantini's life was the death of his mother when he was five years old, and that his art grew out of his love for his lost and idealized mother. Analyzing Segantini's paintings, writings, and the facts of his life, Abraham shows how his various conflicting feelings toward his parents expressed themselves in his life and work: how the jealousy, hostility, and rancor against the father who had abandoned him made of him a lifelong rebel against authority; how the love for his mother and his identification with her, with the homeland and nature, provided the themes for much of his work, while repressed sadistic and aggressive tendencies against this same mother who forsook him in death are also present.

It was Abraham who published, in 1912, the first theoretical study on depression—"Notes on the Psycho-Analytical Investigation and Treatment of Manic-Depressive Insanity and Allied Conditions." Completed the year before and presented to the Third International Psycho-Analytical Congress at Weimar, the paper developed the comparison between mourning and melancholia that Freud had mentioned in passing during remarks delivered to the Vienna Society the previous year (Freud, 1910g). Referring to Freud's statement that what distinguished anxiety from fear was the fact that anxiety grew out of sexual repression, Abraham (1911b) wrote: "In the same way we can distinguish between the affect of sadness or grief and neurotic depression, the latter being unconsciously motivated and a consequence of repression" (p. 137); "depression sets in when he [the subject] has to give up his sexual aim without having obtained gratification. He feels himself unloved, incapable of loving . . ." (pp. 137–138); this is a fundamental thesis whose importance has not dimmed over the years. "We fear a coming evil; we grieve over one that has occurred" (p. 137). Emphasizing how "surprisingly little has been written in the literature of psycho-analysis concerning the psychology of neurotic depression" (p. 138), Abraham broached the subject of manic-depressive psychoses on the basis of six clinical cases he had been following. After comparing their structure to that of obsessional neurosis, he stressed (and was the first to do so) the hostile attitude of the manic-depressive to the external world, which is "so great that his capacity for love is reduced to a minimum" (p. 139). He likewise was the first to demonstrate the manic-depressive's "hostile attitude towards his parents and [his attitude] of jealousy and hatred towards his brothers" (p. 140).

According to Abraham, the conflict underlying the psychosis can be expressed in the formula "I cannot love people; I have to hate them"—whence these patients' pronounced feelings of inadequacy. With the subjects' projection of these feelings outward, the formula becomes "People do not love me, they hate me . . . because of my inborn defects.[1] Therefore I am unhappy and depressed" (p. 145).

But the repressed sadistic impulses do not abate. Rather, they have a tendency to return into consciousness and manifest themselves in many forms—in dreams and symptomatic acts, and especially in tyrannical behavior toward the people around them:

[1] A play on words in German: hässlich = ugly; hass = hatred; "ugly" would be "that which provokes hatred," as Abraham noted.

"New and morbid states, such as *feelings of guilt*, result from the suppression of these frequent impulses of hatred and revenge. . . . As a result of the repression of sadism, depression, anxiety, and self-reproach arise" (pp. 146, 147; italics mine). According to Abraham, the states of depression connected with the period of involution originate in the subject's realization that his erotic life has passed by without gratification, that his life has been wasted. The economy of mania is compared to that of wordplay: "The affect of pleasure in mania is derived from the same source as is that of pleasure in wit" (p. 150).

Abraham was fully aware of the incomplete nature of his study and stressed that "further investigations are very greatly needed . . ." (p. 155). "For instance," he wrote, "although we have been able to recognize up to what point the psychogenesis of obsessional neuroses and cyclical psychoses resemble each other, we have not the least idea why at this point one group of individuals should take one path and the other group another" (p. 156). Abraham's thesis that manic-depressives present obsessional structures during the "free intervals" is no longer widely credited today; indeed, even taking into account the fact that Abraham was referring to psychotic patients, recent studies (Stengel, 1948; Jacobson, 1953; Cohen et al., 1959) have not confirmed it.

Abraham (1924) returned to the subject of obsessive and depressive patients in his "A Short Study of the Development of the Libido, Viewed in the Light of Mental Disorders." In this paper, in which he introduced for the first time the notion of oral fixation, he endeavored to explain and enlarge upon the fundamental distinction Freud made between the obsessional neurotic capable of conserving the object relation and the melancholic who loses it. This leads him to formulate his hypothesis concerning the two subphases of the anal phase (the first, during which the pleasure consists in expulsion, and the second, where the pleasure of retention is foremost). While the melancholic expels the object, the obsessive retains it inside so as to control it. "If the conserving tendencies—those of retaining and controlling his object—are the more powerful, this conflict around the love-object will call forth phenomena of psychological compulsion. But if the opposing sadistic-anal tendencies are victorious—those which aim at destroying and expelling the object—then the patient will fall into a state of melancholic depression" (pp. 430–431). As psychoanalytic experience has shown, in the earlier stage the tendency to destroy the object predominates, while conserving tendencies characterize the latter.

Abraham uses a number of case histories to illustrate the mechanism, described by Freud in "Mourning and Melancholia," whereby the loss is followed by introjection of the love object both in the depressed person and in the individual who has just suffered a bereavement. Nonetheless, the two situations differ in that

> in the normal person it is set in motion by real loss (death); and its main purpose is to preserve the person's relations to the dead object, or—what comes to the same thing—to compensate for his loss. Furthermore, his conscious knowledge of his loss will never leave the normal person, as it does the melancholia. The process of introjection in the melancholic, moreover, is based on a radical disturbance of his libidinal

relations to his object. It rests on a severe conflict of ambivalent feelings, from which he can only escape by turning against himself the hostility he originally felt towards his object. [p. 438]

In Abraham's view, the importance of this introjection had previously been underestimated. He alludes to Freud's conceptions that certain cases of homosexuality can be explained by "the fact that the subject has introjected the parent of the opposite sex" (pp. 438–439). But while the loss of the object (expulsion) and its destruction correspond to an anal mechanism, its introjection, on the other hand, falls within the province of orality. "We can now understand that the patient's desire to eat excrement is a cannibalistic impulse to devour the love-object which he has killed" (p. 444). In an earlier paper on the first pregenital stage (1916), he noted that "in contrast to the sadistic desires of the obsessional neurotic, the unconscious wish of the melancholic is to destroy his love-object by eating it up" (p. 277). In the same paper he delved into fantasies experienced in many melancholics of being transformed into wild man-eating beasts or werewolves, as well as the internal resistances of melancholics to their own impulses to devour the desired object and the links between this psychosis and anorexia. The melancholic attempts to rid himself of his sadistic-oral impulses through recourse to a "pleasurable, sucking activity" (1924, p. 450). It is thus that Abraham explains why eating may alleviate depressive symptoms, as may downing medicine.

Abraham postulated a subdivision of the oral stage into two phases as well, with the more primitive of the two consisting in sucking activity and the second in biting. Ambivalence develops in the second oral stage. For the melancholic, from the minute the object is introjected, ambivalence toward it is likewise directed toward the ego. "Thus melancholia presents a picture in which there stand in immediate juxtaposition yet absolutely opposed to one another self-love and self-hatred, an overestimation of the ego and an underestimation of it—the manifestations, that is, of *a positive and a negative narcissism*" (1924, p. 456).

As to why certain neurotics become melancholics rather than obsessives, Abraham remarks that while a disappointment in love is evidently at the root of any melancholic depression, the disappointment can become pathogenic only to the extent that it is experienced as the "repetition of an original infantile traumatic experience" (1924, p. 456). Abraham was the first to describe the "primal" (or "primary") depression (p. 459) developing in early childhood in reaction to precocious disappointments in the child's relationships with his parents "before the Oedipus-wishes have been overcome" (p. 453).[2] A melancholic depression does not set in without the interaction of a number of factors: first of all, a constitutional factor, in the sense of a "constitutional and inherited . . . over-accentuation of oral erotism" (p. 457) which would favor the libido's fixation at the oral level of development; next, there is "a severe injury to infantile narcissism brought about by successive disappointments in love" (p. 458), giving rise to feelings of total abandonment and loneliness. When this injury occurs

[2] Abraham's description unquestionably inspired some later formulations, including, for example, Melanie Klein's "depressive position."

before the Oedipus complex is resolved, a "permanent association will be established between the Oedipus complex and the cannibalistic stage of his libido" (p. 459). The introjection of the object explains the melancholic's self-reproaches: accusations formulated on the one hand by the introjected object toward the subject, and on the other hand by the subject toward the introjected object. Whereas in melancholia the introjected object represents a superego of excessive severity, during the manic phase the domination of this superego is cast off, the superego becoming, in a way, incorporated into the ego. "For this reason Freud takes the view that in the manic condition the patient is celebrating a triumph over the object he once loved and then gave up and introjected. The 'shadow of the object' which had fallen on his ego has passed away" (p. 471). Using the observations of Róheim, among others, Abraham shows that this mechanism to a certain degree also manifests itself in normal mourning. Thus, after having returned to the study of the pregenital stages of libido development as Freud (1905d) had outlined them in his *Three Essays*, Abraham attributes depression to a regression of the libido to the most primitive stage, which he characterizes as oral or cannibalistic.

## Melanie Klein

Melanie Klein approached the problem of depression from the perspective of the affect, leaving the depressive illness aspect to another line of authors. Her theories, summarized in her conceptualization of the "depressive position," are too well known to re-

quire much elucidation, and we shall confine ourselves in these pages to recalling her first two articles.
In "A Contribution to the Psychogenesis of Manic-
Depressive States," written in 1934, Melanie Klein
further developed the theses formulated in some of
her earlier writings concerning the infant's sadistic
impulses directed "not only against the mother's
breast, but against the inside of her body," and proposes to study "the depressive states in their relations
to paranoia on the one hand and to mania on the
other" (Klein, 1934, p. 283). The anxiety-contents and
projective defense mechanisms constitute the basis
of paranoia, whose essential characteristic is oral sadism. The problem is to destroy the bad, persecuting
objects (bad not only because frustrating, but because
the infant projects his own aggression onto them)
which the infant sees as still dangerous at the time
of incorporation. Furthermore, the good objects are
difficult to maintain safely inside the body because
this inside is itself felt to be dangerous. "The processes which subsequently become clear as the 'loss
of the loved object' are determined by the subject's
sense of failure (during weaning and in the periods
which precede and follow it—to secure his *good, internalized* object, i.e., to possess himself of it. One
reason for his failure is that he has been unable to
overcome his paranoid dread of internalized persecutors" (Klein, 1934, p. 287).

Melanie Klein assumes an early formation of the
superego, emerging on the one hand from the per-
secutions of bad internalized objects and on the other
from the need to protect the good objects. The infant
does not succeed, despite his efforts, in separating
the absolutely good from the absolutely bad objects.

While in the paranoiac "the persecution anxiety is mainly related to the preservation of the ego," in the depressive it is directed to "the preservation of the good internalized objects with whom the ego is identified as a whole" (p. 289), such that "The anxiety lest the good objects and with them the ego should be destroyed, or that they are in a state of disintegration, is interwoven with continuous and desperate efforts to save the good objects both internalized and external" (p. 289). Only a perfect object can be substituted for the destroyed good object. This is the origin of the desire for perfection that will play an essential role in all sublimations. Because of his persecution anxiety, the paranoiac is incapable of identifying with the introjected object with retains its persecutory characteristics. While the depressive strives to reconstitute the good object, for the paranoiac "the disintegrated object is mainly a multitude of persecutors" (p. 292). The same reactional mode manifests itself on the level of food ingestion: while the paranoiac is afraid of absorbing dangerous substances destructive to his inside, the depressive is afraid of destroying the external good object by biting and chewing it or of endangering the internal good object by introducing bad substances into it. Similarly with hypochondriacal symptoms: the paranoiac's pains arise from attacks of internalized persecutory objects against his ego, while the depressive and his good objects suffer from the attacks of his internal bad objects and his id—"an internal warfare in which the ego is identified with the sufferings of the good objects" (p. 293). For Melanie Klein, depression is the result of paranoia: "I consider the depressive state as being the result of a mixture of paranoid anxiety, and those anxiety contents, distressed feelings and defenses which are connected with the impending loss of the whole loved object" (p. 296).

According to her theory, suicide is aimed not solely at the destruction of bad objects, but also at the protection of loved objects, internal or external. Mania is a defense characterized by a sense of omnipotence and the denial of psychic reality, directed both against melancholia and against a paranoid condition the ego is unable to master. Omnipotence makes possible the mastery over objects, keeping them from hurting either the subject or each other, for example during the dangerous coitus of the internalized parents. The manic avidly introjects objects but denies that this introjection can be dangerous, either because the objects are "bad" and can attack him, or because they are "good" and can be destroyed by him. Melanie Klein underscored the importance of the child's good relationship with his mother and the external world: it is through this relationship that he will be able to overcome his paranoid anxieties and attain the depressive position, characterized by a relationship with a total object:

> I have emphasized . . . that, in my view, the infantile depressive position is the central position in the child's development. The normal development of the child and its capacity for love would seem to rest largely on how the ego works through this nodal position. This again depends on the modification undergone by the earliest mechanisms (which remain at work in normal persons) in accordance with the changes in the ego's relations to its objects, and especially on a successful interplay between the de-

pressive, the manic and the obsessional positions and mechanisms. [p. 310]

In her 1940 "Mourning and Its Relations to Manic-Depressive States," Melanie Klein builds on Freud's view that mourning is a reality testing during which the ego allows itself to be "persuaded by the sum of its narcissistic satisfactions in being alive to sever its attachment to the non-existent object" (p. 311). She examines the links between normal mourning and the depressive position, in which the child feels the loss of the maternal breast and all it represents in terms of love and security. The depressive position is further experienced, this time in connection with the fear of loss of the father and the siblings, with the emergence of the oedipal situation. The internal objects constitute the unconscious inner world of the child, partially fashioned from real experiences and partly from his own fantasies. From the time these objects are internalized, the child no longer judges them, which means that he must constantly refer to external objects. "The extent to which external reality is able to disprove anxieties and sorrows relating to the internal reality varies with each individual, but could be taken as one of the criteria for normality" (1940, p. 313). The infant progressively becomes capable of overcoming his depression as he acquires proofs that neither his inner objects nor his external objects have been destroyed. His anxieties of a psychotic nature are thus overcome through a normal infantile neurosis. "In the infantile neurosis the early depressive position finds expression, is worked through, and gradually overcome" (p. 315).

Whereas previously only the fear of persecution by

bad objects manifested itself, with the emergence of the depressive position the fear of losing love objects appears as well: "the introjection of the whole loved object gives rise to concern and sorrow lest that object should be destroyed by the 'bad' objects and the id" (p. 315). Two sets of fears are thus present in the depressive position: first of all, the paranoid fear of being destroyed by bad objects, and then the distressed fear of destroying the good object. It is in order to defend himself against this second fear that the child develops manic defenses based on omnipotence, whose goal on the one hand is to defend himself against the bad object and, on the other, to repair the love objects. The good objects and the bad objects were clearly separated in the child's mind in the earliest phase, but by the time he becomes capable of introjecting the total object, he feels the need to split his "imagos into loved and hated, that is to say into good and dangerous ones" (p. 317). This is the basis for the ambivalence that enables him to trust his real objects even while continuing to utilize his paranoid defenses against the bad objects. "But as the adaptation to the external world increases, this splitting is carried out on planes which gradually become increasingly nearer and nearer to reality" (p. 317). Since the feeling of omnipotence was from the very beginning related to sadistic tendencies, the child persuades himself that his efforts at reparation are ineffective. He then has recourse to "attempted reparations carried out in obsessional ways" (p. 318). Manic and obsessional defenses are joined, with all the sadism and need for mastery they entail. "The objects which were to be restored change again into persecutors, in turn paranoid fears are revived. . . .

As a result of the failure of the act of reparation, the ego has to resort again and again to obsessional and manic defenses" (p. 318). The feelings of triumph and contempt attached to these defenses give rise to guilt, which contributes to thwarting efforts at reparation. "Some people are obliged to remain unsuccessful, because success always implies for them the humiliation or even the damage of somebody else" (p. 319). These mechanisms are contrasted to hypomanic behavior, where the individual goes from idealization to devaluation and uses denial to avoid recognizing that the object has been destroyed and must be repaired. As the child gains confidence in his powers of reparation and in the security provided him by his internal objects, the manic and obsessional defenses lose their *raison d'être*.

During the course of normal mourning, the loss of the external object is accompanied by a total or partial destruction of the inner objects, which revives all the anxieties of the depressive position including the persecution feelings. The essential danger inherent in the mourning situation is that the hatred felt toward a lost object manifests itself "in feelings of triumph over the dead person" (p. 322). With each new death, then, the infantile death wishes against the parents, brothers, and sisters are actually fulfilled. If this hatred gains the upper hand, the lost object becomes a persecutor which destroys the inner world. The work of mourning, as in the depressive position, thus consists in restoring the confidence in external objects, which makes it possible to consolidate the inner world in such a way that the subject can recover his love for the lost object. "That is to say, any pain caused by unhappy experiences, whatever their nature, has something in common with mourning. It reactivates the infantile depressive position; the encountering and overcoming of adversity of any kind entails mental work similar to mourning" (p. 328). There is nonetheless an important difference between the depressive position and mourning: in the first, the object is *experienced* as lost, even if it is still present, whereas in the second it really *is* lost. But it is the infant's success in working through the depressive position, the extent to which he was capable of constructing a benevolent world during that process, that will determine the adult's ability to overcome loss in mourning. In both cases, during the depressive position as at the time of mourning, the restoration of the individual is greatly assisted by the existence of a favorable environment.

> My experience leads me to conclude that, while it is true that the characteristic feature of normal mourning is the individual's setting up the lost loved object inside himself, he is not doing so for the first time but, through the work of mourning, is reinstating that object as well as all his loved internal objects which he feels he has lost. He is therefore recovering what he had already attained in childhood. [p. 330]

Let me draw another conclusion: in normal mourning, as well as in abnormal mourning and in manic-depressive states, the infantile depressive position is reactivated. The complex feelings, fantasies, and anxieties included under this term are of a nature which justifies my contention that the child in his early development goes through a transitory manic-depressive state as well as a state of mourning which becomes modified by infantile neurosis. With the

passing of the infantile neurosis, the infantile depressive position is overcome.

> The fundamental difference between normal
> mourning, on the one hand, and abnormal mourning
> and manic-depressive states on the other, is this: the
> manic-depressive and the person who fails in the
> work of mourning, though their defenses may differ
> widely from each other, have this in common, that
> they have been unable in early childhood to establish
> their internal "good" objects and to feel secure in their
> inner world. They have never really overcome the
> infantile depressive position. In normal mourning,
> however, the early depressive position, which had
> become revived through the loss of the loved object,
> becomes modified again, and is overcome by methods
> similar to those used by the ego in childhood. The
> individual is reinstating his actually lost loved object;
> but he is also at the same time re-establishing inside
> himself his first loved objects—ultimately the "good"
> parents—whom, when the actual loss occurred, he
> felt in danger of losing as well. It is by reinstating
> inside himself the "good" parents as well as the re-
> cently lost person, and by rebuilding his inner world,
> which was disintegrated and in danger, that he over-
> comes his grief, regains security and achieves true
> harmony and peace. [pp. 337-338]

For Melanie Klein, depression is thus the failure of
reparation in the depressive position.

Authors of the Kleinian school (Rosenfeld, 1959;
Wisdom, 1962) describe the depressive as someone
shipwrecked on the rock of ambivalence: the initially
"bad" object is reintrojected as an ideal object, while
the ideal parts of the ego are projected outward (in
contrast to what occurs in the schizophrenic, who

projects the bad parts outward). The primary narcissistic wound, or the loss of the object, is attributed by the patient to a failure of reparation. Wisdom (1962) advances four hypotheses in explanation of this failure: (1) an overwhelming love; (2) delibidinization; (3) incorporation of the bad object in the nucleus of the ego (nuclear embodiment); and (4) envy. In his formulation, the first two factors account for depression, while the third factor explains melancholia.

It is interesting to note that even authors belonging to psychoanalytic currents seemingly little influenced by the views of Melanie Klein have advanced ideas akin to hers. Therese Benedek (1956) of the Chicago school, for example, envisaged a depressive constellation of "a universal nature" representing the "intensification of hostile aggressive components of the ambivalent core in the child" (p. 406). Depression is caused when this "universal organization" is reactivated by certain circumstances. Benedek believes that the child can best be protected against a subsequent aggravation of this depressive constellation through the "basic confidence" consolidated by the good experiences of maternal care, a concept which can be compared with Melanie Klein's idea on the introjection of the good object.

Other authors, while not necessarily subscribing to the totality of Kleinian hypotheses, have described phenomena reminiscent of the depressive position. Thus, Michael Balint (1952), observing individuals just emerging from a paranoid position following a phase of analysis characterized by suspicion and distrust of an entourage perceived as indifferent and uncaring, wrote:

> Behind all that façade, however, there is the feeling
> of a deep, painful, narcissistic wound which, as a
> rule, can be made conscious without serious diffi-
> culty—somehow in this way: "It is terrifying and
> dreadfully painful that *I am not loved for what I am;*
> time and again I cannot avoid seeing that people are
> critical of me; it is an irrefutable fact that no one loves
> me as I want to be loved." [p. 252]

Balint himself likens this to what Melanie Klein calls
the depressive position, even while rejecting the
Kleinian developmental hypothesis of the "paranoid
position–depressive position" sequence and their notion of the death instinct as a driving force. In his
studies on regression, Balint (1952) remarks that when
the analysis proceeds favorably, the patient
"seemed . . . to regress to an as-yet-undefended, naive, i.e., pre-traumatic state, and to *begin anew* to love
and to hate in a primitive way, which was then speed-
ily followed by the development of a mature, well-
adapted, non-neurotic (as far as such a state is think-
able) way of loving and hating" (p. 247).

## Psychoanalytic Literature of the Twenties and Thirties

I would first like to recall the now largely neglected
works of *Eduardo Weiss* (1926, 1932, 1944), who likewise compared melancholia to paranoia (proposing
the term "melancholic *and* paranoid syndrome") on
the basis of the presence in both cases of a "persecutory introjection." For Weiss, the conscience in
melancholia is itself the persecutory introjection which
unleashes its accusations against a "persecuted" in-

troject connected to the repressed instincts. It was Abraham who suggested the existence of this dual introjective process in connection with the superego, while the importance of the repressed instincts (death instincts) for the formation of the superego was developed by Freud in *The Ego and the Id* (1923b). Weiss compared neurotic depressions with melancholic depressions in an article he wrote in 1944, attributing the first to a strong fixation to the object which is rejected but cannot be relinquished, thus blocking a large quantity of libido. As for melancholic depressions, they are of a narcissistic nature: since the melancholic hates himself, his narcissistic satisfactions are obtained from the libido that the superego directs toward the ego. In his view, the reasons for this self-hatred derive essentially from impulses coming from the id.

*Sandor Rado* (1927), using hypotheses of Abraham and Freud as his starting point, characterizes depressed subjects as having an insatiable need for narcissistic gratifications, coupled with an equally deep-rooted narcissistic intolerance and a self-esteem wholly dependent on the object relation. The depressive tirelessly pursues his quest for love, but as soon as he is assured of it he becomes a tyrant over the loved object. He *feeds* on the object without being truly conscious of it, which is why he reacts with extreme violence to any aggression or any threat of withdrawal on the part of the love object. When this revolt ends in failure and object loss occurs, the subject turns this aggression on himself and sinks into melancholia, attempting to regain the object's love by doing penance. By now everything has been transferred into his inner world, and the object relation is transformed into a relation with the superego, whose forgiveness and love he seeks to obtain: In fact, what he is seeking is the love and forgiveness of the internalized parents. We thus end up with the sequence: guilt-atonement-forgiveness. Rado draws a parallel between this sequence and the sequence the infant follows upon awakening hungry: he reacts first with anger, kicks and screams, and then, exhausted, yields wholly to his feeling of hunger, which ends with his being fed when his mother reappears. The "alimentary orgasm" he experiences at that moment becomes the precursor of the genital orgasm. This alimentary orgasm with its sensation of intoxication, exaltation, and ecstasy explains the manic phase, which recalls the psychic experience of fusion with the mother in the nursing situation.

The ego thus passes from a state of rebellion to a state of guilt, this last arising from the aggressive tendencies toward the object. The id is then experienced as more powerful than the ego; it "gangs up" with the superego to crush the ego with the same violence that the ego had used in its aggression against the object. This is why the ego tries to obtain the superego's forgiveness, just as it seeks that of the object. What we are witnessing, then, is a dual incorporation of the object, that is, simultaneously in the superego and the ego. Freud (1915c) already showed that in keeping with the pleasure principle the child's tendency is to incorporate what is good and expel what is bad. But when the child realizes that the object can be a source of both gratification and nongratification, he finds himself confronted with an insoluble problem, a conflict of ambivalence which he is incapable of facing directly but which he resolves by splitting the object into a good object and a bad object. The good object, whose love is desired by the ego, becomes the essential foundation of the superego, while the bad object ("the little boy who cries") is introjected into the ego and becomes the victim of the sadistic tendencies now emanating from the superego. To the extent that the ego is destroyed with the bad object, only the superego with its good object remains, a situation that will lead to the manic phase.[3] Rado concludes that the mechanism of neurotic depression is similar to that of melancholia, with one essential difference: in melancholia, the processes destroy the ego, while in neurotic depression they come up against an ego which, although neurotic, is more or less intact, so that the object and the relation to reality are preserved.

*Fenö Harnik* (1932) goes back to Freud's and Abraham's conceptions on the incorporation and introjection of the lost object in depression. But while Abraham uses the model of defecation for the expulsion of the object preceding introjection, Harnik places the object expulsion at an oral level following the pattern of vomiting. Depression occurs after the devalued narcissistic object has been vomited.

*Helene Deutsch* (1932, 1933) agrees with Weiss on the importance of the paranoid element in manic depressives. In her view, these patients struggle against the guilt feelings arising from their own aggression thanks to a projective mechanism: they complain of being mistreated and hated by the outside world. If this defense mechanism were stabilized, they would

---

[3] In my view, it is not so much the components of the superego as of the ego ideal that are implicated here.

turn toward paranoia. In an article written in 1951, Deutsch brings to light on the basis of clinical data an early tendency in manic-depressives to split parental imagos into an idealized good image and a devalued bad image. During the depressive episodes, the patient identifies with the devalued image, while during the manic episodes he identifies with the good image. The lack of self-esteem in depression stems from the identification with the devalued object.

*George Gerö* (1939) takes up Rado's idea on the melancholic's oral fixation, but extends the notion of orality to include the need for dependence, love, and warmth, a concept shared by the Hungarian school of that time: Bak (1939), Hermann (1943), Balint (1965). Gerö deduces from his clinical experience that depression is in part linked to infantile demands: depressives want love, warmth, body protection, but their libidinal desires are mixed with aggressive tendencies due to their failure to obtain gratification. Their demands to be loved are so immoderate and narcissistic that they cannot be gratified; the consequent disappointment activates an equally immoderate aggression that must be controlled by the ego, and that will thus be turned against the self through the object introjected into the ego. The depressive is incapable of breaking the endlessly repeated vicious circle of infantile demands–disappointments–rage –aggressivity; it is the only path for an object relation in which the pregenital instinctual demands can not be met, where their gratification is doomed from the very outset. The oral and genital drives are profoundly intertwined. For Gerö, Abraham's constitutional predisposition to oral erotism corresponds to a pleasurable experience linked to mucosae of the mouth and other oral experiences—"oral" in the enlarged sense of the term—dating to the beginning of the mother-child relation. Gerö (1936) was the first to question the universality of the obsessional structure in depressed patients.

## Fenichel

According to Otto Fenichel (1945), depression is present in virtually every neurosis (at the very least in the form of neurotic inferiority feelings). The pregenital fixation of depressives manifests itself in a tendency to react to frustrations with violence, while their oral dependence impels them to try to get what they want by ingratiation and submissiveness. The conflict between these contradictory traits is characteristic of persons with a predisposition to depression. Their object relations are mixed with features of identification. What depressives seek from their object is the authorization to merge with it. They demand of the object an understanding of their feelings without ever reciprocating by taking the object's feelings into consideration. Such is their need for the object that they try by any means to deny their ever-present latent hostility. They are "starved for love" but incapable of finding satisfaction because of their fundamental ambivalence linked to their oral tendency. The development of guilt feelings results from the loss of the superego's love:

> the hungry infant remembers having been satisfied previously and tries to force the return of this state by asserting his "omnipotence" in screaming and ges-

> ticulation. Later on, the infant loses his belief in his
> omnipotence; he projects this omnipotence onto his
> parents and tries to regain it through participation in
> their omnipotence. He needs this participation, the
> feeling of being loved, in the same way he previously
> needed milk. [p. 388]

When he feels alone, he feels annihilated; when he
feels loved, he recovers his self-esteem. Later, the
superego develops and takes over the inner economy
of the sense of self-worth it contributed to forming.
The feeling of being loved is no longer enough. The
feeling of having done the right thing becomes a necessity for well-being. A "bad conscience" arouses
states of minor annihilations and small diminutions
of self-esteem in order to warn against the danger of
narcissistic supplies provided, this time, by the superego. Neurotic depressions are desperate attempts
to force the object to furnish vitally necessary narcissistic supplies. In psychotic depressions, this loss is
total and has actually taken place, and regulatory attempts are then aimed exclusively at the superego.
For Fenichel, definite trends of an oral fixation are
always underlying the anal orientation described by
Abraham. The unconscious ideas of these subjects,
and frequently their conscious thoughts as well, are
filled with fantasies about devouring individuals or
parts of individuals. Aims of incorporation also signal
a difference between the anality encountered in
depression and the anality of obsessional neurosis.
The anality of the depressed person aims not at retaining the object but at incorporating it, even if the
object has to be destroyed for this purpose. The experiences that precipitate depressions represent either

a loss of self-esteem or a loss of external supplies which protect or enhance self-esteem: failures, loss of prestige, loss of money, a state of remorse, a disappointment in love, or the death of the loved object. In the phenomenology of depression, there is always in the foreground a greater or lesser loss of self-esteem. Feelings of inferiority are generally rooted in an unresolved Oedipus complex.

Fenichel goes on to link such inferiority feelings to the castration complex, but states that their actual source is an awareness of the impoverishment of the ego due to the unconscious neurotic conflicts. The depressed person can love himself no more than he can love the external object. He is as ambivalent toward himself as he is toward others. In his relation to the object, this need for love appears clearly while the hate is repressed; in his relation to his own ego, the hate bursts out into the open while the primary narcissistic overestimation of the ego remains in the background. Hostility toward the frustrating objects is transformed into hostility, which is turned against one's own ego. This self-hatred takes the form of a sense of guilt: it is then a discord between ego and superego. The ambivalently loved object has been devoured and exists within the body; this introjection is also a sexual fantasy in the patient with an orally-directed sexuality. Because of its sadistic nature, the introjection is perceived as dangerous and bad, and the conflicts previously carried on with the external object are now continued in the patient's "stomach" with the introjected object. Once the introjection is consummated, the sadism takes sides with the superego and attacks the ego, which has already been modified by the introjection. The self-reproaches are intended to destroy the introjected object, but, from the perspective of the ego which stands indicted, they constitute a means of placating the superego by pleading for forgiveness. Suicide is understood as an attempt to blackmail the cruel superego, and is marked in addition by the illusory hope of release. Sometimes it is the hope of joining a dead person, sometimes the oceanic longing to return to the mother, sometimes a libidinous identification with a dead person, sometimes, finally, an orgasm in a life that demands its symbolic realization through death.

Three characteristics are found in subjects predisposed to melancholic depression: an increased narcissistic need, an increased ambivalence, and an increased orality. Melancholic depression is the profoundly erotized prolongation of the struggle against the introjected object, marked by a profound and total regression beyond the later anal phase into orality and the phase of primary narcissism. It is also a loss of self-esteem; the depressive tries to undo this loss, but only succeeds in aggravating it by a pathognomonic introjection of the ambivalently loved object. Feelings of utter annihilation follow. The introjection is intended not only to undo the loss of the object, but is simultaneously "an attempt to achieve the *unio mystica* with an omnipotent external person, to become the lost person's 'companion,' that is, food comrade, through becoming his substance and making him become one's own substance" (p. 396). But the ambivalence gives a hostile significance to this introjection.

Among the probable causes of neurotic and psychotic depression, Fenichel raises the possibility of an as yet unknown organic factor, an accidental factor favoring the development of depression. Predisposition to depression could also be due to injuries to infantile narcissism connected to parental insufficiencies (frustrations that are either too great or not great enough). The depressive has a "specially omnipotent" superego, rigid and strict. To balance the unbearable demands of the superego, he is obliged to call upon narcissistic supplies from the external world.

Depression, Fenichel suggests, may be "nothing but a 'human way of reacting to frustrations and misery' " (p. 406). In his view, unstable times and economic crises, by depriving individuals of their gratifications, as well as of their prestige, increase the number of depressions and suicides. In such periods, self-esteem loses its habitual supports, while narcissistic needs and oral dependency increases. "On the other hand, persons who as a result of childhood experiences have developed an orally dependent character are worse off under such social conditions, since they are unable to take frustrations without reacting in a depressive way" (p. 406).

It seems to me that if the term "superego" is replaced by "ego ideal," Fenichel's conception is very close to that generally accepted today.

## English-Language Contributions of the Post-war Period

*Edward Bibring* (1953) sees depression as a basic affective reaction of the ego, just as anxiety is. The ego of the depressed person is inhibited or paralyzed, incapable of confronting the "danger." Depression involves the reliving of a stage of the ego characterized by helplessness and powerlessness—hence the reactivation of an earlier structural ego state, the primary state of distress experienced in the infantile situation. For Bibring, the depressive affect is a universal experience. Depression represents the affective state corresponding to a partial or complete collapse of the ego's self-esteem, when the ego feels incapable of satisfying its strongly maintained narcissistic aspirations, with a consequent inhibition of its functions. Bibring shows that there are particular narcissistic aspirations corresponding to each level—oral, anal, phallic—and that depression appears when at any level these aspirations are frustrated. Thus, at the oral level, depression follows the discovery of not being loved or of not being independent. At the anal level, it follows the discovery of a loss of mastery over libidinal or aggressive impulses, a loss of mastery over objects, feelings of weakness, or feelings of guilt ("I shall never succeed in being good and loving, but am destined to be hateful, hostile, defiant, and therefore evil"). At the phallic level, depression arises from the fear of being defeated, of being ridiculed, or from the fear of retaliation.

Danger is the potential loss of the object; trauma, the actual loss. The state of distress is a lasting state of object loss.

For Bibring, narcissistic aspirations are intended to build up narcissistic supplies ("adequate stimuli"). For example, the child needs affection ( = aspiration); the affection he receives ( = supplies) enables him to reinforce his self-esteem. Like boredom, depression is the consequence of a lack of narcissistic supplies which frustrates narcissistic aspirations. It is the lack of narcissistic supplies that is responsible for the formation of the original primary state of distress whose reactivation is the essence of depression. The ego ideal, with its underlying narcissistic aspirations, plays a central role in the intrapsychic mechanisms of depression.

*Therese Benedek* investigated the problem of depression in general and in women in particular. In her article "Toward the Biology of the Depressive Constellation" (1956), she stresses the symbiosis between mother and child and discusses the infant's early relation toward his mother in terms of his projection of self. The part of the self projected on the mother is renewed "with each nursing and feeding" (p. 398). Benedek believes there is an introjection of the good mother in situations of satisfaction and an introjection of the bad mother in disagreeable ones:

> The development of confidence does not depend solely upon the mother's ability and willingness to give, but also upon the child's innate or acquired ability to receive, to suck, to assimilate and thrive. If the infant, because of congenital or acquired disability can not be satisfied, he remains frustrated and in turn frustrates the mother. . . . The balance between the positive (libidinal, gratifying) and the negative (aggressive, frustrating) symbiotic events influences the ego organization of the child and also that of the mother. [p. 401]

Benedek shows the central significance of the child's cry and the importance of this cry for the mother's behavior toward the child: "It is up to the mother to make an effort to reestablish the child's ego and, in doing so, she becomes an object of the diffuse, aggressive discharge" (p. 403). Thus, the child develops hatred toward the object so as to be able to distance himself and succeed in establishing his self. "With the memory traces of frustration, and with the accompanying diffuse aggression, the infant introjects his own aggressive impulses, which then become a part of his psychic organization. Thus, just as there are memory traces of satisfying, good mother and frustrating, bad mother, so are there also memory traces of good (satisfied) self and bad (angry) self. By this the core of ambivalence is established within" (p. 404). The child's difficulties will reawaken in the mother similar problems from her own infantile past. Thus, the symbiotic mother-child relationship will be disturbed, and the nuclear conflict described as the "depressive constellation" will be in place. The conflicts of ego aspiration will lead to regressive processes which will activate deep layers of developmental fixations, for example oral feeding complexes which can thus mobilize the depressive constellation. The emotional condition is more serious if the conflict includes within the self not only the bad mother, but also the hated and bad self. "The woman hates in herself the child who still harbors a hostile dependence" (p. 415). If anxiety and aggression necessitate a libidinal provision during certain phases of development, the depressive constellation will make its appearance in men as well as in women. But Benedek believes that this constellation is more frequent in women (a fact she attributes to hormones). Her ideas recall one of Melanie Klein's views on the reactivation of the depressive position at certain phases of infantile development and adulthood, and still more certain ideas of Winnicott, who laid stress on the importance of the mother's response to the child. Nonetheless, Benedek does not clearly explain whether she considers these phenomena pathological or universal.

For *Bertram Lewin* (1961), the appearance of depression in the course of analysis signals conflicts between the superego and the ego, whereas anxiety is indicative of conflicts between the ego and the id. Depression, like anxiety, is thus the sign of an inner conflict of the personality. The superego of the depressive orders him to relinquish the breast, but for all the secret or unconscious reprimands he receives, he maintains his regressive place there. The admonishment is treated in the same way the dreamer treats a stimulus from within or without: he registers it, but the narcissistic regression is preserved.

The studies of *John Bowlby* (1960, 1961a,b, 1963) dealing with the mourning process have already been outlined in the chapter on depressive affect.

*Joseph Sandler and Walter G. Joffe* (1965) consider depression to be a basic affective response of the same type as anxiety, and in no way prejudge either the developmental phase or the clinical picture in which it occurs. Attributing the same conceptual status to depression as to anxiety makes it possible to integrate the literature on the subject more effectively. Sandler and Joffe emphasize the connection between the depressive reaction and loss: the depressive reaction follows the loss of a state of well-being, even when the object is already constituted. What is lost is the biological and psychological state, a consequence of the object relation, which is why there can be a depressive response even before the formation of the object. The loss of a state of well-being is experienced as the loss of something essential to narcissistic integrity; nar-

cissistic integrity being linked to feelings of helplessness, its loss triggers a depressive response. Sandler
and Joffe's conception is close to Bibring's: depression
is the emotional expression of the ego's state of weakness and results from the ego's awareness of its powerlessness in regard to its aspirations. Sandler considers
the depressive response as a response of a biological
nature akin to pain, the opposite of the state of well-
being. In this, he claims to differ from Bibring, who
uses the more elaborated concept of "self-esteem."

Pain, in the sense that Freud used it in Addendum
C of "Inhibitions, Symptoms and Anxiety" (1926d),
is a reaction to the loss of the strongly cathected object. The depressive reaction is a state of impotent
resignation in the face of this pain. The state of well-
being is defined as the maximal approach to the ideal
state thanks to the presence of a love object; thus, the
consequence of the loss of the object will be the wid-
ening of the gap between the state of the self and the
ideal state, whence the appearance of pain and, secondarily, depression once the feelings of resignation
and helplessness enter in. For Sandler, the aggressiveness that follows pain is directed against the
source of the pain. If this aggressiveness cannot be
expressed, the impression of powerlessness, helplessness, and resignation will be reinforced. The superego intervenes on several levels: (1) first of all, by
holding up to the ego an unrealizable ideal, which
accounts for the guilt during instinctual gratifications;
and (2) by repressing the aggressiveness. Normally,
the child in the course of development becomes progressively capable of decathecting the lost ideal object
with a minimum of suffering, and of recathecting in
the outside world; a point of vulnerability results

when this transition proves impossible. According to Sandler and Joffe, this process should be understood not as a position or a developmental phase, but rather as a line of development beginning early in life and continuing throughout.

Sandler and Joffe consider simplistic the idea that aggression is simply turned against the self through identification with the hated object. Far more frequently, in their view, the child either inhibits his aggression or directs his anger against the actual self, which is not loved because it is unsatisfying. The essence of the depressive reaction consists in the feeling that the ideal state of the self is unattainable; hence the feeling of powerlessness.

*D.W. Winnicott* (1954) describes a normal stage within the affective development of the child which occurs between the age of five months and the end of the first year, immediately following the stage of absolute dependence. Principal among the preconditions of this stage, the child must already be a total person and have relationships with total persons. Winnicott calls this stage the "stage of anxiety" or "the stage of concern," because it is then that the child begins to feel anxiety or concern about the possible consequences of the instinctual impulses he feels toward the external object (in contrast to the infant under six months, who is "ruthless," utterly unconcerned with the consequences of his feelings). In this stage of concern, the child experiences as simultaneous and coexisting the opposing feelings of love and hate, and calm and excitement regarding the frustrating or gratifying mother, who begins to be recognized as being one and the same. It is only when the mother, as the gratifying object, proves capable of surviving the child's assaults and aggression that he is finally able to make the distinction between the destructiveness of his fantasies and the actual outcome, between his inner fears and the external reality (the stress is thus placed on the environment as well). The elaboration of the depressive anxiety passes through guilt and leads to reparation. What Winnicott envisages is a stage reached at a certain moment rather than a position such as that formulated by Melanie Klein.

*Edith Jacobson* (1946) holds oedipal difficulties or disappointments responsible for reviving unresolved pregenital conflicts. Depending on the resonance these disappointments have on the organization of the personality, which in turn will depend on earlier disappointments, they will be decisive in predisposing the subject to the expectation of disappointment, powerlessness, hopelessness. One of the fundamental psychoanalytic hypotheses is that introjected, cumulative experiences define the manner in which later events will be experienced. This hypothesis also finds expression in the repetition compulsion, which among other things is an aspect of the timelessness of the unconscious.

According to Jacobson (1954, 1964), our concept of the self is initially not very firm. It emerges from sensations hardly distinguishable from perceptions of the gratifying part-object (the breast), and at first is fused and confused with images of the object. Rather than a stable and durable concept, the self is composed of a constantly changing series of self-images which reflect mainly the incessant fluctuations of the primitive mental state. Jacobson postulates that the most fundamental goals of development are the integration, organization, and unification of these images into a stable and consistent self-image and the establishment of clear and lasting boundaries between the representations of the self and the object along with the optimal cathexis of these representations. For that, the individual must be able to differentiate clearly between the self and the object, and to develop and maintain his self-esteem at an optimal level thanks to an atmosphere of parental care and affection in which tolerable frustrations are experienced in manageable doses. The dangers come from two directions: on the one hand, overgratification with an undue prolongation of the mother-child unity will retard the establishment of clear boundaries between the images of self and the object; it will also hinder the development of independence and the formation of a realistic view of the external world. On the other hand, excessive frustrations which are too much for the developing ego to master will lead to the immoderately aggressive cathexis of the images of the object and the self, resulting in unsatisfactory interpersonal attitudes and feelings of inferiority and self-depreciation. Frustration, deprivation and separation from the mother compel the child to become conscious of himself as an entity separate from her. This also leads to fantasies and wishes for reunion, which are gratified when the child is at the breast or near his mother, when the images of the self and the mother are thought to fuse again. "Thus the hungry child's longing for oral gratification is the origin of the first, primitive type of identification, an identification achieved by refusion of self- and object-images and founded on wishful fantasies of oral incorporation of the love object" (Jacobson, 1954, p. 99).[4]

The preoedipal period of the child's life is marked by belief in the omnipotence of his thoughts and the magic of words. The residue of the magical belief in the omnipotence and value of the love objects becomes separated from the realistic appreciation of their power and becomes part of the ego ideal, even if this is vaster, for Jacobson, than the image of the idealized parents. Magic fantasies and images contribute to forming the ego ideal, making possible the distinction between the real parents and their idealized images. These idealizations will be extended to abstract values in general, to ideas, ideals, and ideal goals. Jacobson believes that self-esteem, which is the emotional expression of the evaluation of self, reflects the degree of either divergence or harmony between the representation of self and the desired conception of self. Annie Reich (1953, 1954) and Rochlin (1953) describe patients in whom fluctuations or lowering of self-esteem bring about fluctuations of mood, confirming in a number of aspects the theories of Bibring and Jacobson. These patients do not feel unloved or guilty, but weak and inadequate. Jacobson believes that the loss of self-esteem (in other words, feelings of inferiority, weakness, impoverishment, and powerlessness) represents the central psychological problem of depression. She distinguishes between neurotic and psychotic depressions: self-esteem is diminished in both, but in psychotic patients there is in addition

[4] Therese Benedek (1956) describes the nursing process in the same way: "the mother becomes, with each nursing and feeding, part of the self again" (p. 398).

a severe regressive process in the entire organization of the personality.

Moreover, psychotic depressions have somatic components and cannot be explained solely on a psychological basis; psychotics are predisposed to these severe regressions through a flaw of the ego and of the superego fixated at an immature preoedipal level. In her view, this insufficient development is the result of a combination of inherited constitution and emotional frustrations and privations in early infancy. Indeed, serious disappointments in the early years of life lead to a premature devaluation of the love objects. If the parent is precociously devalued, the child experiences a collapse of the magical world and can oscillate between an optimistic illusion and a pessimistic illusion which, once again, distorts reality. This premature and excessive disappointment in relation to the parents, with the concomitant devaluation of them and the self, explains the fixation of the ego and superego of depressive patients at preoedipal levels of identification.

Prepsychotic personalities present a number of developmental characteristics belonging to the preoedipal magic stage: among other things, their way of dealing with their conflicts is characteristic of this stage, with the massive withdrawal or displacement of aggressive and libidinal cathexis from the object onto the ego or from one object to another. Jacobson shows the unusual degree of dependence of these cyclothymic patients. Their objects do not necessarily have to be persons. They are capable of establishing intense emotional relationships with causes or organizations—political, scientific, or religious. This type of exaggerated dependency is closely related to what

Jacobson considers a specific weakness of the ego in these patients, namely, their extreme intolerance to injuries and frustrations. The failures of the love object or the self plunge them into depressive states. One defense against this tendency to be disappointed by the love object is the mechanism of denial, denial of the weakness or inadequacy of the love object. Jacobson points out that this denial mechanism can be so powerful that the patient can lose contact with reality and enter a manic state. He will react by mood swings, or will prove incapable of recathecting the object which will lead to an aggressive devaluation of himself and the object. The "primal depression" consists of a pessimistic, disillusioned, uninterested attitude toward life and the self, such that everything appears empty, without interest or pleasure. In order to rebuild his depleted libidinal resources, the depressive will seek narcissistic supplies from a new love object, adopting an attitude of submission and petition. In transference, he turns to his analyst for such supplies. Sometimes he gives up hope of finding an infinitely good and loving object and accepts anyone, provided the person is strong and powerful; he will then revive the image of an all-powerful and unloving primitive sadistic object. If this fails, he may seek refuge in withdrawal from the object world. It might be mentioned that Jacobson's description here is very close to that of Rado (1927).

As we have already seen, Freud (1917e) recognized the melancholic's self-reproaches as accusations directed against the abandoned love object now identified with the self. The ego, in seeking to appease the superego, tries to regain the love not only of the original love object but also of the latest love object whose good aspects he introjected into the superego. For Rado, the abandoned love object was split into two parts: the bad aspects or the bad object were introjected into the ego and punished, while the good aspects previously loved were introjected into the superego whose forgiveness is being sought. Jacobson (1953) postulates that in the melancholic psychotic phase, "This reanimated, inflated image will now be dissolved as a representation in the system ego and will be absorbed by the superego, whereas the deflated worthless object-image merges with the self-representations" (pp. 79–80). These fusions are facilitated by the inadequate separation of the images of self and object on the one hand and of the superego on the other. In other words, Jacobson believes that the melancholic psychotic process consists of a regressive dissolution of the identifications which had been precariously built up in the prepsychotic, a dissolution which leads to a fusion of the love objects' good and bad images with the self-image and with the superego. Whence the pathological conflicts between the self and the ego. Freud had spoken of a "narcissistic identification" in the melancholic process. For Jacobson it is not an identification of the ego with the object, but of a total or partial fusion of the images of the self and the object within the ego system. In this type of identification, the ego does not assume the characteristics of the love object. This process represents the continuation of earlier attempts at restitution and defense, by withdrawing from the object world and internalizing the conflict, the manic depressive is still trying to reconstitute in the superego the powerful love object he lost in the external world. Within the psyche, the self continues the struggle with the love object feeling itself helpless and powerless, like a small dependent child punished by a cruel parent. The feelings of helplessness and inadequacy are further aggravated by the inhibition of the ego functions. Jacobson attributes this first and foremost to an insufficient maturation, with an unsatisfactory differentiation of images of the self and the object and of the ego ideal–superego systems, and secondly to a regressive dissolution of these identifications.

*Margaret Mahler* (1961) studied the reactions to the loss of the symbiotic object in psychotic children. She demonstrated how, at the time of the separation from this object, the fused symbiotic representations of self and object prevent progress toward individuation. Catastrophic rage-panic reactions, described as typical of the symbiotic psychotic syndrome, accompany the separation. Next there is a regression to a secondary autism and other primary symbiotic and secondarily autistic mechanisms in various combinations. Mahler defined grief as a reaction specific to object loss, and anxiety as a reaction specific to the danger the loss entails. Restoration of the libidinal object makes small children capable of feeling sadness and grief. In fact, once there is a dent in their autistic armor, they become particularly vulnerable to emotional frustration, helplessness, and despair.

Mahler describes the period of grief and mourning (rarely brought out in the literature) which inevitably precedes the complete psychotic break with reality and the secondary autistic withdrawal. Clinical examples show that sadness and grief are the first signs of a progressive development in psychotic children and that these emotions seem of necessity to accompany the child's leaving the inanimate autistic world through restoration of the libidinal object. It is only when the children retained the memory trace of the first satisfactions of their needs—resulting in a confident expectation that their needs can be satisfied—that they become capable of restoring the symbiotic object after its loss.

In a 1966 article, Mahler shows how the vicissitudes of the separation-individuation phase determine any potential depressive reactivity to come. The narcissistic pleasures linked to the mastery of new skills (secondary narcissism) awaken in the child a feeling akin to magic omnipotence. If, in the period of rapprochement which follows the practicing period (subphases 2 and 3 of the separation-individuation phase), there is a significant lack of acceptance on the part of the mother, a substantial narcissistic vulnerability will result which will give rise to the helplessness that creates the basic depressive affect or mood. Children with a deficit in narcissistic or emotional supplies are characterized by a diminution of the "confident expectation," with an affect of irritation and the tendency to succumb to an angry mood. The depressive affect consists in an ensemble of separation and grief reactions marked by temper tantrums and continual attempts to coerce the mother even while clinging to her and wooing her, then giving up these efforts in despair, abdication, and resignation. This negative depressive affective responsiveness leads to a precocity of superego structuralization.[5] For Mahler,

[5] Mahler, like the Kleinians, believes that the discovery of anatomical sexual differences is made much earlier than previously believed, and attributes the proclivity of girls to depressive moods to this factor, among others.

then, the depressive response is a basic affective reaction comparable to anxiety. In her view, it is the
depletion of "confident expectation" and the diminution of self-esteem, combined with a deficit in neutralized aggression that create the libidinal economic
basis for the depressive mood. This vulnerability to
the sense of helplessness following the depletion of
basic trust is due to the collapse of the child's belief
in his own omnipotence and to the impossibility of
restoring it, since his belief in his parents' omnipotence has likewise collapsed. Furthermore, on the
basis of identification with the aggressor (the mother),
the child, as the aggressor's victim, turns the aggression against himself (and this before the superego
persecutors are consolidated into a superego structure).

The basic depressive reaction is thus a particular
response to a painful situation, accompanied by feelings of helplessness and incapacity to restore a satisfying condition. Mahler (1968) defines individuation
as the progressive development of ideals that are increasingly better adapted to reality coupled with the
renunciation of infantile aims of dependence on external objects. During the separation-individuation
phase, the child separates the mental representations
of his self from those of his mother, and at the same
time consolidates the autonomous ego functions. He
can feel anxiety as a result; for Mahler, this anxiety
is due to the danger of losing the object, in contrast
to the conception of Joffe and Sandler (1965), for
whom this anxiety was related to the renunciation of
ideal states of the self as experienced during the symbiotic phase. For these two authors, individuation includes not only a renunciation of the past and an

acquisition of ideals adapted to reality, but also the satisfying experience of functioning and mastering, a process which continues to develop throughout adult life.

*John Klauber* (1967) uses three constants to characterize neurotic depressives in their object relations: (1) they are afraid to love for fear of disappointments or failures; (2) they are doomed to experience their current objects as unsatisfying because they have shifted onto these their anger against their first disappointing objects; (3) they feel their objects disappointed them because they themselves are unworthy of being loved, which leads them to doubt themselves and idealize their objects, thus assuring further disappointments. The self-image of the neurotic depressive is split into an ideal, omnipotent image and an (aggressive) devalued image, with the divergence between the two images being such as to make any hope of rapprochement futile. This split in the self-image reflects a division in the object images: the objects having been idealized and devalued by turns, the depressive attempts to resolve the ambivalence which is unbearable to him by incorporating the devalued part-object into his ego and idealizing the remaining part.

According to Klauber, the patient during psychoanalysis begins by showing the devalued representations of self and denying his fantasies of omnipotence while provoking the analyst into assuming the role of ego ideal, of all-powerful savior. The analyst's interpretation of the ambivalence, that is, of aggression intermingled with the desires for love, makes the patient conscious of the object loss; these frustrated wishes for love express themselves during transference. The release of aggression leads to a rapprochement between the self-image and the images of objects, which no longer appear unattainable. As an example, the analysand looks for weak points in his analyst and compares his image of the analyst and of all-powerful objects against reality.

*David Rubinfine* (1968) worked out a theory of depression akin to that of Jacobson. He stressed the importance of unexpected frustrations arising in a satisfying climate. In his view, disappointment entails awareness of being separate, rejected and abandoned, which necessitates the splitting of the object so as to preserve the good part.

## Contemporary Francophone Authors

*Serge Lebovici* (1955), relying on his clinical experience, remarks that "contrary to classical opinion, attacks of depression (like episodes of excitation), are observed in children, and the cycles of manic-depressive psychosis can appear very early" (p. 503). Alluding to Germaine Guex's 1950 book on the neurosis of abandonment, he comments:

> One of the most interesting points to pursue in studying the ego of melancholics is what G. Guex brought to light in abandonics: that it is not so much the affective traumas determined by actual family inadequacies as the constitutional factor that lies at the root of this particular structure, where self-depreciation is linked to frustrations experienced on the level of fantasy. . . . The description by Swiss authors of what they call—contestably in my view—the neurosis of abandonment makes it possible to recognize this par-

ticular organization of the ego where the craving to love and be loved ill conceals a profound masochism, evidently accompanied by very primitive aggressive tendencies. Thus the ego organization of the melancholic can be understood without reference to regression. Regression is acceptable here only to a very limited extent, in that it attests the sensitivity of melancholic patients to the slightest frustration, which triggers in them this aborted work of mourning. . . . In the final analysis, the ego of melancholics appears dominated by a very primitive organization wherein the fantasmatically elaborated mechanisms of incorporation play a fundamental role. Their voracity vis-à-vis the object, chosen on a highly narcissistic basis, accounts for the seriousness of the least frustration, which dangerously lowers the feeling of self esteem. . . . The attempt to clarify this psychogenesis is not to deny the often constitutional—and indeed even hereditary—aspect of the illness. Nor is it to reduce the study of the illness to a study of its motivations, which are pathogenic only in this particular organization of the ego in the melancholic. [pp. 525-526]

*Jean Mallet* (1955) likewise believes that neurotic depressions originate in disappointments experienced as a loss of self-esteem or a loss of the external supplies buttressing self-esteem. Attacks of melancholia, on the other hand, follow the loss of the object, real or ideal, total or part-object. In his formulation, the neurosis underlying melancholic depression is hysteria; he considers the depressive episodes of obsessionals and phobics to be aggravations of the neurosis itself rather than true depressions. Mallet sees the loss of self-esteem that accompanies decompensations as being due (1) to punishment for a fault actually committed (when the guilt, repressed or attributed to others, could no longer be avoided by the hysteric's succumbing to despair); (2) to the relinquishment of the object, seen as depreciating by these subjects for whom the sole purpose of love experiences is to bring narcissistic satisfactions; (3) to the devaluation of the object, whose shortcomings are seen as devaluing for the subject himself.

Mallet believes that, appearances to the contrary, libidinal regression is virtually nonexistent in either neurotic depression or hysteria. In his view, even though the drives may express themselves regressively, they are still genital and nondefused. In melancholia, on the other hand, there is a true and profound instinctual regression with defusion and the release of nongenitalized, purely oral urges. During recovery from the melancholic episode, the subject's character takes on obsessional traits even to its mechanisms, its defenses protecting the objects against new dangerous tendencies of the subject.

For Mallet, the point of fixation for neurotic depression is in the genital phase, while for melancholia the experience responsible for the fixation occured in a narcissistic phase. This experience could have been the actual (or simply affective) abandonment by the parent of the opposite sex (a circumstance even more serious if the parent of the same sex to whom the child has turned in his distress likewise leaves him). Alternatively, it could be the implication of the parent of the opposite sex in circumstances entailing the parent's devaluation in the child's eyes, these last two scenarios taking place in the postoedipal stage. Finally, it could be an infirmity or the lack of a penis. Mallet, like other authors, calls attention to the high frequency of oral regressions and certain anal regressions in depressed patients, and lastly to the depressive predisposition among women and those suffering from hysteric neurosis.

*Sacha Nacht and Paul Claude Racamier* (1959) distinguish the depressed person—a patient in a state of depression—from the depressive—a subject exposed or predisposed to depression. They define "depression as a pathological state of conscious psychic suffering and guilt accompanied by a marked lowering of the sense of self-worth and a nondeficitary diminution of mental, psychomotor, and even organic activity" (p. 568). Nacht and Racamier express reservations concerning the terms "depressive position" and "anaclitic depression" coined respectively by Melanie Klein and René Spitz, because of the confusion introduced by using the term "depression" when referring to normal states. They stress the fundamental unity of depressive states for all their apparent diversity. "The loss of love is the fundamental depression-causing situation. . . . The rupture of a close and mutual bond of love is at the root of all states of depression . . ." (p. 570). Depression is thus triggered by

> the estrangement of an object which the depressive was determined to hold close to him, not to say to keep tightly clutched to him, and by the more or less total defusion of the libidinal and aggressive drives (with the aggressive drive taking a more or less marked precedence over the libidinal drive). . . . The depressed person, instead of truly converging these opposing tendencies on the person and image of the object, makes a compromise of love and hate and seeks to deflect his aggression from the object he

wants to safeguard. . . . On the instinctual level, depression consists of the transformation of a close mutual love relationship into a no-less close aggressive relationship, of which the subject makes himself the victim by turning the aggression against himself. For the depressive, his feelings of being aggressive, guilty, and threatened somehow assure that he will continue to love and be loved. Through his moral suffering, he attempts to remain tightly attached to his object and to bind it to him. Through his suffering and conscious guilt, he seeks to make amends. [p. 573]

The authors stress the force of the superego in depressive patients.

They *insist* that the frustrating and punitive object, internalized in the form of the superego, is *all-powerful*. . . . They had originally aspired to an omnipotently good object that protects them from everything, including themselves, and in depression the internalized object becomes on the contrary completely aggressive, but it remains in any case all-powerful. [p. 574]

The depressed subjects' feelings of powerlessness originally have reference to the object (reproaches of powerlessness addressed to the analyst). Their attitude toward others is truly aggressive through the intermediary of their depression.

His suffering is an accusation. His feeling of incurability is a reproach. His demands are humble . . . but devastating. His dependence is tyrannical. He sinks into suffering and tries to drag his object into it as well. He makes himself slave to the object, but attempts to enslave it. He clings to the object in a desperate embrace wherein it is difficult to distinguish between love and hate. [p. 575]

The structures of the depressed person's object relations involve the introjection of the object, internalization of the sadistic object; the depression is comparable to an acute crisis of moral masochism. "But in masochism, the object and the subject are experienced and presented as existing independently of one another," while "in depression and especially in melancholia . . . the paths of aggression have been 'short-circuited.' . . . the reversal of the aggression is not even necessary since the attacked object was unconsciously introjected by the patient," and the patient, in destroying himself, aims at destroying the incorporated object (p. 576). Nacht and Racamier draw a parallel with certain psychosomatic ailments such as asthma, and in fact, psychosomatic manifestations during depressive states are numerous and significant. But in psychosomatic ailments, the aggressive drives are turned against "the body of the subject through defense mechanisms that, ontogenetically speaking, antedate the constitution of an integrated psychic ego . . ." (p. 577).

According to these authors, the notion of "organic primary masochism" (Nacht) can account for certain aspects of the depressive predisposition. Depression is situated between psychosomatic aggression and moral masochism, but is relatively less developed than this last since the separation between subject and object is less pronounced. It can be distinguished (1) from schizophrenic psychosis, in that the regression does not reach the point of complete fusion between subject and object (although it can constitute a preliminary stage to schizophrenic psychosis); and (2) from psychosomatic disorders, in that the libidinal and aggressive impulses remain tied up in the object relationship. "What is specific in the dynamic of depressive states is the mechanism of aggressive identification with the object" (p. 577): "the aggressive introjection of the frustrating object, originally maternal, at once loved and detested" (p. 578) to which the subject is bound by an oral fixation. "The defusion of the representations of self and object is not entirely achieved in the depressive and . . . is not sustained in the depressed person" (p. 579). Depressives display a hypersensitivity to frustration; their desires are insatiable, unquenchable, of the all-or-nothing variety; their demands are exorbitant and by this very fact doomed to frustration; they are concrete and ever ready to be renewed and increased; nothing seems to give depressives the definite, sufficient proof that they are loved. The object must be perfectly good or perfectly evil, the fact that the object can be both gratifying and disappointing is intolerable to them. Moreover, these objects are completely anonymous. The criteria of the relationship are not qualitative, but above all quantitative.

Nacht and Racamier classify depressive states by the degree of defusion of the love relationship and by the degree of internalization of the object relation and of the introjection of the object. Antidepressive defenses include inhibition, obsessiveness, and oral affective recovery.

For them, suicide is sometimes a dream, "the return to a whole, shadowless, boundless, and limitless love with the ideal mother, the object which has been lost or tarnished by aggression but which is now restored and made completely good again by suicide: the depressive commits suicide in order to love and be loved. His fantasy is that of nirvana" (p. 123). Or again,

> Divided, tormented and paralyzed by his ambivalence, the depressed person who kills himself seeks and thinks to find in the act of suicide the unification of his ego, unification with the object and the unification of his drives. For him, suicide represents the only means of reconciling and fusing the libido and aggression he was incapable of forging together on the anvil of his object relation, which is why suicide can bring to an end the depression whose onset marked the instinctual defusion. [pp. 124-125]

*Francis Pasche* (1969) chose to deal with the inferiority depression, which in his view is not merely the most frequent but also the only depression worthy of the name.

> The inferiority depression is defined by the devaluation of the self, a painful self-depreciation which is devoid of conscious ideas of guilt: the depressive is incapable of doing evil because he is incapable of doing anything at all, so depression is situated this side of guilt. Depression is a feeling of deficiency, inadequacy, helplessness. . . . On the surface, it is concerned with *having*—beauty, wealth, strength, acuity, knowledge, and with *doing*—agility, skill, competence, efficiency, comprehension, creativity. . . . He (the depressed person) does not reproach his parents for not having sufficiently nourished him, caressed him or petted him, . . . but for not having made him handsome enough, strong enough, intel-

ligent enough. . . . "I must change," he tells his analyst in a thousand different ways. . . . What the depressed person fears is to live diminished, to live . . . a third-rate existence. . . . It is as if he had been not engendered but *created* by his parents, with all that implies in terms of the omnipotence he can bestow upon them and, consequently, the potential devaluation or accusations he can level at them if he turns out to be a failure. But while seeing himself as the creature of his parents, he aspires simultaneously to be a creator; the nondepressed person is far less ambitious. . . . From the relative, we move to the absolute. . . . He must either create from nothing or undertake nothing. . . . What he needs is not to have more, but to be more. . . . [p. 182]

Pasche thus lays emphasis on the depressed person's megalomania. He makes a distinction between the "ego" and the "I." "The ego is a complex agency whose very nature it is to divide itself in a continuous dehiscence, enabling it to detach itself from itself, to watch itself, to gain awareness of itself and to feel itself the cause of its own acts" (p. 185). Pasche uses the word "I" to designate the subject of intentionality. "The total conversion of the I by the superego, with which it makes common cause, and its total dissociation from the ego are the essential characteristics of depression which distinguish it from obsessional neurosis. It remains for the ego to be put on trial and pilloried" (p. 185).

Pasche examines the relationships between the four elements of the psyche—I, ego, superego, and ego ideal—in the depressive syndrome.

The ego concentrates all its cathexes on its

injury . . . and in appearance cares for no one. The superego overwhelms the ego with its contempt, the unending reminder of its inadequacies. . . . To all indications, the superego directs all its love to the ego ideal . . . as if each time it brought out a deficiency of the ego it was to the benefit of the ego ideal, which, inflated with this new gratification, became all the more perfect and thus all the more inaccessible for the ego, with the I ratifying the new promotion of the ideal since it is here always in agreement with the superego. [p. 191]

In the depressive "there is a regression of the ego, since it introjects the deteriorated object massively—ravenously, one might say—according to an oral defense mode" (p. 193). The ego ideal is regressive, megalomanic; "the libidinal drives are not so much regressed as quite simply emptied in favor of the superego, the ego, and the ego ideal; the aggressive impulses are used in the highly sublimated form of denial and countercathexis" (p. 193).

For Pasche there are different major precipitating causes of depression. First is devaluation of a close object, the object always being narcissistic, annexed by the subject in order to enhance itself ("it doubtless represents a phallus"). Or it can be a testing "comparison between the ideal [the depressed subject] strives for and the imperfection inherent in every achievement" (it is this that explains depression following success). Finally, depression can be triggered by an internal modification (a bodily weakening, due for example to sickness, overwork, etc.).

"As to the more distant genesis of depression," Pasche advances several hypotheses.

The child at times behaves as if he felt he had certain qualities of the prestigious parent, qualities such as stature, voice, strength, and so on, and this through a kind of immediate participation, a magic spell, without, naturally, these qualities having been in the least acquired and before they were synthesized into a real representation of the fascinating object. . . . This identification takes place prior to the constitution of the object and consequently precedes object attachment. There is no question of love . . . on the part of the child. It is then merely a question of being. . . . If this megalomania remains more or less profoundly repressed in the form of the ego ideal, it would be . . . at the expense of the effective realization of identification and the possibilities of loving. . . . That is the depressed person's ego ideal and it is in keeping with this ideal that he chooses his complementary object, which in combination with him constitutes a potential concrete ideal. [pp. 194-195]

A number of conditions must be present if the child is to be able to develop the primitive ego ideal: reality must "offer him enough love so that he can find object compensations for lowering his narcissistic ambitions," he must be "loved independently of his performances," and in addition to the

always conditional love-esteem, he must be given simple, unconditional love. Parental demands concerning scholastic, sports, and finally social accomplishments must not be exorbitant, even while being continuous enough and strong enough to keep him motivated and convince him that he is also loved for what he does. If this is not the case, the child will have no other means of being loved than making himself appreciated for his success, and neither his mere existence nor even his moral qualities will suffice to procure him the love of others. . . . The megalomania underlying depression goes hand in hand with a micromania which is not merely superficial. [pp. 164-165]

For Pasche, the mode of civilization also acts upon the mental pathology of a given era. Concerning our own, he writes:

The extension of various offshoots of gnosis, these varied forms of secularization of magic with lead both to deifying and mechanizing man, threaten to submerge the humanism of Judaeo-Christian origin and, in so doing, increasingly to favor the proliferation of depressive and manic-depressive syndromes by placing us before the alternative of being God or nothing. [p. 199]

*Béla Grunberger* (1971) endeavors to make the connection between narcissism and drive theory by assuming in melancholia a disequilibrium between the original narcissism and instinctual maturation. At the source of melancholia he places the cataclysmic memory of the narcissistic trauma represented by birth. "In depression," he writes, "it is life itself that becomes the source of malaise . . ." (p. 219).

The depressive . . . has succeeded in developing a psychic ego and a body ego that are coherent and integrated, but he lacks narcissistic revaluation and confirmation. When such confirmation is equal to the task, it endows the ego forever with a special, pleasurable euphoria growing out of an enhanced functional plenitude *(joie de vivre)*, but in the depressive . . . this euphoria takes a negative direction, that is, it is *reversed*. . . . This affect, depression, is the psychic expression of a lack not of narcissistic investment but of its confirmation by the ego ideal, which is, in the last analysis, narcissism itself. When it has not been properly integrated into the instinctual system, narcissism remains infantile, unadapted, anachronistic. . . . The depressive has a need to be loved; however, he can use to that end, for narcissistic gratification, *all sources of narcissistic pleasure*, from no matter what psychological level. . . . Depression is a disorder of the ego. . . . It involves not only suffering resulting from the discrepancy between the ego and the ego ideal, . . . but veritable conflict between the ego and the narcissistic ego ideal, perceived as a psychic agency in the same sense as the superego, but different from it. . . . The ego's sole concern from then on will be to recover that lost narcissistic ideal, trying to prove itself worthy before that agency, which possesses and personifies its projected narcissism, trying to make itself loved by that agency. . . . The primary object, which should provide narcissistic confirmation when the ego is being formed, is what enables the subject to leave the world of primary narcissism, an oceanic world marked by boundlessness, timelessness, and omnipotence, and to move toward new possibilities of narcissistic gratification, which are inherent in normal development and in satisfactory instinctual maturation. . . . If it [the primary object] fails in its task, the child projects his absolute primary narcissism—in my view, prenatal narcissism—wholly onto his ego ideal, and there will be only one possible way to attain that ego ideal, which will be to return to the same level, that is, the level of prenatal narcissism. [pp. 223-233]

Grunberger shows the protest aspect of the depressive's aggressive affect, which he interprets as a pro-jection of self-directed aggression rather than as masochism (and is thus of depressive nature).

> Depressives frequently commit suicide in a state of physiological elation, induced or not, not to mention the suicidal impulses that occur at the height of sexual ecstasy. . . . In all these states, there is a kind of meeting between a libidinal component and a narcissistic component, a meeting that would be likely to lead to a synthesis. Yet such a synthesis seems to be impossible; in fact, the two factors behave like explosive substances when they come in contact with one another. . . . *The body ego dies, but narcissism triumphs;* it alone is responsible for the subject's optimistic outlook and plans. . . . [At the moment when the change makes] the ego regress to a point at which it will cede its dominance to the ego-cosmic narcissistic formation, *it would automatically return to an earlier state without conflicts, which means nullification of the narcissistic wound,* but also, of course, the elimination of the ego. . . . The melancholic's regression derives from the conflict between the ego and narcissism, and the ego is in effect abandoned and condemned by the narcissistic agency. In neurotic depression, however, the schism between the two protagonists is not yet complete, and the ego can defend itself against the troubles that befall it and hence avoid regression. . . . [For the melancholic, the abhorred ego is the body ego.] For, irrespective of the importance that classic descriptions attribute to the sadism factor, the elative factor unquestionably always shows through the suicidal gesture, to the exclusion of any other component. . . . The melancholic's suicide is always marked by a certain inner radiance, even if externally it ap-

pears to us as a sad and shocking slide to self-de-
struction [pp. 258-264].

The depressive will always seek an object in keeping with a certain narcissistic identity, which seems
to open for him the only avenue to his real object
relation, but since he hates himself, he will immediately turn away from it.

*Nicolas Abraham and Maria Torok* (1975) use as their
starting point three cases of important object loss following a death or precocious separation. The object
having been introjected, "encrypted," the authors
show how a conflict develops as a result of the ambivalent relation with the wounding object, thus pre-
venting the mourning from taking place. The object
was transformed into the ego ideal after the wound
caused by the disappointment was eliminated from
consciousness. The object had replaced the ego to the
extent that the analysand spoke of himself as if he
were the object, giving rise to difficulties in transference. Transference could not take hold until the analyst gave the interpretation that the speaker was the
object that had replaced the ego.[6]

*Jean Bergeret* (1975, 1976; for a more detailed bibliography, see 1976) laid stress on conflicts at the level
of anal receptivity. While from the economic point of
view, such conflicts impede the articulation between
narcissism and genitality, from the dynamic stand-

---

[6] I only learned of the remarkable text by Braunschweig and
Fain (1975) after completing this manuscript. I am aware that
many problems remain to be discussed in connection with this
subject.

point it is the aggressive drives and the sexual instincts that are considerably inhibited. From the topical point of view, "the infantile ego ideal conserves its power of aspiration linked to the early period (phallic and maternal) of the castration threat"; at the same time, the paternal superego is not sufficiently individualized and developed. Bergeret's original contribution is summarized in his 1976 report, which likewise concerns itself with the notion of *essential* depression (see Marty, 1968) and sheds light on crucial points of reference in the system of the defensive economy of depressivity, on the border between neuroses and psychoses.

Numerous ideas and reflections have contributed to illuminating the problem of depression, constituting so many lights in a darkness that has not yet entirely lifted. Certain points of impact, certain nodes, strike me as apprehensible, others escape us still. But the pioneers of psychoanalysis—Freud, Abraham, Klein, and others—have bequeathed to us a methodology elucidating the pathological through the commonplace, the sublime through the desperate, the adult through the child. With the use of this methodology, by attempting to understand and deepen the hidden meaning of phenomena, I believe that a broadening of the study of depression can, in this domain as in others, prove fruitful.

# References

Abraham, K. (1911a), Giovanni Segantini: A psycho-analytical study. In: *Clinical Papers and Essays on Psychoanalysis*. New York: Basic Books, 1955, pp. 210–261.

———— (1911b), Notes on the psycho-analytical investigation and treatment of manic-depressive insanity and allied conditions. In: *Selected Papers of Karl Abraham, M.D.* London: Hogarth Press, 1949, pp. 137–156.

———— (1916), The first pregenital stage of the libido. In: *Selected Papers of Karl Abraham, M.D.* London: Hogarth Press, 1949, pp. 248–279.

———— (1924), A short study of the development of the libido, viewed in the light of mental disorders. In: *Selected Papers of Karl Abraham, M.D.* London: Hogarth Press, 1955, pp. 418–501.

Abraham, N. & Torok, M. (1972), Introjecter-incorporer: Deuil ou melancolie. *Nouv. Rev. Psychanal.*, 6:111–122.

———— (1975), L'objet perdu—moi. *Rev. fr. Psychanal.*, 39:409–426.

Alexander, F. (1960), *The Western Mind in Transition*. New York: Random House.

Anthony, S. (1940), *The Child's Discovery of Death*. London: Paul Kegan.

Anzieu, D. (1974), Vers une metapsychologie de la création. *In*: D. Anzieu, M. Mathieu, M. Besdine, E. Jaques, E., & J. Guillaumin, Psychanalyse du génie créateur, *Paris*: Dunod, pp. 1–30.

———— (1975), *L'auto-analyse de Freud*. Paris: Presses Universitaires de France.

240

Bak, R.C. (1939), Regression of ego-orientation and libido in schizophrenia. *Internat. J. Psycho-Anal.*, 20:64–71.

Balint, M. (1952), New beginning and the paranoid and depressive syndromes. In: *Primary Love and Psycho-Analytic Techniques.* London: Hogarth Press, 1952.

—— (1959), *Thrills and Regressions.* New York: International Universities Press.

—— (1961), *Psychotherapeutic Techniques in Medicine.* London: Tavistock.

—— (1965), *Primary Love and Psycho-Analytic Techniques.* London: Hogarth Press.

—— (1968), *The Basic Fault: Therapeutic Aspects of Regression.* London: Tavistock.

Barande, I. (1975), Bref historique à propos de la mélancolie. *Rev. fr. Psychanal.*, 39:403–407.

Beck, A.T. (1967), *Depression: Clinical, Experimental and Theoretical Aspects.* New York: Hoeber.

Benedek, T. (1956), Toward the biology of the depressive constellation. *J. Amer. Psychoanal. Assn.*, 4:389–427.

Beres, D. (1966), Superego and Depression. In: *Psychoanalysis: A General Psychology,* ed. R.M. Loewenstein et al. New York: International Universities Press, pp. 479–498.

Bergeret, J. (1975), *La dépression et les états limites.* Paris: Payot.

—— (1976), *Dépressivité et dépression dans le cadre de l'économie defensive.* Rapport au Congres des Psychanalystes de Langues romanes. Paris: Presses Universitaires de France.

Bibring, E. (1953), The mechanism of depression. In: *Affective Disorders,* ed. P. Greenacre. New York: International Universities Press, pp. 13–48.

Binitié, A. (1975), A factor-analytical study of depression across cultures (African and European). *Brit. J. Psychiat.*, 127:559–563.

Bion, W.R. (1965), *Transformations.* London: Heinemann.

—— (1967), Notes on memory and desire. *Psychoanal. Forum*, 2:271–280.

Blatt, S.J. (1974), Levels of object representation in anaclitic and introjective depression. *Psychoanal. Study Child*, 29:107–157. New Haven: Yale University Press.

Bolk, L. (1926), Le problème de la génèse humaine. Reprinted in: *Rev. fr. Psychanal.*, 25 (1961): 243–279.

Bowlby, J. (1946), *Forty-Four Juvenile Thieves, Their Characters and Home Life.* London: Bailliere, Tindall & Cox.

—— (1952), *Maternal Care and Mental Health.* Geneva World Health Organization.

—— (1960), Grief and Mourning in infancy and early childhood. *Psy-*

*choanal. Study Child*, 15:9–52. New York: International Universities Press.

—— (1961a), Process of mourning. *Internat. J. Psycho-Anal.*, 42:317–340.

—— (1961b), "Note on Dr. Max Schur's comments on grief and mourning in infancy and early childhood. *Psychoanal. Study Child*, 16:206–208. New York: International Universities Press.

—— (1963), Pathological mourning and childhood mourning. *J. Amer. Psychoanal. Assn.*, 11:500–541.

—— (1970), Self reliance and some conditions that promote it. In: *The Making and Breaking of Affectional Bonds*. London: Tavistock, 1979.

Braunschweig, D. & Fain, M. (1975), *La nuit, le jour: Essai psychanalytique sur le fonctionnement mental*. Paris: Presses Universitaires de France.

Brierley, M. (1942), "Internal Objects" and Theory. *Internat. J. Psycho-Anal.*, 22:107–112.

Brill, A.A. (1911), Ein Fall von periodischer Depression psychogenen Ursprungs. *Zentralblatt f. Psychoanal.*, 1:158–164.

Burton, I. & Derbyshire, A.J. (1958), "Sleeping fit" caused by excruciating pain in an infant. *A.M.A. J. Dis. Children*, 95:258–260.

Byck, R. & Freud, A. (1974), *The Cocaine Papers by S. Freud*. New York: Stonehill.

Chasseguet-Smirgel, J. (1973), Essai sur l'idéal du moi. *Rev. fr. Psychanal.*, 37:735–931.

Cohen, M.B., Baker, G., Cohen, R.A., Fromm-Reichmann, F., & Weigert, E.V. (1959), An intensive study of twelve cases of manic-depressive psychosis. *Psychiatry*, 17:103–138.

Darwin, C. (1872), *The Expression of the Emotions in Man and Animals*. New York: Greenwood Press, 1969.

David, C. (1971), *L'état amoureux: Essais psychanalytiques*. Paris: Payot.

Deutsch, H. (1929), The genesis of agoraphobia. *Internat. J. Psycho-Anal.*, 10:51–69.

—— (1932), *Psychoanalysis of the Neuroses*. Hogarth, London.

—— (1933), The psychology of manic-depressive states, with particular reference to chronic hypomania. In: *Neuroses and Character Types*. New York: International Universities Press, 1965.

—— (1937), Absence of Grief. *Psychoanal. Quart.*, 6:12–22.

—— (1951), Abstract of panel discussion on mania and hypomania. *Bull. Amer. Psychoanal. Assoc.*, 7:265–276.

—— (1965), *Neuroses and Character Types: Clinical Psycho-Analytic Studies*. New York: International Universities Press.

Donnet, J.L. & Green, A. (1973), *L'enfant de ça*. Paris: Minuit.

Eissler, K.R. (1955), An unusual function of an amnesia. *Psychoanal. Study Child*, 10:75–82. New York: International Universities Press.

—— (1971), *Talent and Genius*. New York: Quadrangle Books.

Ellenberger, H.F. (1970), *The Discovery of the Unconscious: The History and Evolution of Dynamic Psychiatry*. New York: Basic Books.

Engel, G.L. (1962), Anxiety and depression-withdrawal: The primary affects of unpleasure. *Internat. J. Psycho-Anal.*, 43:89–97.

Erikson, E.H. (1950), *Childhood and Society.* New York: Norton.

—— (1968), The life cycle: Epigenesis of identity. In: *Identity, Youth and Crisis.* New York: Norton.

Fairbairn, W.R.D. (1940), Schizoid factors in the personality. In: *Psychoanalytic Studies of the Personality.* London: Tavistock; Routledge & Kegan Paul, 1952, pp. 3–27.

Federn, P. (1952), *Ego-Psychology and the Psychoses.* New York: Basic Books.

Fenichel, O. (1926), Identification. In: *Collected Papers.* New York: Norton, 1953, pp. 97–113.

—— (1934), Zur Psychologie der Langeweile. Reprinted in: *Psychoanalyse und Gesellschaft.* Frankfurt: Druckstock, 1972, pp. 110–121.

—— (1945), Depression and mania. In: *The Psychoanalytic Theory of Neurosis.* New York: Norton, 1945, pp. 387–414.

Ferenczi, S. (1909), Introjection and transference. In: *Contributions to Psycho-Analysis.* Boston: Richard G. Badger, 1916.

—— (1913), Stages in the development of the sense of reality. In: *Contributions to Psycho-Analysis.* Boston: Richard C. Badger, pp. 181–203.

—— (1924), *Thalassa: A Theory of Genitality.* New York: Psychoanalytic Quarterly, 1938.

—— (1933), Confusion of tongues between adults and the child. In: *Final Contributions to the Problems and Methods of Psycho-Analysis.* London: Hogarth Press, 1955, pp. 156–157.

Field, M.J. (1958), Mental disorder in rural Ghana. *J. Ment. Science*, 104:1043—1051.

Fischer-Homberger, E. (1968), *Das zirkulare Irresein.* Zurich: Juris.

Fleming, J. (1972), Early object deprivation and transference phenomena. *Psychoanal. Quart.*, 41:23–49.

Flournoy, O. (1975), "Le moi ideal: vecteur de vide." *Nouv. Rev. Psychanal.*, 11:45–62.

Foucault, M. (1972), *Histoire de la Folie à l'Âge classique.* Paris: Gallimard.

Freud, A. (1958), Adolescence. *Psychoanal. Study Child*, 13:255–278.

—— (1960), Discussion of Dr. John Bowlby's Paper. *Psychoanal. Study Child*, 15:53–62.

—— (1965), *Normality and Pathology in Childhood.* London: Hogarth Press and the Institute of Psychoanalysis.

—— (1967), Eine Diskussion mit Rene Spitz. *Psyche*, 21:4–15.

Freud, S. (1895d) (with J. Breuer), Studies on hysteria. *Standard Edition*, 2:1–306. London: Hogarth Press, 1956.

—— (1896b), Further remarks on the neuro-psychoses of defence. *Standard Edition*, 3:157–186. London: Hogarth Press, 1962.

———— (1897a), Draft N (dated 31 May 1897). In: *The Origins of Psycho-Analysis*. New York: Basic Books, 1954, pp. 207–210.

———— (1897b), Letter 70 to W. Fliess, 3 October 1897. In: *The Origins of Psycho-Analysis*. New York: Basic Books, 1954, pp. 218–220.

———— (1899), Letter 102 to W. Fliess, 16 January 1899. In: *The Origins of Psycho-Analysis*. New York: Basic Books, 1954, pp. 272–274.

———— (1900a), The interpretation of dreams. *Standard Edition*, 4/5:1–622. London: Hogarth Press, 1953.

———— (1901b), The psychopathology of everyday life. *Standard Edition*, 6:1–290. London: Hogarth Press, 1960.

———— (1905a), On psychotherapy. *Standard Edition*, 7:257–258. London: Hogarth Press, 1953.

———— (1905b), Psychical (or mental) treatment. *Standard Edition*, 7:281–302. London: Hogarth Press, 1953.

———— (1905d), Three essays on the theory of sexuality. *Standard Edition*, 7:123–243. London: Hogarth Press, 1953.

———— (1905e), Fragment of an analysis of a case of hysteria. *Standard Edition*, 7:1–122. London: Hogarth Press, 1953.

———— (1907a), Delusion and dreams in Jensen's "Gradiva." *Standard Edition*, 9:1–93. London: Hogarth Press, 1959.

———— (1908e), Creative writers and day-dreaming. *Standard Edition*, 9:141–154. London: Hogarth Press, 1959.

———— (1910g), Contributions to a discussion on suicide. *Standard Edition*, 11:231–232. London: Hogarth Press, 1957.

———— (1911c), Psycho-analytic notes on an autobiographical account of a case of paranoia (dementia paranoides). *Standard Edition*, 12:1–84. London: Hogarth Press, 1958.

———— (1911f), Great is Diana of the Ephesians. *Standard Edition*, 12:342–344. London: Hogarth Press, 1958.

———— (1912–1913), Totem and taboo. *Standard Edition*, 13:1–161. London: Hogarth Press, 1955.

———— (1913f), The theme of the three caskets. *Standard Edition*, 12:289–302. London: Hogarth Press, 1958.

———— (1914c), On narcissism: An introduction. *Standard Edition*, 14:67–104. London: Hogarth Press, 1957.

———— (1915a), Letter to K. Abraham dated 4 May. In: *A Psycho-Analytic Dialogue: The Letters of Sigmund Freud and Karl Abraham, 1907–1926*, ed. H. Abraham & E. Freud. New York: Basic Books, 1965, pp. 220–222.

———— (1915b), Thoughts for the times on war and death. *Standard Edition*, 14:273–300. London: Hogarth Press, 1957.

———— (1915c), Instincts and their vicissitudes. *Standard Edition*, 14:109–140. London: Hogarth Press, 1957.

―――― (1916a), On transience. *Standard Edition,* 14:303–308. London: Hogarth Press, 1957.

―――― (1916d), Some character types met with in psycho-analytic work. *Standard Edition,* 14:309–336. London: Hogarth Press, 1957.

―――― (1917a), A difficulty in the path of psycho-analysis. *Standard Edition,* 17:135–144. London: Hogarth Press, 1955.

―――― (1917b), A childhood recollection from *Dictung und Wahrheit. Standard Edition,* 17:145–146. London: Hogarth Press, 1955.

―――― (1917e), Mourning and melancholia. *Standard Edition,* 14:237–258. London: Hogarth Press, 1957.

―――― (1918b), From the history of an infantile neurosis. *Standard Edition,* 17:1–122. London: Hogarth Press, 1955.

―――― (1919h), The "uncanny." *Standard Edition,* 17:217–252. London: Hogarth Press, 1955.

―――― (1920g), Beyond the pleasure principle. *Standard Edition,* 18:1–64. London: Hogarth Press, 1955.

―――― (1921c), Group psychology and the analysis of the ego. *Standard Edition,* 18:67–144. London: Hogarth Press, 1955.

―――― (1923b), The ego and the id. *Standard Edition,* 19:1–59. London: Hogarth Press, 1961.

―――― (1923d), A seventeenth century demonological neurosis. *Standard Edition,* 19:67–108. London: Hogarth Press, 1961.

―――― (1924e), The loss of reality in neurosis and psychosis. *Standard Edition,* 19:183–190. London: Hogarth Press, 1961.

―――― (1925h), Negation. *Standard Edition,* 19:235–240. London: Hogarth Press, 1961.

―――― (1926d), Inhibitions, symptoms and anxiety. *Standard Edition,* 20:75–176. London: Hogarth Press, 1959.

―――― (1927c), The future of an illusion. *Standard Edition,* 21:1–56. London: Hogarth Press, 1961.

―――― (1927d), Humour. *Standard Edition,* 21:159–166. London: Hogarth Press, 1961.

―――― (1927e), Fetishism. *Standard Edition,* 21:147–158. London: Hogarth Press, 1961.

―――― (1933a), New introductory lectures on psycho-analysis. *Standard Edition,* 22:1–182. London: Hogarth Press, 1964.

―――― (1936a), A disturbance of memory on the Acropolis. *Standard Edition,* 22:239–250. London: Hogarth Press, 1964.

―――― (1937c), Analysis terminable and interminable. *Standard Edition,* 23:209–254. London: Hogarth Press, 1964.

―――― (1939a), Moses and monotheism. *Standard Edition,* 23:1–138. London: Hogarth Press, 1964.

―――― (1940a), An outline of psycho-analysis. *Standard Edition,* 23:139–208. London: Hogarth Press, 1964.

——— (1941c), A premonitory dream fulfilled. *Standard Edition*, 5:623–625. London: Hogarth Press, 1953.

——— (1941f), Findings, ideas, problems. *Standard Edition*, 23:299–300. London: Hogarth Press, 1964.

——— (1950a), Draft G, undated (?7–1–1895): Melancholia. In: *The Origins of Psycho-Analysis*. New York: Basic Books, 1954, pp. 101–108.

Friedman, T., ed. (1967), *On Suicide: Discussions of the Vienna Psychoanalytic Society, 1910*. New York: International Universities Press.

Fries, M.E. & Woolf, P.J. (1953a), Some hypotheses on the role of the congenital activity type in personality development. *Psychoanal. Study Child*, 8:48–62.

——— (1953b), Some remarks on infant observation. *Psychoanal. Study Child*, 8:9–19.

Fromm, E. (1971), Instinctive versus characterological sources of human aggression. In: *Proceedings of the Fifth World Congress of Psychiatry in Mexico* (no. 26).

Furman, R.A. (1964a), Death and the young child: Some preliminary considerations. *Psychoanal. Study Child*, 19:321–333.

——— (1964b), Death of a six-year-old's mother during his analysis. *Psychoanal. Study Child*, 19:377–397.

Galenson, E. & Roiphe, H. (1972), The impact of early sexual discovery on mood, defensive organization and symbolisation. *Psychoanal. Study Child*, 26:195–216.

Garma, A. (1947), Psychoanalytic investigations in melancholias and other types of depressions. In: *Yearbook of Psychoanal.*, vol. 3. New York: International Universities Press, pp. 75–108.

Gerö, G. (1936), The construction of depression. *Internat. J. Psycho-Anal.*, 17:423–461.

——— (1939), Zum Problem der oralen Fixierung. *Internat. Zeitschr. f. Psychoanal. und Imago*, 24(3):240–257.

Gide, A. (1951), Journal 1889–1939. Paris: Gallimard.

Gitelson, M. (1958), On ego distortion. *Internat. J. Psycho-Anal.*, 39:245–257.

Glover, E. (1955), *The Technique of Psychoanalysis*. New York: International Universities Press.

Granoff, W. (1961), Ferenczi: faux problème ou vrai malentendu. *La Psychanalyse*, 6:255–282.

Green, A. (1967), Le narcissisme primaire: structure ou état. *L'Inconscient*, 1:127–156; 2:89–116.

——— (1970), L'affect. *Rev. fr. Psychanal.*, 34:885–1169.

——— (1973), *Le discours vivant*. Paris: Presses Universitaires de France.

——— (1974), L'analyste, la symbolisation et l'absence dans le cadre analytique. *Rev. fr. Psychanal.*, 38:1191–1230; *Nouv. Rev. Psychanal.*, 10:225–258.

Greenson, R. (1949), The psychology of apathy. *Psychoanal. Quart.*, 18:290–302.

―― (1953), On boredom. *J. Amer. Psychoanal. Assn.*, 1:7–21.

―― (1959), Phobia, trauma and the ego. Abstracted in Panel Report, Phobias and their Vicissitudes, rep. L. Ferber. *J. Amer. Psychoanal. Assn.*, 7:182–192.

Gregory, I. (1966), Retrospective data concerning loss of a parent: I. Actuarial estimates vs recorded frequencies of orphanhood. *Arch. Gen. Psychiat.*, 15: 354–361; II: Category of parental loss by decade of birth, diagnosis and MMPI, *Arch. Gen. Psychiat.*, 15: 362–367.

Gressot, M. (1973), L'Idéal du moi entre une illusion créatrice et une illusion aliénante. *Rev. fr. Psychanal.*, 37:973–978.

Grunberger, B. (1965), A study of depression. In: *Narcissism.* New York: International Universities Press, 1979, pp. 219–240.

―― (1966), Suicide of melancholics. In: *Narcissism.* New York: International Universities Press, 1979, pp. 241–264.

―― (1971), *Narcissism.* New York: International Universities Press, 1979.

Guex, G. (1950), *La névrose d'abandon.* Paris: Presses Universitaires de France.

Guntrip, H. (1969), *Schizoid Phenomena, Object Relations and the Self.* New York: International Universities Press.

Harnik, J. (1932), Introjection and projection in the mechanism of depression. *Internat. J. Psycho-Anal.*, 13:425–431.

Hartmann, H. (1939), Psychoanalysis and the concept of health. In: *Essays on Ego Psychology: Selected Problems in Psychoanalytic Theory.* New York: International Universities Press, 1964.

Haynal, A. (1968), Le syndrome de couvade. *Ann. medico-psychol.*, 126(1):539–571.

―― (1971), Transsexualisme et identité sexuelle. *Med. et hygiene*, 29:2040–2042.

―― (1975), The role of the father in reproduction as a transcultural problem. In: *Proceedings of the Symposium on Neurological Sciences in Developing Countries.* Kuala Lumpur, Malaysia.

Hermann, I. (1943), *L'instinct filial.* Paris: Denoel, 1972.

Jacobson, E. (1946), The effect of disappointment on ego and superego formation in normal and depressive development. *Psychoanal. Rev.*, 33:129–147.

―― (1953), Contribution to the metapsychology of cyclothymic depression. In: *Affective Disorders*, ed. P. Greenacre. New York: International Universities Press.

―― (1954), The self and the object world: Vicissitudes of their infantile cathexes and their influences on ideational and affective development. *Psychoanal. Study Child*, 9:75–127. New York: International Universities Press.

———— (1961), Adolescent moods and the remodeling of psychic structures in adolescence. *Psychoanal. Study Child*, 16:164–183. New York: International Universities Press.

———— (1964), *The Self and the Object World*. New York: International Universities Press.

———— (1971), *Depression: Comparative Studies of Normal, Neurotic and Psychotic Conditions*. New York: International Universities Press.

Joffe, W. & Sandler, J. (1965), Notes on pain, depression and individuation. *Psychoanal. Study Child*, 20:394–424.

Jones, E. (1926), The origin and structure of the super-ego. In: *Papers on Psycho-Analysis*. 4th ed. London: Bailliere, Tindall & Cox, 1938.

———— (1927), The early development of female sexuality. *Internat. J. Psycho-Anal.*, 8:459–472.

———— (1953), *The Life and Work of Sigmund Freud*, Vol. 1. New York: Basic Books.

———— (1955), *The Life and Work of Sigmund Freud*, Vol. II. New York: Basic Books.

Kanzer, M. (1952), Manic-depressive psychoses with paranoid trends. *Internat. J. Psycho-Anal.*, 33:34–42.

———— (1953), Writers and the early loss of parents. *J. Hillside Hosp.*, 2:148–151.

Katan, A. (1972), The infant's first reaction to strangers: Distress or anxiety? *Internat. J. Psycho-Anal.*, 53:501–503.

Kernberg, O. (1975), *Borderline Conditions and Pathological Narcissism*. New York: Aronson.

Khan, M.M.R. (1963), The concept of cumulative trauma. *Psychoanal. Study Child*, 18:286–306.

———— (1964), Ego distortion, cumulative trauma and the role of reconstruction in the analytic situation. *Internat. J. Psycho-Anal.*, 45:272–279.

———— (1974), Ego-ideal, excitement and the threat of annihilation. In: *The Privacy of the Self*. New York: International Universities Press, pp. 181–202.

Kierkegaard, S. (1849), *The Concept of Dread*, London: Oxford University Press, 1944.

———— (1935), *Le Concept d'l'Anjoissi*. Paris: Gallimard.

Kiev, A. (1972), *Transcultural Psychiatry*. New York: Free Press.

Klauber, J. (1966), An attempt to differentiate a typical form of transference in neurotic depression. *Internat. J. Psycho-Anal.*, 47:539–545.

———— (1967), "Drei typische Stadien der Uebertragung in der Analyse neurotischer Depressionen," in: *Jahrbuch der Psycho-analyse*, ed. G. Scheunert. Huber, Band 4, Berne, pp. 202–216.

———— (1975), Ueber einige Schwierigkeiten, Psychoanalytiker zu sein.

*Psyche*, 29:835–839.

Klein, M. (1934), A contribution to the psychogenesis of manic-depressive states. In: *Contributions to Psycho-Analysis 1921–1945.*London: Hogarth Press, 1948, pp. 282–310.

—— (1940), Mourning and its relation to manic-depressive states. In: *Contributions to Psycho-Analysis 1921–1945*. London: Hogarth Press, 1948, pp. 311–338.

—— (1957), *Envy and Gratitude*. New York: Delacorte Press/Seymour Lawrence, 1975.

Kohut, H. (1971), *The Analysis of the Self*. New York: International Universities Press.

Kris, E. (1938), Ego development and the comic. *Internat. J. Psycho-Anal.*, 19: 77–90.

—— (1955), Neutralization and Sublimation: Observations on Young Children. *Psychoanal. Study Child*, 10:30–46. New York: International Universities Press.

Lacan, J. (1949), The mirror stage as formative of the function of the Id. In: *Écrits: A Selection*, transl. A. Sheridan. New York: Norton, 1977.

—— (1966), *Écrits:* transl. Alan Sheridan. New York: Norton, 1977.

Lagache, D. (1956), Deuil pathologique. *La psychanalyse*, 2: 45–74.

Lambo, T.A. (1956), Neuropsychiatric observations in the western region of Nigeria." *Brit. Med. J.*, 11:1388–1394.

Lampl–de Groot, J. (1960), On Adolescence. *Psychoanal. Study Child*, 15: 95–103. New York: International Universities Press.

Laplanche, J. (1970), *Life and Death in Psycho-Analysis*, transl. J. Mehlman. Baltimore: Johns Hopkins University Press, 1976.

—— Pontalis, J.B. (1967), *The Language of Psycho-Analysis*, transl. D. Nicholson-Smith. London: Hogarth Press, 1973.

Lebovici, S. (1955), Contribution psychanalytique à la compréhension et au traitement de la mélancolie. *Evol. psychiat.*, 20:502–529.

Leighton, A.H. et al. (1963), *Psychiatric Disorders Among the Yoruba*. Ithaca: Cornell University Press.

Levi, L.D. et al. (1966), Separation and attempted suicide. *Arch. Gen. Psychiat.*, 15:158–164.

Levi-Strauss, C. (1949), *Elementary Structures of Kinship*, transl. J.H. Bell, J.R. von Sturmer, & R. Needham. Boston: Beacon Press, 1969.

—— (1955), *Tristes Tropiques*, transl. J. & D. Weightman. New York: Atheneum, 1978.

Levy-Bruhl, L. (1910), *Les fonctions mentales dans les sociétés inférieures*. Paris: F. Alcan.

Lewin, B.D. (1932), Analysis and structure of a transient hypomania. *Psychoanal. Quart.*, 1:43–58.

—— (1937), A type of neurotic hypomanic reaction. *Arch. Neurol. Psychiat.*, 37:868–873.

—— (1950), *The Psychoanalysis of Elation.* New York: Norton.

—— (1961), Reflections on depression. *Psychoanal. Study Child*, 16:321–331. New York: International Universities Press.

Lewis, W.C. (1974), Hysteria: The consultant dilemma. *Arch. Gen. Psychiat.*, 30:145–151.

Lidz, T. (1968), *The Person: His Development Throughout the Life Cycle.* New York: Basic Books.

Lin, T.-Y. (1953), A study of the incidence of mental disorder in Chinese and other cultures. *Psychiatry*, 16:313–336.

Lincke, H. (1971), Der Ursprung des Ichs. *Psyche*, 25:1–30.

Lindemann, E. (1944), Symptomatology and management of acute grief. *Amer. J. Psychiat.*, 101:141–148.

Luquet, P. (1962), Les identifications précoses dans la structuration et la restructuration du moi. *Rev. fr. Psychanal.*, 26:117–301.

—— (1973), Les idéaux du moi et l'idéal du je, *Rev. fr. Psychanal.*, 37:1007—1013.

McConville, B.J. & Boag, L.C. & Purohit, A.P. (1972), Mourning depressive responses of children in residence following sudden death of parent figures. *J. Amer. Acad. Child Psychiat.*, 11:341–364.

McDougall, J. (1972), L'anti-analysant en analyse. *Rev. fr. Psychanal.*, 36:167–184.

Maeder, A. (1911), Psychoanalyse bei einer melancholischen Depression. *Jahrbuch fur psychoanalytische und psychopathologische Forschungen, III/I*, pp. 479–480.

Mahler, M.S. (1961), On sadness and grief in infancy and childhood: Loss and restoration of the symbiotic love object. *Psychoanal. Study Child*, 16:332–351. New York: International Universities Press.

—— (1966), Notes on the development of basic moods: The depressive affect. In: *Psychoanalysis: A General Psychology*, ed. R.M. Loewenstein et al. New York: International Universities Press, pp. 152–168.

—— (1967), Problems of over-idealization of the analyst and analysis (discussion of Phyllis Greenacre's paper). Abstr. in *Psychoanal. Quart.*, 36:637.

—— (1968), *On Human Symbiosis and the Vicissitudes of Individuation*, Vol. I. New York: International Universities Press.

—— (1972), On the first three subphases of the separation-individuation process. *Internat. J. Psycho-Anal.*, 53:333–338.

—— Pine, F. & Bergman, A. (1975), *The Psychological Birth of the Human Infant.* New York: Basic Books.

Mallet, J. (1955), La dépression névrotique. *Evol. psychiat.*, 20:483–501.

Marmor, J. (1974), *Psychiatry in Transition.* New York: Brunner/Mazel.

Marris, P. (1974), *Loss and Change.* London: Routledge & Kegan Paul.

Marty, P. (1968), La dépression essentielle. *Rev. fr. Psychanal.*, 32:595–598.

—— Fain, M. (1955), Importance du role de la motricité dans la relation d'objet. *Rev. fr. Psychanal.*, 19:205–284.

Mead, M. (1956), The implications of culture change for personality development. In: *Anthropology: Collected Works*, ed. D. Haring. 3rd ed. Syracuse: Syracuse University Press.

Meissner, W.W. (1972), Notes on identification: III. The concept of identification. *Psychoanal. Quart.*, 41:224–260.

Melges, F.T. & Bowlby, J. (1969), Types of hopelessness in psychopathological process. *Arch. Gen. Psychiat.*, 20: 690–699.

Meltzer, D. (1967), *The Psycho-Analytical Process.* London: Heinemann Medical Books.

Mendels, J. (1970), *Concepts of Depression.* New York: Wiley.

Mendelson, M. (1974), *Psychoanalytic Concepts of Depression.* 2nd ed. New York: Spectrum.

Michaux, H. (1972), *Emergences-résurgences.* Genève: A. Skira.

Modell, A.H. (1963), Primitive object relationships and the predisposition to schizophrenia. *Internat. J. Psycho-Anal.*, 44:282–292.

Moellenhoff, F. (1939), Ideas of children about death: A preliminary study. *Bull. Menn. Clin.*, 3:148–156.

Moore, B.E. & Fine, B.D. (1968), *A Glossary of Psychoanalytic Terms and Concepts.* New York: American Psychoanalytic Association.

Muensterberger, W. (1962), The creative process. In: *The Psychoanalytic Study of Society*, Vol. 3. New York: International Universities Press, pp. 161–185.

Murphy, H. et al. (1967), Cross-cultural inquiry into the symptomatology of depression: A preliminary report and critical evaluations. *Internat. J. Psychiat.*, 3:1–22.

Nacht, S. & Racamier, P.C. (1959), Les états dépressifs. In: *La présence du psychanalyste*, ed. S. Nacht. Paris: Presses Universitaires de France, 1963, pp. 96–137.

Nagera, H. (1970), Children's reactions to the death of important objects. *Psychoanal. Study Child*, 25:360–400.

Nagy, M. (1948), The child's view of death. *J. Gen. Psychol.*, 73:3–27.

Nunberg, H. & Federn, E. (1967), *Minutes of the Vienna Psychoanalytic Society*, Vol. II. New York: International Universities Press.

Pasche, F. (1963), De la dépression. *Rev. fr. Psychanal.*, 27:191–222; reprinted in À partir de Freud. Paris: Payot, 1969, pp. 181–199.

—— (1969), *À partir de Freud.* Paris: Payot.

Peto, A. (1972), Body image and depression. *Internat. J. Psycho-Anal.*, 53:259–263.

Piaget, J. (1936), *The Origins of Intelligence in Children.* New York: International Universities Press, 1952.

Pollock, G.H. (1961), Mourning and adaptation. *Internat. J. Psycho-Anal.*, 42: 341–361.

——— (1975), On mourning, immortality and utopia. *J. Amer. Psychoanal. Assn.*, 23:334–362.

Rado, S. (1927), The problem of melancholia. *Internat. J. Psycho-Anal.*, 9:420–438.

——— (1933), The psychoanalysis of pharmacothymia (drug addictions). *Psychoanal. Quart.*, 2:1–23.

Raimbault, G. (1975), *L'enfant et la mort.* Toulouse: Privat.

Rank, B. (1949), Aggression. *Psychoanal. Study Child*, 3/4:43–48.

Rapaport, D. (1951), *Organization and Pathology of Thought.* New York: Columbia University Press.

——— (1959), On the psychoanalytic theory of motivation. In: *Collected Papers.* New York: Basic Books, 1967, pp. 853–915.

——— (1967), Edward Bibring's theory of depression (1959). In: *Collected Papers.* New York: Basic Books, 1967, pp. 758–773.

Reich, A. (1953), Narcissistic object choice in women. *J. Amer. Psychoanal. Assn.*, 1:22–44.

——— (1954), Early identifications as archaic elements in the superego. *J. Amer. Psychoanal. Assn.*, 2:218–238.

Reik, T. (1929), Zur Psychoanalyse des judischen Witzes. *Imago*, 15:63–88.

Rentchnick, P. (1975), Les orphelins menent le monde: Une nouvelle théorie sur la génèse de la volonté de puissance politique. *Méd. et hygiène*, 33:1754–1764.

Ribble, M.A. (1943), *The Rights of Infants: Early Psychological Needs and Their Satisfactions.* New York: Columbia University Press.

Rie, H.E. (1966), Depression in childhood: A survey of some pertinent contributions. *J. Amer. Acad. Child Psychiat.*, 5:653–685.

Roch, M. (1967), Du Surmoi "heritier du complexe d'Oedipe." *Rev. fr. Psychanal.*, 31:913–1060.

Rochlin, G. (1953), The disorder of depression and elation. *J. Amer. Psychoanal. Assn.*, 1:438–457.

——— (1959), The loss complex. *J. Amer. Psychoanal. Assn.*, 7:299–316.

——— (1965), *Grief and Discontents: The Forces of Change.* Boston: Little, Brown.

——— (1967), How young children view death and themselves. In: *Explaining Death to Children*, ed. E. A. Grossman. Boston: Beacon Press, pp. 51–88.

Róheim, G. (1943), *The Origin and Function of Culture.* Nervous and Mental Disease Monographs, no. 69.

——— (1950), *Psychoanalysis and Anthropology.* New York: International Universities Press.

Ronsard, P. de (1938), *Oeuvres complètes*, V. 2. Paris: Bibliotèque de la Pléjade, p. 921.

Rosenfeld, H. (1959), An investigation into the psycho-analytic theory of depression, *Internat. J. Psycho-Anal.*, 40:105–129.

Rosolato, G. (1975), L'axe narcissique des dépressions. *Nouv. Rev. Psychanal.*, 11:5–34.

Rubinfine, D.L. (1968), Notes on a theory of depression. *Psychoanal. Quart.*, 37:400–417.

Rycroft, C. (1968), *Anxiety and Neurosis*. Baltimore: Penguin Books.

Sandler, J. (1960), On the concept of the superego. *Psychoanal. Study Child*, 15:128–162.

———— et al. (1963), The ego ideal and the ideal self. *Psychoanal. Study Child*, 18:139–158.

———— & Joffe, W.G. (1965), Notes on childhood depression. *Internat. J. Psychoanal.*, 46:88–96.

———— (1972), Round Table Conference, Meeting of the European Psycho-Analytical Federation, London.

Sartre, J.-P. (1964), *The Words*, transl. I. Clephane. Harmondsworth: Penguin Books.

Sauguet, H. (1969), Le processus analytique (notes pour une introduction). *Rev. fr. Psychanal.*, 33:913–927.

Saussure, J. de (1971), Some complications in self-esteem regulation caused by using an archaic image of the self as an ideal. *Internat. J. Psycho-Anal.*, 52:87–97.

———— (1972), Round Table Conference, Meeting of the European Psycho-Analytical Federation, London.

Saussure, R. de (1934), Les sentiments d'inferiorité. *Rev. fr. Psychanal.*, 7:655–664.

Schilder, T. & Wechsler, G. (1935), The attitude of children toward death. *J. Genet. Psychol.*, 45:406–420.

Schmale, A.H. (1972a), Depression as affect, character style and symptom formation. In: *Psychoanalysis and Contemporary Science*, ed. R.R. Holt & E. Peterfreund. New York: Macmillan, pp. 327–351.

———— (1972b), Giving up as a final common pathway to changes in health. In: Psychosomatical Aspects of Physical Illness, ed. Z.J. Lipowski. *Abs. Psychosom. Med.*, 8:20–40.

———— & Engel, G.L. (1967), The giving-up complex. *Arch. Gen. Psychiat.*, 17:135–145.

Schneirla, T.C. (1959), An evolutionary and developmental theory of biphasic processes underlying approach and withdrawal. In: *Nebraska Symposium on Motivation*, ed. M.R. Jones. Lincoln: University of Nebraska Press.

———— (1965), Aspects of stimulation and organisation in approach-withdrawal processes underlying vertebrate development. In: *Advances in the Study of Behaviour*, Vol. I, ed. D.S. Lehrman et al. New York: Academic Press.

Schur, M. (1966), *The Id and the Regulatory Principles of Mental Functioning.* New York: International Universities Press.

───── (1972), *Freud Living and Dying.* New York: International Universities Press.

Segal, H. (1958), Fear of death. *Internat. J. Psycho-Anal.,* 39:178–181.

Smirnoff, V. (1966), *La psychanalyse de l'enfant.* Paris: Presses Universitaires de France.

Smith, J.H. (1971), Identificatory styles in depression and grief. *Internat. J. Psycho-Anal.,* 52/53:259–266.

Spira, M. (1968), A proposito dei meccanismi di evoluzione e di regressione in relazione con la memoria. *Riv. Psico-anal.,* 4:221–233.

Spitteler, C. (1906), *Imago.* Jena: E. Diederichs.

Spitz, R. & Wolf, K.M. (1946), Anaclitic depression: An inquiry into the genesis of psychiatric conditions in early childhood. *Psychoanal. Study Child,* 2:313–342.

───── Cobliner, W. (1965), *The First Year of Life.* New York: International Universities Press.

Starobinski, J. (1960), *Histoire du traitement de la mélancolie des origines à 1900.* Basle: Geigy.

───── (1966), Le concept de nostalgie. *Diogene,* 54:92–115.

Stein, M. (1953), Premonition as defence. *Psychoanal. Quart.,* 2:69–74.

Stengel, E. (1948), Some clinical observations on the psychodynamic relationship between depression and obsessive-compulsive symptoms. *J. Ment. Sci.,* 94:650–652.

Sterba, R. (1948), On Hallowe'en. *Amer. Imago,* 5/3:213–224.

Stern, M. (1972), Trauma, Todesangst und Furcht von dem Tod. *Psyche,* 26:901–928.

Stierlin, H. (1970), The functions of "inner objects." *Internat. J. Psycho-Anal.,* 51:321–329.

Stone, L. (1961), *The Psychoanalytic Situation: An Examination of Its Development and Essential Nature.* New York: International Universities Press.

Strachey, J. ed. (1955), *The Standard Edition of the Complete Psychological Works of Sigmund Freud,* Vol. 18. London: Hogarth Press.

───── ed. (1957), *The Standard Edition of the Complete Psychological Works of Sigmund Freud,* Vol. 14. London: Hogarth Press.

───── ed. (1966), *The Standard Edition of the Complete Psychological Works of Sigmund Freud,* Vol. I. London: Hogarth Press.

Szondi, L. (1956), *Ich-Analyse.* Berne: Huber.

Tausk, V. (1919), On the origin of the "influencing machine" in schizophrenia. *The Psycho-Analytic Reader,* ed. R. Fliess. New York: International Universities Press, 1948, pp. 31–64.

Teja, J.G., Narang, R.L. & Aggarwal, A.K. (1971), Depression across cultures. *Brit. J. Psychiat.,* 119:253–260.

Toffler, A. (1973), The future of law and order. *Encounter*, 41(1):13–23.

Torok, M. (1968), Maladie de deuil et fantasme du cadavre exquis. *Rev. fr. Psychanal.*, 32:715–733.

Van der Waals, H.G. (1949), Le narcissisme. *Rev. fr. Psychanal.*, 13:501–526.

Venkoba, R.A. (1966), Depression: A psychiatric analysis of thirty cases. *Indian J. Psychiat.*, 8:143–154.

Virgil, *Aeneid*, In: Publii Virgilii Maronis Opera. Paris: Hachette, 1873.

Wagner, R. (1971), *Siegfried*. Paris: Aubier-Flammarion.

Wahl, C.W. (1958), The fear of death. *Bull. Menn. Clin.*, 22:214–223.

Weiss, E. (1926), Der Vergiftungswahn im Lichte der Introjektions- und Projektionsvorgange. *Internat. Zeitschr. f. Psychoanal.*, 12:466–470.

———— (1932), Regression and projection in the superego. *Internat. J. Psycho-Anal.*, 13:449–478.

———— (1944), Clinical aspects of depression. *Psychoanal. Quart.*, 13:445–461.

Winnicott, D.W. (1954), The depressive position in normal emotional development. *Brit. J. Med. Psychol.*, 28:89–100.

———— (1957a), *Mother and Child: A Primer of First Relationships*. New York: Basic Books.

———— (1957b), *The Child and the Outside World*. London: Tavistock.

———— (1958), The capacity to be alone. *Internat. J. Psycho-Anal.*, 39:416–420.

———— (1960), The theory of the parent-infant relationship. *Internat. J. Psycho-Anal.*, 4:585–595.

———— (1963a), The mentally ill in your caseload. In: *Maturational Processes and the Facilitating Environment*. New York: International Universities Press, 1965, pp. 217–229.

———— (1963b), Psychiatric disorder in terms of infantile maturational processes. In: *Maturational Processes and the Facilitating Environment*. New York: International Universities Press, 1965, pp. 230–241.

———— (1971), *Playing and Reality*. London: Tavistock Publications.

———— (1958), *Collected Papers: Through Paediatrics to Psycho-Analysis*. London: Tavistock.

Wisdom, J.O. (1962), Comparison and development of the psychoanalytic theory of depression. *Internat. J. Psycho-Anal.*, 43:113–132.

Wittgenstein, L. (1975), *Philosophical Remarks*. Chicago: University of Chicago Press.

Wolfenstein, M. (1973), The image of the lost parent. *Psychoanal. Study Child*, 28:433–456.

Wyrsch, J. (1965), Preface to J. Oeschger, *Melancolie*. Basle: Geigy.

Yap, P.M. (1958), *Suicide in Hong-Kong*. London: Oxford University Press.

———— (1965), Phenomenology of affective disorder in Chinese and other cultures. In: *Transcultural Psychiatry*, ed. A.V.S. de Reuck & R. Porter. Boston: Little, Brown.

Zetzel, E. (1953), The depressive position. In: *Affective Disorders*, ed. P. Greenacre. New York: International Universities Press, pp. 84–116.

———— (1970), *The Capacity for Emotional Growth*. New York: International Universities Press.

# Name Index

Abraham, K. xi, xii, xiv, xvi, 3, 14, 15, 16, 22, 28, 34, 46, 49, 62, 88, 93, 105, 106, 108, 115, 124, 164, 165, 166, 171, 173, 174, 181-188, 199, 201, 202, 204, 239
Abraham, N., xxvii, 71, 95, 99, 238
Adler, A., 170
Aggarwal, A. K., 118
d'Alembert, J. R., 145
Alexander, F., 58, 136
Anthony, S., 43, 44
Anzieu, D., xi, 7, 146, 165, 166
Aristotle, 1, 3, 70, 145
Aretea of Cappadocia, 2
Augustine, 1, 142
Aurelius, M., 145

Bacon, F., 145
Bak, R. C., xiii, 88, 202
Balint, Alice, 39, 88
Balint, M., xiii, 32, 39, 55, 88, 94, 138, 197, 198
Barande, I., 34
Baudelaire, C., 2, 145
Beck, A. T., 132
Benedek, T., xiii, 16, 77, 197, 209-211, 216
Beres, D., 116
Bergeret, J., 34, 238-239
Bergman, A., xiii
Bibring, E., 14, 27, 38, 49, 87, 88, 207-209, 212

Binitié, A., 100
Binswanger, L., xiii, 86
Bion, W. R., xxii, 117
Blatt, S. J., 33
Boag, A. C., 42
Bolk, L., 147
Bowlby, J., 16, 22, 29, 40, 41, 42, 43, 47, 65, 73, 74, 88, 122, 211
Braunschweig, E., 238
Brazelton, T. Berry, viii
Brierley, M., 99
Brill, Z. Z., 181
Brontë, C., 145
Brontë, E., xiv, 145
Buber, M., 147
Buddha, 146
Burton, I., 28
Byck, R., 165
Byron, G., 145

Calderon, P., 64
Camus, A., 145
Chasseguet-Smirgel, J., 21, 138
Cohen, M. B., 184
Coleridge, S. T., 145

Dante, A., 145
Darwin, C., 56
David, C., 72
Derbyshire, A. J., 28
Descartes, R., xiv, 145
Deutsch, H., 26, 44, 66, 126, 201-202

Dickens, C., 145
Diderot, D., 145
Dostoevsky. F. M., 145
Donnet, J. L., 158
Drinkwater, J., 146
Dumas, A., 145
Dürer, A., 3

Eissler, K. R., 66-67, 68
Ellenberger, J. F., 90
Engel, G. L., xxx, 54, 72, 77
Erasmus, 145
Erikson, E. H., 16, 40, 90, 147

Fain, M., 238
Fairbairn, W. R. D., 122
Federn, E., 171
Federn, P., 8, 31
Fenichel, O., 22, 26, 34, 86, 87, 88,
    90, 102, 112, 133-134, 203-207
Ferenczi, S., xiii, xvii, 55, 97, 102,
    106, 110, 148
Field, M. J., 119, 150
Fine, B. D., 99
Fischer-Homberger, E., 2
Fliess, W., xii, xix, 19, 70, 81, 90,
    164, 169, 171
Fleming, J., 94
Flournoy, O., 23
Foucault, M., xviii
Fraiberg, S., viii, x
Freud, A., 26, 41, 45, 54, 156
Freud, E., 166
Freud, J., vii, 166
Freud, S., vii, ix, xi-xiii, xv, xvi,
    xviii, xix-xx, xxiii, xxiv, 3, 4-5,
    7, 8, 15, 16, 18-22, 24, 27, 28,
    30, 33, 42, 49, 53-61, 66-72, 79,
    81-83, 85-90, 92, 93, 98-103,
    106, 107, 109, 110, 112, 114,
    121-123, 125, 126, 131-132, 138,
    143, 144, 146, 148, 150, 152,
    156, 157, 159, 163-179, 182,
    184-186, 188, 192, 199, 200,
    201, 212, 218, 219, 239
Friedman, T., 171
Fries, M. E., 28
Fromm, E., 131, 147
Furman, R. A., 41

Galenson, E., 154
Gandhi, 145
Garma, A., 181
Geor, G., xiii, 111, 202-203
Gibbon, E., 145
Gide, A., xix, 132
Ginsberg, A., 90
Gitelson, M., 27
Glover, E., 23
Goethe, J.-W., 2, 81
Green, A., 31, 33, 158
Greenson, R., 26, 30, 135
Gregory, I., 145
Gressot, M., 138
Grünberger, B., xxix, 6, 22, 36, 47,
    77, 117, 120, 148, 152, 157,
    235-238
Guex, G., 46, 70, 125, 224
Guntrip, H., 116

Harnik, J., xiii, 106, 201
Hartmann, H., 39, 117
Haynal, A., vii, viii, ix, xi-xxxii,
    100
Heraclitus, xvi, xxv, 65
Hermann, I., xiii, 28, 39, 60, 61,
    88, 141, 202
Hofer, J., 136
Hugo, V., 145

Jacobson, E., 8, 15, 17, 18, 30, 46,
    47, 74, 89, 95, 110, 112, 113,
    116, 117, 125, 139, 184, 214-
    220
Jensen, W., 82
Joffe, W., xxv, 24, 39, 44, 211-213,
    222

Jones, E., xi, 17, 81, 164, 171, 172
John of the Cross, Saint, 2
Joyce, J., 146
Jung, C. G., 166

Kafka, F., 146
Kant, Immanual, 136
Kanzer, M., xiv, 121, 145
Katan, A., 26, 49
Keats, J., 145
Kernberg, O., 6, 23
Kestenberg, E., vii, x
Khan, M. M. R., 121, 156
Kierkegaard, S., xviii, 4, 52, 145, 146
Kiev, A., 119, 123
Klauber, J., 34, 76, 96, 106-107, 223-224
Klein, M., xiv, 4, 6, 15, 17, 18, 20, 46, 47, 58, 77, 89, 141, 142, 158, 187, 188-198, 210, 214, 227, 239
Kohut, H., xxvii, xxviii-xxix, 6, 17, 21, 22-23, 35, 47, 101, 107, 110, 135
Kris, E., 126

Lacan, J., xiv, 54
Lagache, D., 23, 68, 69
Lambo, T. A., 150
Lampl-de Groot, J., 45
Laplanche, J., xv, 49, 59, 70, 97, 99, 110
Lebovici, S., vii-x, 224-225
Leighton, A. H., 119
Leonardo da Vinci, 146
Levi, L. D., 75
Levi-Strauss, C., 62, 143
Levy-Bruhl, L., 110
Lewin, B. D., 90, 110, 118, 126, 211
Lewis, W. C., 138
Lidz, T., 49
Lin, T.-Y., 118
Lincke, H., 98, 123

Lindemann, E., 87
Luquet, P., 21-22, 49, 100, 117, 133

McConville, B. J., 42
McDougall, J., 65-66
Maeder, A., 181
Mahler, M. S., xiii, xiv, xvi, xxvii, 6, 16, 20, 34, 40, 43, 47, 60, 109, 156, 220-223
Mallet, J., 225-227
Mann, T., xviii
Marcel, G., 145
Marmor, J., 71
Marris, P., 149
Marty, P., vii, x, xxx, 239
Maupassant, G. de, 145
Mead, M., 149
Meissner, W. W., 105
Melges, F. T., 47
Meltzer, D., 90
Mendels, J., 181
Michaux, H., xxiv
Michelangelo, 3, 146
Modell, A. H., 26
Moellenhof, F., 122
Moliére, J.-B., 145
Montaigne, 163
Montale, E., 97, 114
Moore, B. E., 99
Muensterberger, W., 144
Murphy, W., 119
Musset, A. de, 140

Nacht, S., 16, 227-231
Nagera, H., 44, 47
Nagy, M., 42, 44
Narang, R. L., 118
Nerval, G. de, 1
Nestroy, J., 1
Nietzsche, F., 58, 155
Nunberg, H., 171

Paracelsus, P. A., 145
Pascal, Blaise, 145, 146

Pasche, F., 8, 231-235
Péguy, Ch., 145
Petö, A., 109
Piaget, J., 39, 98
Picasso, P., 144
Pine, F., xiii
Plato, 1, 65, 80, 145
Poe, E. A., xiv, 145
Pollock, G. H., 87, 146
Pontalis, J. B., xv, 49, 59, 97, 99, 110
Pope, A., 2
Proust, M., 96, 146, 148
Puccini, G., 146
Purohit, A. P., 42

Racamier, P. C., 15, 227-231
Racine, J., 145
Rado, S., xiii, xxix, 15, 16, 22, 24-25, 74, 90, 111, 112, 115, 150, 199-201, 202, 218, 219
Raimbault, G., 43
Rank, B., 16
Rapaport, D., 100, 111, 158
Reich, A., 216
Reik, T., 126
Renan, E., 145
Renard, J., 145
Rentchnick, P., 145
Ribble, M. A., 28
Rie, H. E., 43-44, 45
Rochlin, G., 42, 43, 47, 65, 116, 216
Róheim, G., 141, 142, 143, 147, 188
Roiphe, H., 154
Ronsard, P. de, 2, 3
Rosenfeld, H., 103, 181, 196
Rosolato, G., 116
Roth, P., 94
Rosseau, J. J., xiv, 145
Rubinfine, D. L., 224
Rubens, P. P., 146
Russell, B., 145, 151
Rycroft, C., 30, 99

Sand, G., 145
Sandler, J., xxv, 24, 39, 44, 77, 105, 211-213, 222
Santayana, G., 148
Sartre, J.-P., 2, 44, 145, 153
Sauguet, H., 91
Saussure, J. de, 21, 72
Saussure, R. de, 23
Schilder, T., 44
Schmale, A. H., 49, 54
Schneirla, T. C., 88-89
Schopenhauer, A., 145
Schur, M., xi, xxiii, 70, 79, 86, 89, 164, 165
Segal, H., 81
Segantini, G., 115, 181, 182
Seneca, L. A., 13, 160
Sévigné, M. de, 145
Shakespeare, W., xxix, 3, 79, 80, 131-132, 149
Smirnoff, V., 254
Smith, J. H., 104
Socrates, 1, 80
Spira, M., xvii
Spitteler, C., xxvi
Spitz, R., 15, 32-33, 45, 88, 119, 227
Stael, Mme. de, 140
Starobinski, J., 2, 136
Stein, M., 68
Stekel, W., 170
Stendhal, H. B., 145
Stengel, E., 184
Sterba, R., 122
Stern, M. D., viii, x
Stern, N., 84
Stierlin, H., 102
Stone, L., 90
Strachey, H., 15, 58, 168
Swift, J., 145
Szondi, L., 110

Tausk, V., 8, 34
Teja, J. G., 118

Toffler, A., 64
Tolstoy, L., xiv, 145
Torok, M., xxviii, 71 95, 99, 238
Toynbee, A., 148

Valéry, P., 132
Van der Waals, H. G.,
Venkoba, R. A., 118
Verlaine, P., 2, 128
Virgil, xix
Vogelweide, W. von der, 2
Voltaire, F., 145

Wagner, R., xxiv
Wahl, C. W., 122
Weber, M., 146
Wechsler, G., 44

Weiss, E., 198-199, 201
Whitehead, A. N., xv, 1
Winnicott, D. W., viii, x, xiv, xviii,
    xxvii, 2, 20, 24, 39, 40, 61, 77,
    91, 137, 140-141, 143, 150, 153,
    210, 213-214
Wisdom, J. O., 196, 197
Wittgenstein, L., 180
Wolf, K. M., 15, 32-33
Wolfenstein, M., 42, 46
Woolf, P. J., 28
Wordsworth, W., 145
Wyrsch. J., 2

Yap, P. M., 118

Zetzel, E., 26, 39, 77, 113

# Subject Index

Abandonment, 52, 70, 224-225
Acute grief reaction, 87
Addiction and depression, 150
Adolescence/adolescents
    boredom and violence of, 130
    as mourning, 45-46
Affective states
    depression vs other, xxv-xxvi
    lifestyles and disorders of, 151
Aggression, 16, 47-48, 77, 212-213,
        227-228, 229, 237
    disappointment and , 47-48
    loss of love and, 227-228
    mourning and, 77
    object relations and, 229
    pain and, 212-218
Ambivalence, 16, 87, 88, 123, 187,
        193, 196-197
Anaclitic depression, 15, 227
    definition of, 32-33
Anal receptivity, 238
Anality, 204-205
Analysis, see Psychoanalysis
Ancestor worship, 144
Anthropologists, 149
Anxiety, 13-14
    depression and, xi, xxv, 19, 20,
        26-27
    depression vs, xvi, 27
    depressive, xxv
    helplessness and, 55-56
    persecution, 190
    primary, 26-27

sadness vs, 18
stage of, 213
Apathy, see Boredom
Attachment, 73

Behaviorism, 124
Biology of depression, 30, 89
Birth trauma, 235-236
Body image, disturbances in, 109
Borderline cases, 95
Boredom, xxv-xxvi, 72, 128-139
    adolescent violence and, 130
    definition of, 129
    disillusionment and, 138
    of drug addicts, 136
    as emptiness, 135
    family romance and, 130-131
    inhibition and, 134-135
    nostalgia and, 136-137
    as painful solitude, 135-136
    thrill seeking and, 131-132
Budapest school, xiii

Castration, fear of, 111
Castration complex, 205
Cathexis, loss of capacity for, 72
    early separation and, 66
Change
    problem of, xvi-xviii, 6, 157
    stress in, 64-65
    of structure, 32
Character, 107
Children/childhood, 36-48

adolescence, 45-46, 130; *see also*
    Adolescence/adolescents
death in, knowledge of, 42-44,
    81-82
depression in, 45
mourning in, 40-45
narcissistic injury in, 36-37
primary depression in, 46-47
psychotic, 220-223
self-representation, 45
separation-individuation in, *see*
    Separation-individuation
Civilization, 235; *see also* Creativ-
    ity, culture and civilization
Cognitive function in depression,
    31
Communication of depression, 28,
    138-139
Conflict, depression as sign of, 211
Constitutional factor, 28-29
Creative suffering, 2-3
Creativity; *see also* Creativity, cul-
    ture and civilization
death and, 146, 148
as defense, 144-145
early loss of parents and, 145
midlife crisis and, 146
Creativity, culture and civiliza-
    tion, 140-154; *see also* Civili-
    zation; Creativity; Culture
ancestor worship and, 144
Greek tragedy and, 144
incest taboo at root of, 143
lifestyles and affective disorders
    and, 151
nostalgia and, 147-148
Culture, 118-120, 123; *see also* Crea-
    tivity, culture and civilization

Death; *see also* entries beginning
    Death
as aggression, 80
as castration, 81
child's conception of, 42-44, 81-
    82

creation and, 146, 148
denial of, 82-83
fear of mastering, 84
guilt following, creativity and,
    148
immortality and, 79-84
love and, 81, 149
mourning and trauma of, 71
narcissistic elation in, 80
as nuptial celebration, 80
object loss following, 238
realization of, 146-147
as sleep, 80
Death compulsion/demonic factor,
    58-60
Death instinct, 115
Death of parents, vii, xi, xix, xxiii,
    165-166, 170, 182
creativity after, 146
famous orphans, xiii-xiv
Death theme, xii, xiii, xxiii, 58-60,
    79, 81-83
Death wish, xii, 166
Death wish against others, 115-
    116
Decathexis, process of, 29-30
Defense(s) against depression, 121-
    127, 230
creation as, 144-145
denial, 122-123, 125-126, 218
fantasy as, 68
humor as, 126-127
idealization as, 127
manic, 121-122
schizoid organization, 122-123
sleep as, 125
Defense against disappointment,
    218-219
Demonic factor, 58-60
Denial, 218
as defense against depression,
    122-123, 125-126
in fantasy, 90
mourning and, 68
Dependence, need for, 202-203

Dependency, 73
Depressed person vs depressive, 227
Depression, 20; *see also* Melancholia
　acceptance of limitations in, 92
　addiction and, 150
　anaclitic, 15, 32-33
　anaclitic vs adult, 15
　of analyst, 95
　anxiety and, xiv, 19, 20, 26-27
　anxiety vs., xvi, 19, 20, 27
　basic, 39
　basic structure of, 67-68
　biological significance of, 30, 89
　borderline cases of, 95
　case reports of, xxx-xxxii
　causes of, 206-207, 233-234
　change of structure in, 32
　classic neurosis vs, 116-117
　clinical, 87
　cognitive functions in, 31
　communication of, 28, 138-139
　conflict and, 211
　constitutional factor in, 28-29
　in course of analysis, 211
　cultural aspects of, 118-120, 123
　defenses against, *see* Defenses against depression
　developmental aspects of, 213-214
　essential, notion of, 239
　evolution of ideas on, *see* Evolution of ideas on depression
　Freud, on, *see* Freud on depression
　guilt and, xxv
　history of, 1-2
　infantile, 21
　inferiority, 231-235
　introjections of, 103-104
　lack in, 30-31
　narcissistic inadequacy and, sense of, 62

neglect of topic of, 14
neurotic, xxvii, 34, 223-224
neurotic vs melancholic, 34, 199, 201, 225-226
neurotic vs psychotic, 216-217
nosology of, 32-35
object relations in, 107
obsession and, 3
obsessional character and, 34
obsessional structure in, 203
other affective states vs, xxv-xxvi
pain vs, 27
physical illness and, 72, 150
powerlessness and, xxv
predisposition/vulnerability to, 15-18, 46-47, 206-207, 229-230
primal, 218
primary, 26-27, 46-47, 187-188
psychosomatic disorders vs, 230
resignation and, 159
in retired persons, 136
sadness vs, xv
schizophrenic psychosis vs, 204, 229-230
simple or normal, 87
sociogenetic theories of, 125
sub-depression, 132; *see also* Boredom
symptoms of, 2
trauma and, 20, 54, 55, 65-66, 69- 71, 156, 208; *see also* Trauma
wide spectrum of, 35
Depressive
　depressed person vs, 227
　quest for unity in, 75-76
Depressive affect, 6, 13-35
　trigger of, 32
　types of, 50-51
Depressive personality, xxvii-xxviii
Depressive position, 4-5, 6, 15, 20, 46, 27-28, 77, 187, 193, 194-196, 198, 227

Depressive predisposition/vulner-
ability, 15, 18, 46-47, 206-207,
229-230
Depressive structure, xxvi, xxvii
Deprivation, 16
Despair, vii, viii, ix, 3-5, 50-51
definition of, 51
guilt in, 4-5
Detachment and working through,
42
Developmental aspects of depression, 213-214
Differentiation, 38-39
Disappointments, 76, 187, 214, 224
defense against, 218-219
early, 46-47
oedipal imagos and, 17-18
at oedipal level, 15
Disillusionment and boredom, 138
Dreams
helplessness in, 58
restorative function of, 142
Drive theory, narcissism and, 235
Drives, destructuring forces inherent in, 60-61
Drug addicts, 136
Dual union, 39-40, 53
growth and, 39-40
inferiority feelings and, 53

Ego, 23, 132-133
affective reaction of, 207-208
discrepancy between ego and,
132-133
impoverishment of, 205
introjects and functions of, 100-
101
maturation of, 38-39
superego development before,
117-118
weakness of, 212
Ego ideal, 21-22, 132-133, 209, 234-
235
conditions for development of,
234-235

discrepancy between ego and,
132-133
two levels of, 21-22
Elation, 38
Emptiness, 54, 72, 135
Eudaemonia, xxiv
Evolution of ideas on depression,
180-239
Abraham, 181-188
Abraham and Torok, 238
Benedek, 209-211
Bergeret, 238-239
Bibring, 207-209
Bowlby, 211
contemporary francophone au-
thors, 224-239
Deutsch, 201-202
early works, 181-198
Fenichel, 203-207
Gerö, 202-203
Grunberger, 235-238
Harnik, 201
Jacobson, 214-220
Klauber, 223-224
Klein, 188-198
Lebovici, 224-225
Lewin, 211
Mahler, 220-223
Mallet, 225-227
Nacht and Racamier, 227-231
Pasche, 231-235
post-war English-language, 207-
224
Rado, 199-201
Rubinfine, 224
Sandler and Joffe, 211-213
twenties and thirties, 198-207
Weiss, 198-199, 201
Winnicott, 213-214

Family romance and boredom,
130-131
Family situation, helplessness and,
56-57

Fantasy/fantasies
    child's, xv
    as defense, 68
    denial of loss, 90
    hypochondriacal, 150
    of omnipotence, xxviii-xxix
Fatigue, 133
Fear of death, mastering, 84
Francophone authors, contemporary, 224-229
French authors, contemporary, xiii
Freud on depression, vii, ix, xi-xiii, xv, xvi, xviii, xix-xx, xxiii, xxiv, 3, 4-5, 7, 8, 15, 16, 18-22, 24, 27, 28, 30, 33, 42, 49, 53-61, 66-72, 79, 81-83, 85-90, 92, 93, 98-103, 106, 107, 109, 110, 112, 114, 121-123, 125, 126, 131-132, 138, 143, 144, 146, 148, 150, 152, 156, 157, 159, 163-179, 182, 184-186, 188, 192, 199, 200, 201, 212, 218, 219, 239
    addiction of Freud and, 165
    aggression, 16, 131-132
    anxiety, 18-19, 20, 27
    biological significance of depression, 30
    death of father, vii, xi, 165-166
    death theme, xii-xiii, xxiii, 58-60, 79, 81-83
    decathexis, 66
    defenses, 121-123, 125, 126
    despair, 4-5
    disillusionment, 138
    ego, 21
    foreshadowing of oedipus complex in, 168-169
    helplessness, 53, 54, 56, 57, 58
    hysteria, 168, 170
    identification and introjection, 98-103, 171-172, 199, 200, 201
    knowledge of death, 42
    love, being in, 72
    melancholia and obsessional neurotic conflicts, 171
    mourning and melancholia, xv, 18, 67, 170-171
    mourning and psychoanalytic process/working through, 85-90, 92, 93, 166-168, 170-178
    mourning as reality testing, 67, 192
    narcissism, 156-157
    normal vs pathological mourning, 173-174
    nosology, 33
    obsession, 3, 171, 184-185
    oedipus complex, discovery of, 166
    as subject of depression, 164-166
    suicide, 173
    superego in melancholia, 114, 178
    term melancholia, 163-164
    trauma, 55, 57, 69-71
    boredom, 131-132

Greek tragedy, 144
Grieving, see Mourning
Growth, 38-40
Guilt, xxv, 115-116
    in despair, 4-5
    in depression, 115-116
    following death, creativity and, 148
    in grief, 172
    internalization of, 149
    in non-Western cultures, 118-120
    problem of, 95-96

Happiness, xxiv
Health, loss of, 72
Healthy personality, 74
Helplessness, xv, xviii, 49-63, 222
    anxiety and, 55-56

in adult undergoing analysis, 53
in dream states, 58
in grief, 56, 57
and prisoner of family situation,
  56-57
repetition and, 56-57
Hope, 28
Hopelessness, xviii, 50-51
Human symbiosis, 39
Humor as defense, 126-127
Hungarian school, 202
Hypochondria, 150
Hysteria, 86, 168-170, 225-227
  bereavement and, 86
  Freud on, 168-170
  Mallet on, 225-227

Idealization as defense, 127
Identification, 16, 87-88; see also
  Introjection and identification
  Freud on, 98, 171-172
  object choice vs, 100-101
  object relations mixed with, 203
  object relations replaced by, 107
  projective, 99
  regressive dissolution of, 219
  superego and, 101-102
Imago, 99
Imagoic world, xxvi
Immortality, 79-84
  feeling of, 82-83
Impotence, 53
Impulsiveness, 94
Incest taboo, 143
Incorporation, 97
  introjection vs, 99
Independence, growing up and,
  39-40
Individuation, see Separation-in-
  dividuation
Infantile demands, 202-203
Infantile depression, 21
Inferiority feelings
  in depression, 231-235

dual union and, 53
Inhibition and boredom, 134-135
Inner object, 99
Inner and internal world, 100
Intersexual victimization, 94
Introjection; see also Introjection
  and identification
  complex cases of, 99
  of depression vs mourning, 103-
    104
  dual introjective process, 199,
    200-201
  dual nature of process of, 111-
    112
  ego functions and, 100-101
  as hypercathected memory, 111
  incorporation vs, 99
  loss followed by, 185-186
  memory and, 102
  sadistic nature and, xxix
  superego and, 117
  transference and, 106
Introjection and identification, 97-
  113; see also Identification; Introjection
  definition of, 97-98
  object relations and, 105-106
  mourning and, 113
  narcissistic cathexes and, 103
  overidealization of psychoanal-
    yst and, 109
  self-image, 110
Isolation, 149-150

Kleinians, xiii, xxvi, 4-5, 46-47, 221

Lack in depression, 30-31
Lifestyles and affective disorders,
  151
Limitations, acceptance of, 92
Loneliness, 149-150
Loss; see also Loss and mourning
  of feeling of omnipotence, 90,
    91, 92

followed by introjection, 185-186
of health, 72
problem of, 157
problem of change and, xvi-xviii
of mother, xiii-xiv
in mourning vs melancholia, 67
of object, see Object loss
of parents, 93-94; see also Death of parents
of self, 72
of self-esteem, 87, 88
of sense of well-being, 24
Loss and mourning, 64-78; see also Loss; Mourning
ability to cathect objects and, 66
in early separation, 65-66
in midlife crisis, 71-72
object loss in, 74-75
in separation-individuation, 68-69
Love
being in, 71-72
and death, 81, 149
need for, 202-203
self-esteem and, 24-26

Mania, 177, 191
Manic defenses, 121-122
Manic-depressive psychoses, 183-184
Megalomania, 232
Melancholic depression/ melancholia; see also Depression
mourning and, xv, 18, 67, 170-178
neurotic depression vs, 34, 199, 201, 225-226
object relation in, 107
obsessional neurotic conflicts and, 171
paranoia and, 198-199, 201-202
predisposing characteristics of, 206

term melancholia, 163-164
Memory, xvii, 102
introjection and, 102
Mental breakdown, 140-141
Midlife crisis, 71-72, 146
Mother/mothering, viii, 76, 209-211
depressed mother, viii
depressive vulnerability and, 47
loss of mother, xiii-xiv
narcissistic cathexes and object relation with, 103
separation from, see Separation-individuation
Mourning, xv, 18; see also Loss and mourning; Mourning and psychoanalytic therapy/ working through
aggression during, 77
biological meanings of, 89
capacity for, 66-67
in childhood, 40-45
danger inherent in, 194-195
denial and, 68
false, 94
guilt in, 172
helplessness in, 56, 57
introjection and identification and, 113
introjection of, 103-104
melancholia and, xv, 18, 67, 166-168, 170-178
melancholia vs, 67
normal vs abnormal/pathological, 177-178, 196
obsessive, 78
and reality testing, 67, 192
renunciation of oedipal wishes and, 78
synonyms for, 87
trauma of death, 71
Mourning and psychoanalytic therapy, xix-xxiii, xxv, 85-96, 141-142, 166-168, 170-173

detachment and, 42
guilt following death, creativity
    and, 148
loss of feelings of omnipotence,
    90, 91, 92
hysteria and, 86

Narcissism, 6, 17, 21, 22-23, 156-
    157
drive theory and, 235
primary, 36-37, 49
Narcissistic, term, 104
Narcissistic aspirations, 208-209
Narcissistic cathexes, object rela-
    tion with mother and, 103
Narcissistic inadequacy, sense of,
    62
Narcissistic injury, 36-37
Narcissistic neuroses, 35
Narcissistic regression, 118
Narcissistic support, need for, 16
Narcissistic trauma of birth, 235-
    236
Neurosis
    depression vs 'classic', 116-117
    narcissistic, 35
Neurotic depression, xxvii, 34, 223-
    224
    melancholia vs, 34, 199, 201,
        225-226
    object relations in, 223-224
    self-image in, 223-224
Nonsatisfaction of needs, 153; *see
    also* Disappointment
Nosology, 32-35
Nostalgia, xxv-xxvi, 136-137, 147-
    148, 149

Object choice, identification vs,
    100-101
Object images, self-images and,
    110
Object loss, 74-75, 94-95, 173
    danger of, 18

early, 89-90
mourning and, 74-75
powerlessness and reconstruc-
    tion of lost object, 62-63
Object metabolization, theory of,
    29
Object relations, 229
    identification mixed with, 203
    incorporation, introjection and
        identification and, 105-106
    in neurotic depressives, 223-224
Object restoration
    powerlessness and, 62-63
    in therapy, xvii-xix
Obsession, depression and, 3
Obsessional character, 34
Obsessional neurotic conflicts, 171
Obsessional structure in depres-
    sion, 203
Obsessive mourning, 78
Obsessive patients, 184-185
Oedipal problem and depression,
    108, 148-149, 157-159, 166, 214
    Freud's discovery of, 166
    overcoming, 52
    renunciation of oedipal wishes,
        78
Omnipotence
    fantasy of, xxviii-xxix
    feelings of loss of, 90, 91, 92
    limitation of, 104-105
Oral dependence, 203
Oral fixation, 204
Oral-narcissistic gratification, 22
Oral stage, subdivision of, 186-187
Orphans, famous, xiii-xiv

Pain, psychic, *see* Psychic pain
Paranoia and melancholia, 198-199,
    201-202
Paranoiac, 190
Parent, loss of, 93-94; *see also* Death
    of parents
    creativity and early, 145

Persecution anxiety, 190
Personality, healthy, 74
Phallic stage and depression, 108
Physical illness and depression, 150
Powerlessness, xxv, 20, 26, 62-63, 213, 228-229; see also Helplessness
reconstruction of lost object and, 62-63
Pregenital fixations, 111, 203
Prepsychotic personalities, 217-218
Preoedipal period, 216
Primal depression, 218
Primary depression, 26-27, 46-47, 187-188
Psyche, four elements of, 232-233
Psychic pain, 27-28, 212
depression vs, xxv, 27
Psychoanalysis/analysis
depression and, 165-166
depression in course of, 211
fundamental question of/ultimate aim of, 158
mastering fear of death in, 84
mourning and process, see Mourning and Psychoanalytic process/working through
object restoration in, xviii-xix
overidealization of, 109
relinquishing old objects and ideals in, 92
time needed for, 91
Psychoanalyst, depression of, 95
Psychoanalytic literature, evolution of ideas on depression in, see Evolution of ideas on depression
Psychosis
in children, 220-223
prepsychotic personalities, 217-218
schizophrenic, 229-230

Psychosomatic disorders vs depression, 230
Psychotherapeutic technique, nonpunitive
listening in, 124-125
Punishment, fear of, 149
Rapprochement, 38
Reality testing and mourning, 67, 192
Regression, 99, 112
narcissistic, 118
Reparation, 152-153
failure of, 197
Repetition and helplessness, 57-59
Resignation, 159
Retired persons, depressive problems in, 136

Sadness, xv, xxv, 18, 27-28, 182
anxiety vs, 18
Schizoid organization, 122-123
Schizophrenic psychosis vs depression, 229-230
Self; see also Death, immortality and
loss of, 72
sense of, 214-215
Self-esteem, 24-26
loss of, 87, 88, 112
low, 109
Self-hatred, 205-206
Self-image, 110
in neurotic depressive, 223-224
Self-representation, child's, 45
Separation
precocious, 238
trauma of early, 65-66
Separation anxiety, 69-71
Separation-individuation, xiii-xv, xvi, xxvi, 6, 38, 68-69, 156-157, 221-223
Sleep, 125
Sociogenetic theories, 125
Solitude, 149-150

boredom as painful, 135-136
Somatic illness, 72, 150
Stage of anxiety, 213
Stage of concern, 213
Suicide, xxix, 120, 170-171, 177, 191, 206, 230-231, 237-238
  cultural determinants of, 120
  Grunberger on, 237-238
  Nacht and Racamier on, 230-231
Superego, 17, 114-120, 207, 228
  classic neurosis vs depression and, 116-117
  cultural aspects of, 118-120
  death wishes and, 115-116
  development before ego of, 117-118
  Freud on, 178
  guilt and, 115-116, 118-120
  identification and, 101-102
  introjections that comprise it, 117
  severity of, 114-115

Technique, psychotherapeutic, see Psychotherapeutic technique
Techniques to diminish unpleasant experiences, 154

Therapeutic relationship, establishing, 94
Thrill seeking and boredom, 131-132
Transference
  difficulties in, 238
  introjection and, 106
  object relation, 107
Trauma, 20, 156, 208
  of death, 71
  definition of, 54, 55
  of early separation, 65-66
  separation anxiety and, 69-71

Unity, desperate quest for, 75-76

Violence, boredom and, 130

War, impacet of, xii
Warmth, need for, 202-203
Well-being
  definition of, 212
  loss of sense of, 24
Working through, mourning and, see Mourning and psychoanalytic process/working through